220

Essays on the History of British Sociological Research

This book traces the history of British sociology and empirical social research over the last hundred years. Its coverage includes the census of population, the classic poverty surveys of Booth and Rowntree, the slow growth of social science between the wars, Mass-Observation, the rise of the Government Social Survey, the establishment of academic sociology after 1945 outside Oxford and Cambridge, and independent initiatives such as the foundation of the Institute of Community Studies. A concluding section considers the uses made of British sociology, the place of the citizen as the subject of research, social surveys for policy-making, and the success of social science in predicting the future.

These essays reflect the interests of the distinguished British sociologist, the late Philip Abrams. In addition to him the contributors include a number of distinguished sociologists such as A.H. Halsey, Hannan C. Selvin, Edward Shils, Peter Townsend and Peter Willmott as well as several well-known younger scholars.

To the memory of

PHILIP ABRAMS,
1933–1981

Essays on the History of British Sociological Research

edited by
MARTIN BULMER
Senior Lecturer in Social Administration, London School of Economics

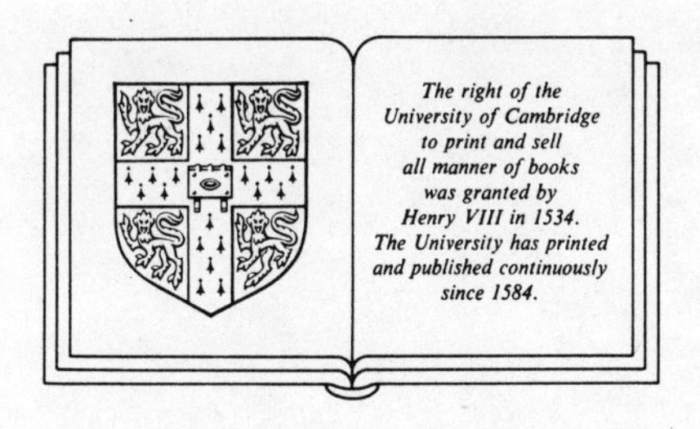

CAMBRIDGE UNIVERSITY PRESS
Cambridge
London New York New Rochelle
Melbourne Sydney

Published by the Press Syndicate of the University of Cambridge
The Pitt Building, Trumpington Street, Cambridge CB2 1RP
32 East 57th Street, New York, NY 10022, USA
296 Beaconsfield Parade, Middle Park, Melbourne 3206, Australia

First published 1985

Printed in Great Britain at the University Press, Cambridge

Library of Congress catalogue card number: 84-11371

British Library Cataloguing in Publication Data

Essays on the history of British sociological research.
1. Sociology – Great Britain – Research – History
I. Bulmer, Martin
301′.092041 HM48

ISBN 0 521 25477 9

BO

Contents

Preface

This volume commemorates two aspects of the work of the distinguished British sociologist, the late Philip Abrams, on the history of sociology and on the uses of sociology. Philip Abrams's sudden death on 31 October 1981 followed only two months after the 150th Anniversary Meeting at York of the British Association for the Advancement of Science, held from 31 August to 4 September. At that meeting, Philip was the President of Section N, Sociology. The core of this book is made up of papers delivered there, including Philip's Presidential Address to the section on 'The Uses of British Sociology 1831–1981' and several papers delivered at a Section N symposium on the British Survey Tradition. Dr Stuart S. Blume, Recorder of Section N, suggested that a selection of these papers was suitable for publication, and the resulting volume includes these with the addition of several other papers on related subjects in the history of British social research.

Philip Abrams's interest in the history of sociology reflected his academic origins as a historian.[1] Born in 1933, he took a first in history at Peterhouse, Cambridge, in 1955, followed by three years as a research student and three years as a research fellow. In 1961 he was awarded his Ph.D. for a thesis on 'John Locke as a conservative'.[2] These six postgraduate years were also spent in the study of sociology, particularly political sociology, and his first teaching appointment in 1961 was as Assistant Lecturer in Sociology at L.S.E. He returned to Cambridge the following year as Assistant Lecturer, teaching political sociology in the Faculty of Economics and Political Science. In 1965 he was appointed University Lecturer and Fellow and Tutor at Peterhouse. Between 1968 and 1970 he was Chairman of the Social and Political Sciences Committee, which was responsible for setting-up and then running the new Part II Tripos in Social and Political Sciences, which became the main instrument for introducing substantial sociology teaching into the university. Philip Abrams pushed hard for the establishment of this Tripos against considerable resistance, discussed in the introduction and in chapter 10 by Edward Shils. In January 1971 he took up the appointment as Professor of Sociology at the University of Durham which he held at his death.

Philip Abrams's scholarly interests ranged widely, among which the two which are the subject here were only a part. Political sociology was his first love and remained a major centre of interest. Historical sociology proper was an abiding interest, reflected in his membership of the editorial board of *Past and Present*, which he helped to found; in a collection on *Towns in Societies* which he edited with E.A. Wrigley;[3] and in his posthumous *Historical Sociology.*[4] In Durham he initiated a series of research projects spanning sociology and social policy including studies of regionalism and regional development, communes as alternative families (Abrams and McCulloch, *Communes, Sociology and Society*[5]) and neighbouring and patterns of social care in the community.[6] He also commissioned and edited a wide-ranging survey of contemporary British society.[7] An early interest, too, was in the sociology of the military,[8] which led to an invitation from Morris Janowitz to spend the year 1966–7 at the University of Chicago. There he wrote *The Origins of British Sociology 1834–1914*,[9] a classic essay and standard source of reference.

His interests in the history of the discipline and in the uses of sociology were therefore only a part of his work, and this volume is in no sense a reflection of all his interests in the round. Nevertheless, his strong commitment to the development of sociology as a discipline indicates how central these interests were. He continued to work on the development of British sociology after 1914, and in 1979–80 received a personal research grant from the S.S.R.C. to investigate the utilisation of British sociology in the present century. This work was not completed, but a part appears as his Presidential address in chapter 11. His professional involvement in the British Sociological Association, notably as the editor of its journal *Sociology* from 1976 to 1981, was reflected in the retrospective theme of its 1980 Thirtieth Anniversary conference, which he suggested, and in the resulting proceedings, *Practice and Progress: British sociology 1950–1980* which included a characteristically thoughtful contribution of his own entitled 'The collapse of British sociology?'[10] In recognition of his contribution to the discipline, the British Sociological Association has established from 1984 the Philip Abrams Memorial Prize for a piece of work by a younger sociologist in any one of nine fields in which he worked. The first of these is the History of Social Research.

The appearance of this volume also recognises the contribution which the British Association for the Advancement of Science has made to the public recognition and acceptance of sociology among the other social sciences, particularly in the last twenty-five years since the creation of Section N, Sociology. Over 150 years, the role of the British Association has changed. In its early years it functioned to raise collective consciousness among Britain's natural scientific elites and to raise standards to the level of competitors such as France.[11] In the mid-Victorian period, it became the premier public forum for scientific debates (such as that between Wilberforce and Huxley in 1860), as well as fostering a good deal of research. After the beginning of the twentieth century, scientific specialisation reduced this role, and it became much more a vehicle for science education and popularisation, as well as the oracle, public relations advocate and (on occasion) apologist of science. Its leading statesmen see it as the parliament of science,[12] though perhaps inevitably it is more like the European Parliament than Westminster.

The increasing attention paid by the British Association to social science was reflected in the creation of Section N in 1960, the presidency of which has until recently alternated annually between a sociologist and a social anthropologist.[13] Philip Abrams was its twenty-second incumbent. The B.A.A.S. annual meetings provide one of the most visible opportunities for British sociologists to speak to a wider lay audience. Sociologists have shown over the years that they are capable of taking such an opportunity. The 1981 meeting was no exception, the proceedings of Section N receiving considerable press coverage. In a contribution to a plenary symposium at York, Philip Abrams paid tribute to the role that the British Association had played.

> Sociology is saddled with a special problem of unavoidable, subjective involvement in its own subject-matter. The question it must always face is whether its scientific pretensions can survive such an involvement – and the partial, relative character which it necessarily gives to sociology's problems, observations and proposals. The history of British sociology since 1831 is a history, first, of the discovery of the urgency of that question; then of two bold but mistaken attempts to answer it by way of empiricism (science as facts) and positivism (science as laws); of an ensuing and far-reaching intellectual crisis as those mistakes worked themselves out; and perhaps now of a hesitant movement towards more modest answers asserting the possibility of sociology as a *reasonably* scientific enterprise. In that history the British Association has had a constant and significant part, providing a forum in which the possibility, scope and nature of a science of the social has been debated, a platform from which successive foolish positions have been adopted (and discarded), a forcing house for the withdrawal of sociology from science (mistakenly conceived) and its gradual advancement as science (more sensibly conceived). The problem for sociology is not that of being a science like other sciences but of being a science *appropriate* to the peculiar nature of the social and of sociology's own place in it. I think we are slowly getting there.

> And the way in which the British Association has carried forward the relevant debates and prodded us along has definitely helped.[14]

In recognition of Philip Abrams's presidency of Section N and the origin of the papers by C. Hakim, Frank Whitehead, Angus Calder, Catherine Marsh, L.F. Barić and Peter Townsend at the York meeting, royalties from this book have been donated to Section N of the British Association for the Advancement of Science to use for the advancement of sociology.

This volume, then, is both a selective tribute to Philip Abrams's scholarly contribution in two areas, and a demonstration of the historical strength of the tradition of British sociology and social research to which he, like his father Dr Mark Abrams, contributed so notably. Most, though not quite all, of the other contributors to this book would regard themselves as sociologists, reflecting the fact that in Britain 'sociology' and 'social research' are not coterminous. A good deal of social research – particularly survey-based inquiries of a factual kind – are carried out beyond universities in independent institutes, for profit or non-profit research organisations, central or local government research divisions or quangos. Thus Frank Whitehead's chapter on the Government Social Survey and Gerald Hoinville's on methodological research on social surveys are not written by sociologists, while Angus Calder's study of Mass-Observation is concerned with a body of amateurs who were distant from the academic sociology and anthropology of their day. The title of this book reflects the fact that empirical social inquiry in Britain was not in the past and is not now the exclusive preserve of sociologists. All the same, there are good grounds for the view that sociology is the academic discipline with the closest affinity with social research of all types, with a special contribution to make. As Philip Abrams put it at York in 1981:

> Sociology should not revert to being just a diffuse practice of social research, least of all one responding directly to the perceived needs of government, or of any other authorities, but should have an institutional space of its own from which its special scientific task can be pursued. It is a task – the pursuit of argumentative knowledge, the refusal of authoritative knowledge – peculiarly possible, perhaps only possible within the sort of space provided by an academic discipline. It involves the cultivation of respect for the rigorous interpretation of rigorously assembled evidence about the social world coupled always with the cultivation of scepticism about the objectivity of the knowledge yielded by such work. Insofar as such a combination of respect and scepticism is achieved both science and politics, both social knowledge and social debate can flourish.[15]

Issues relating to the social function of sociological knowledge and the uses to which sociology can be put are addressed specifically in the second part of the book.

For the original suggestion to edit the York papers for publication, I am greatly indebted to Professor Stuart S. Blume of the University of Amsterdam, then Recorder of Section N. For advice and assistance of various kinds in preparing the manuscript for publication I am grateful to the contributors and to Sheila Abrams, Mark Abrams, Richard K. Brown, Robert Moore, John Barnes, Jack Goody, George E.C. Paton, Jennifer Platt and E.A. Wrigley. Valerie Campling typed parts of the manuscript. The responsibility for selecting papers for inclusion and for the overall balance of the book remains my own.

October 1983 MARTIN BULMER

NOTES

1 For appreciations of the career of Philip Abrams, see 'Obituary: Philip Abrams', *Network: the newsletter of the British Sociological Association*, No. 22, January 1982, p.2; Richard K. Brown, 'Philip Abrams, 1933–1981', *Sociology* 16(1), February 1982, pp.i–iii, and Andrew McCulloch, 'Philip Abrams – a tribute', *Sociology* 16(1), February 1982, pp.iii–iv.
2 Cf. also Philip Abrams (ed.), *John Locke: Two Tracts on Government* (Cambridge: Cambridge University Press, 1963).
3 E.A. Wrigley and Philip Abrams (eds.), *Towns in Societies* (Cambridge: Cambridge University Press, 1977).
4 Philip Abrams, *Historical Sociology* (Shepton Mallet, Somerset: Open Books, 1982). The general theme was first addressed in his inaugural lecture at Durham; Philip Abrams, *Being and Becoming in Sociology* (Durham: University of Durham, 1972).
5 Philip Abrams and Andrew McCulloch, *Communes, Sociology and Society* (Cambridge: Cambridge University Press, 1975).
6 An account of this aspect of Philip Abrams's work is currently being prepared for publication by the editor.
7 Philip Abrams (ed.), *Work, Urbanism and Inequality* (London: Weidenfeld & Nicolson, 1978).
8 Cf. Philip Abrams, 'Democracy, technology and the retired British officer', in S.P. Huntingdon (ed.), *Changing Patterns of Military Politics* (Glencoe, Ill.: Free Press, 1965); 'The late profession of arms: ambiguous goals and deteriorating means in Britain', *Archives européens de sociologie* 6(2):238–61; 'Armed forces and society: problems of alienation', in J.N. Wolfe and J. Erickson (eds.), *The Armed Forces and Society: alienation, management and integration* (Edinburgh: Edinburgh University Press, 1970).
9 Philip Abrams, *The Origins of British Sociology 1834–1914: an essay with selected papers* (Chicago: University of Chicago Press, 1968). The book appeared in the 'Heritage of Sociology' series edited by Morris Janowitz.

10 Philip Abrams, Rosemary Deem, Janet Finch and Paul Rock (eds.), *Practice and Progress: British Sociology 1950–1980* (London: Allen & Unwin, 1981), pp. 53–70. The complete papers of this conference are collected in P. Abrams and P. Lewthwaite (eds.), *Development and Diversity: British Sociology 1950–1980: Transactions of the 1980 Annual Conference of the British Sociological Association*, 3 volumes (London: British Sociological Association, 1980) (available in the British Library of Political and Economic Science).
11 Jack Morell and Arnold Thackray, *Gentlemen of Science: the early years of the British Association for the Advancement of Science* (Oxford: Clarendon Press, 1981).
12 Roy Macleod and Peter Collins (eds.), *The Parliament of Science: the British Association for the Advancement of Science 1831–1981* (London: Science Reviews, 1982).
13 The first president of the section, at Cardiff in 1960, was David Glass; the second, at Norwich in 1961, was Max Gluckman (information from George Paton, Recorder of Section N).
14 Philip Abrams, 'Sociology: could there be another 150 years?', contribution to Social Sciences Symposium no. 9 at York, 2 September 1981 (London: British Association for the Advancement of Science, 1981, mimeo).
15 ibid., pp. 15–16.

Contributors

The late Philip Abrams *Professor of Sociology, University of Durham*

Lorraine F. Barić *Professor of Sociology and Anthropology, University of Salford*

The late Christopher Bernert *Graduate student in Sociology, State University of New York at Stony Brook*

Martin Bulmer *Senior Lecturer in Social Administration, London School of Economics and Political Science*

Angus Calder *Staff Tutor in Arts, The Open University in Scotland*

C. Hakim *Principal Research Officer, Department of Employment, London*

A.H. Halsey *Professor of Social and Administrative Studies, University of Oxford*

Gerald Hoinville *Co-Director, Social and Community Planning Research; Visiting Professor of Statistics, The City University*

Raymond Kent *Lecturer in Sociology, University of Stirling*

Catherine Marsh *Lecturer in Social and Political Sciences, University of Cambridge*

Hannan C. Selvin *Professor of Sociology, State University of New York at Stony Brook*

Edward Shils *Distinguished Service Professor of Social Thought and of Sociology, University of Chicago and Honorary Fellow of Peterhouse, Cambridge*

Peter Townsend *Professor of Social Policy, University of Bristol*

Frank Whitehead *Deputy Director, Office of Population Censuses and Surveys, London*

Peter Willmott *Senior Fellow, Policy Studies Institute; Visiting Professor of Social Policy and Administration, London School of Economics and Political Science.*

INTRODUCTION

1 The development of sociology and of empirical social research in Britain

MARTIN BULMER

There are many famous British names in the Pantheon of empirical social and statistical inquiry, such as Edwin Chadwick, William Farr, Charles Booth, Seebohm Rowntree, and A.L. Bowley. Sociologists, too, have made a considerable contribution to the British tradition of social research (cf. Raison 1979). Yet the historical study of the growth of social research does not display any unified pattern. Rather it is characterised by episodic bursts, intellectual and disciplinary fragmentation, lack of cumulation and profound weaknesses of institutionalisation. In *The Origins of British Sociology 1834–1914*, Philip Abrams emphasised at the same time the strength of the tradition and the profound discontinuities which were apparent by the outbreak of the First World War.

This collection of essays takes the story forward into the twentieth century, with several backward glances to the nineteenth. Its focus upon empirical sociological research reflects its origins in a symposium on the British Survey Tradition. The theme of the book is at once broader and narrower than the history of sociology in general. Some of the antecedents of British sociology are identified, but also some developments – such as Mass-Observation and the Government Social Survey – which have stood at some distance from academic sociological inquiry are discussed. On the other hand, the aim is not to provide a rounded picture of twentieth-century British sociology. This still awaits its historian, though there are a number of useful essays and surveys which provide a partial account (Rumney 1945; Sprott 1957; Krausz 1969; MacRae 1972; Eldridge 1980; Abrams 1981a; Kent 1981; Rex 1983). The focus in this collection is primarily upon aspects of twentieth-century empirical sociological investigation. The account given here is only a partial one, highlighting important areas and issues, but leaving others unexplored. The period up to 1950 receives the main attention.

Terminological differences between 'social research', 'sociology' and 'social science' are indicative of underlying intellectual tensions.

> Already by 1906 [Philip Abrams observed] one could find as many divergent definitions of sociology as there were sociologists. Already one could hear loud complaints about the uselessness of this variety of sociology, the arid pedantry of that, the misty philosophizing of another, the political tendentiousness of yet another . . . The nature and province of the emergent discipline were the heart of the problem. That a social science was desirable was widely agreed. But what *was* the social and just what would be involved in studying it scientifically? . . . On the one hand, the hope of building a science to close the gap between social knowledge and social action encouraged ambitious quests for the philosophical foundations of authoritative knowledge about the social, construed in the widest possible sense. On the other hand, the effort to create intellectual and institutional space for sociology by establishing it as a science in the eyes of other scientists encouraged a drastic narrowing of both substance and method. Prevailing empiricist conceptions of science, the appetite for definitive information about poverty, industrial conflict, town planning and a host of other current social problems, and the mere practicalities of academic politics persuaded many to see sociology as little more than a battery of research techniques (for social observation and measurement) occupying a province of substantive problems which had a purely ad hoc existence, either as what happened to be politically 'important' at any given moment, or as those matters which happened to have been left over, as it were, by the disciplines that already existed. The social came to be defined as a miscellaneous residual category grouping-together whatever economics, history and psychology between them had not already appropriated. Trapped thus, between contrary expectations and possibilities, sociology was, by 1906, already busy sowing the seeds of its own subsequent crises (1981b:5).

For the first half of the century 'social science' only meant 'sociology' to a quite limited extent, and 'sociology' did not in general mean 'empirical social research'. If the difference between 'social science' and 'sociology' tended to be blurred in the nineteenth century (cf. Goldman 1983: 587–9, 615–16; Soffer 1978; Collini 1978), in the first half of the twentieth, sociology was overshadowed by other social sciences such as economics, political science and social anthropology, which grew more sturdily. One contributory factor was the enduring amateur tradition of social investigation. Booth, Rowntree and Lady Bell are usually remembered, but at a slightly later period Patrick Geddes and Victor Branford, and (in a different way) Mass-Observation, represented research not only done outside the university, but antipathetic to academic discipline; Geddes through eclectic multidisciplinarity, Mass-Observation through the recruitment of volunteers for mass social ornithology. It is hardly an exaggeration to say that almost all of the empirical social research undertaken in Britain between the wars went untouched by what then passed for academic sociology. Some of this research was of doubtful quality, but then the orientation of academic sociologists also left something to be desired.

The discontinuity between 'sociology' and 'empirical social research' is not resolved by treating the latter as a sub-set of the former. Not only were there clear intellectual differences, but the activities were institutionalised in different ways. In the inter-war period empirical research was largely organised in a series of ad hoc, local, survey projects. During the war the Government Social Survey was created (chapter 5) and the Government Statistical Service established. After the war there developed independent institutes, social and market research organisations and 'in-house' government research divisions, one or two of which are discussed later in the book. To a large extent they and academic sociology have passed each other by, to the detriment of each. These developments underline the fact that sociology has no monopoly over the systematic empirical study of contemporary Britain.

The history of academic sociology, at least up to 1950, is the story of sociology at L.S.E. Sociology began its official academic existence in Britain at L.S.E. in 1903, followed in 1907 by L.T. Hobhouse's appointment to the Martin White Chair there. For a long period it was the only centre, though later Liverpool played a minor subsidiary role. Hobhouse retired in 1929 and was succeeded by Morris Ginsberg, who carried on the philosophical tradition which Hobhouse had begun. Neither, it is fair to say, was particularly interested in systematic empirical research, and they did rather little to foster it before 1945. Only after 1945 did the situation begin to change at the School, particularly through the influence of Edward Shils, David Glass and T.H. Marshall in a period evoked by A.H. Halsey in chapter 9. The slow pace of institutionalisation of the subject is evident by the late date of the founding of the British Sociological Association: 1951 (cf. Banks 1967).

Much has been made, in the long run, of the curious strength of positivism in English social thought (cf. Annan 1959). In the case of sociology what is much more striking before 1950 is the enduring strength of idealism (cf. Collini 1978). This was particularly so at L.S.E., where Hobhouse and Ginsberg were much more social philosophers than empirical sociologists. Since so much of the history of sociology is written as the history of social thought, this has not seemed odd or curious. Yet it is surely remarkable that for forty years the standard bearers of the discipline in Britain were devoted to the primacy of armchair reflection. The discontinuities between academic sociology and empirical research remain marked in a different way if one looks at the relation between social survey research and social science. There the very strong links evident in the United States and some European countries are lacking, though many sociological surveys were carried out. Connections between survey research and academic statistics are rather stronger (for a visitor's view see Selvin 1965). In Britain 'sociology' and 'empirical social research' have not been, and are not, coterminous.

The story told here has both threads which run through from start to finish, and episodic developments which left their mark for a time. One of the strongest continuing threads is provided by government fact-gathering by the General Register Office set up in 1837 (since 1970 part of the Office of Population Censuses and Surveys) and particularly the census of population, discussed by Hakim in chapter 2. Hakim contends that the census is properly seen as a survey of social conditions and a means of tracing changing social conditions over nearly a century and a half, since the first self-enumeration census in 1841. Moreover, as Marsh points out in chapter 12, the census was relying on citizens to act as respondents long before most other forms of social investigation.

The characteristic source of information for the nineteenth-century parliamentary committees and Royal Commissions whose 'Blue Book sociology' shed so much light on the social conditions which accompanied urbanisation and industrialisation (cf. Bulmer 1982: 1–9) was the *informant*, usually a middle-class professional person with knowledge of the working classes, who was questioned to provide data and impressions at second hand. Individual citizens were not thought reliable witnesses. At the end of the century, Booth still relied on School Board visitors to gather the data for his great survey of London. In certain respects 'Blue Book sociology' was an antecedent of twentieth-century government social inquiry, the main differences lying in the amateur and value-laden approach often prevalent in the nineteenth century. There is marked continuity between the statistical inquiries of the early and mid nineteenth century (cf. Cullen 1976) and the role of the Government Statistical Service today. One difference, of course, lies in the character of leading public servants. Men of the character of Edwin Chadwick would have a hard time in the contemporary civil service, where independence of spirit and bulldozing reforming zeal are kept well in check (cf. Finer 1952). Peter Townsend's call in chapter 13 for greater social responsiveness on the part of government researchers hankers after the stronger meat of nineteenth-century administration.

William Farr (1807–1883), statistician at the General Register Office for 35 years, is a good case in point. Though most honoured by medical statisticians today, Farr made important contributions to the study of morbidity, mortality and marriage patterns, both in the work which he directed and in the introductions he wrote to the Registrar General's Annual Reports from 1843 to 1878. It has been said of him that if 'vital statistics are figures with the tears wiped off', Farr never forgot the tears. In the twentieth century a man with such an inquiring mind would probably have held an academic post; in the nineteenth, he found scope for his inquiries within government (Eyler 1979; Alderson 1983; Lewes 1983). His importance for sociology lay perhaps most of all in the work he began on occupational mortality, which was followed in the early twentieth century by the development of the Registrar General's Social Class classification (Leete and Fox 1977; McDowall 1983).

If social research had its origins in statistical inquiry, by the late nineteenth century the social survey was developing in its own right, under the influence of other independent-minded individuals. Charles Booth and Seebohm Rowntree, unlike Chadwick and Farr, were businessmen who used their own wealth to pursue investigations into topics which concerned them, notably urban poverty and its relationship to employment and housing conditions. Kent in chapter 3 discusses their work and its continuation by others in the first four decades of the twentieth century. Theirs is perhaps the best known contribution to the early history of sociological research, yet some of the most interesting questions are counterfactuals. Why did Booth not become involved in the early twentieth-century sociological movement? What would have happened if Rowntree had not turned increasingly to research in the cause of the Liberal Party? Why did neither of them draw on the parallel work of Durkheim in France, and apparently remain in ignorance of the breakthroughs in statistical analysis made around the same time in Britain by G. Udny Yule? This last question is tackled effectively by Hannan Selvin in chapter 4, though the lack of contact between British statisticians and sociologists deserves further study (see Marsh 1982:40–6; MacKenzie 1981).

By the beginning of the twentieth century, for both intellectual and institutional reasons British sociology was in a curiously fragmented condition. It is perhaps a little strong to talk of 'the rise and collapse of the first effort to establish sociology in Britain' (Abrams 1968:144), for empirical social research was becoming more developed and several innovations had been made which were of lasting significance. Yet the pattern evident around 1900 was to persist for at least another half century. Individual initiatives of note were taken – for example, Bowley's introduction of random sampling, the inter-war surveys of social conditions, Hogben's work on population – without cumulation, cross-fertilisation or significant impact upon academic sociology. Several major developments took place outside universities altogether. By 1950 extra-academic empirical social inquiry was in a fairly healthy condition. For example, the Government Social Survey, described by Whitehead in chapter 5, was growing in size and influence, the Royal Commission on Population was completing its work backed by an impressive range of demographic research. Yet academic sociology, as

Halsey's account emphasises, was really still in its infancy. It is easy to forget how recent is the growth of the discipline in Britain. Even during the 1950's, it was not obvious that growth was likely. '[I]f anything a brief post-war momentum seemed to be evaporating. Few would have thought it obvious in 1956 that a great intellectual and institutional explosion of sociology was imminent' (Abrams 1981b:7–8). The first half of the twentieth century was, for British sociology, a period of slow, partial and fragmentary advance.

This uncertain history contrasts both with sociology in certain other countries and with other disciplines in Britain. In the United States, not only was sociology securely established much earlier in a wide range of universities (Shils 1980:183–99) but in the Chicago School between 1915 and the early 1930's developed an integrated and cumulative programme of theoretically-informed locally-based, empirical research which was particularly impressive for its time (cf. Faris 1967; Bulmer 1984). To be sure it had weaknesses, but as a stage in the institutionalisation of sociology and of empirical social research it had long-term significance and impact. Columbia University was a lesser centre at the beginning of the century, and a major centre from 1940 under Paul Lazarsfeld and Robert Merton. In France, Durkheim created in the late nineteenth and early twentieth century a notably successful school of sociology, centred on his own person and the journal *Année Sociologique* which he founded. The group of pupils and collaborators, which included Mauss, Halbwachs, Davy, Bouglé, Simiand and Granet constituted a strong scholarly collective for the promotion of the discipline. Though the impact of the Durkheim school weakened considerably after his death, it had a lasting impact upon French sociology and was in marked contrast to the intellectual and institutional weaknesses of the subject in Britain (Shils 1980:173–6; Besnard 1983).

In Britain, other disciplines showed greater signs of stronger development around dominating scholars than did sociology. In economics, the influence of Alfred Marshall in Cambridge was historically of signal importance. In the 1930's and 1940's, the group of younger economists under the influence of Maynard Keynes, if they did not exactly constitute a 'school', did have a major impact subsequently in carrying through and developing their master's ideas. The nearest equivalent to a 'school' (cf. Tiryakian 1979) in disciplines cognate to British sociology between the wars was the group of anthropology students around Bronislaw Malinowski at L.S.E. Strongly committed to empirical research, and with a dominant personality leading them, they were perhaps the nearest equivalent at the time, if there was one in Britain, to the Chicago School.

Six strands may be discerned in the history of British social investigation in the thirty years after 1914. Each was fairly distinct from the others, and their separateness, and the different directions in which they led, help to account for the weak intellectual and institutional impact of sociology before 1945. The tradition of the social survey, discussed by Kent in chapter 3, was perhaps the strongest of the six. The example of Booth and Rowntree was followed diligently, and the inter-war period saw a flowering of the survey of social conditions, with which social research was more or less equated (cf. Wells 1935). *The New Survey of London Life and Labour*, carried out at L.S.E. between 1927 and 1932, was merely the largest of a considerable number of local surveys, concerned particularly, though not exclusively, with the social consequences of structural unemployment and the Great Depression (for a useful summary, see Stevenson 1977). Some of the survey work was carried out by professional researchers, others by local volunteers. This was the era in which the popularity of the community 'self-survey' was also at its peak. The inter-war surveys were conceived of as rigorously factual and empirical, without any reference to general ideas or social theory. The main aim of such surveys was 'to make an accurate and impartial collection and presentation of the facts' (Jones 1948) with government and public opinion as the main audience. Their impact on sociology was negligible (Marsh 1982:30), but they maintained continuity with the nineteenth-century inquiries of the statistical societies and 'blue-book sociology'.

Another strand is represented by the specifically statistical contribution to survey work, notably that of A.L. Bowley. Here the theme of Selvin's chapter is again pertinent. In the inter-war period statistics and survey work, though continuing to be largely separate and in ignorance of each other, were brought together through Bowley's pioneering work to use random sampling in survey work, particularly in two major studies of poverty (Bowley and Burnett-Hurst 1915; Bowley and Hogg 1925). He first drew attention to the possibilities of what he called 'the representative method' in his presidential address to Section F of the British Association in 1906 (Bowley 1906; Maunder 1972:19, 22–4). In *The Measurement of Social Phenomena* (1915), he was ahead of his time in suggesting the need for standard definitions of variables such as income, poverty and household. He carried out other work on index numbers and national income accounting, contributing to improved measurement in economics. Bowley's work brought the social survey into the university, in the sense that he was an academic researcher. He also brought statistical ideas of random sampling to bear upon survey practice, though it took a long time for these ideas to germinate in Britain and they were first taken up by government statisticians and market researchers in the United States in the 1930's. Survey sampling was not adopted widely in Britain until after World War Two (Moser and Kalton 1971:7–20; Teer and Spence 1973:12–17; Marsh

1982:33–6; chapter 6 below). Bowley's influence upon the history of social survey research requires fuller treatment than is possible here. His work on sampling provides an instructive case-study in the factors facilitating and hindering cross-fertilisation between academic disciplines and between academic and non-academic survey research (cf. Stephan 1948; Hansen and Madow 1976; Duncan and Shelton 1978:32–73; Kruskal and Mosteller 1980; O'Muircheartaigh and Wong 1981). A forthcoming history of American survey research by Jean Converse will also throw important light on the extent of Bowley's influence.

Social inquiry between the wars continued to be dominated by amateurs who lacked university posts or did not desire them. The most notable influence at this period from this third strand was undoubtedly Patrick Geddes, a mercurial figure who was trained as a biologist and had taught for a time at Edinburgh University in the late nineteenth century. Geddes's ideas spanned many subjects including biology, architecture and sociology (Boardman 1978; Kitchen 1975). He and his associate Victor Branford were instrumental in founding the Sociological Society of London in 1903. Lord Bryce was its first president, Branford secretary and Martin White treasurer. The council included Geddes, H.G. Wells, J.A. Hobson, Graham Wallas, H.J. MacKinder (who had recently become Director of L.S.E.), L.T. Hobhouse and E.A. Westermarck. The Society established *The Sociological Review*, initially edited by Hobhouse. For a brief period it appeared that the subject might be successfully institutionalised, because the Society brought together Geddes's school of civic sociology, eugenicists, ethical social work teachers represented by E.J. Urwick, and comparative and philosophically-oriented sociologists (Halliday 1968). It did not endure. The eugenicists and social work teachers left within a few years, and coolness between Geddes and Hobhouse on intellectual matters, sharpened by competition for the Martin White chair in sociology at L.S.E., led to Hobhouse's withdrawal after 1911. The Society and the *Review* became a vehicle for Geddes's ideas on cities and civics, with the peculiar connotations that did a good deal to give sociology a bad name in Britain between the wars. The most important influence upon Geddes was Le Play and his theory that the environment and mode of livelihood of an area shape its social characteristics (Silver 1982). The trilogy of place/work/folk was the centrepiece of Geddes's sociological ideas, within an overall organic and evolutionary intellectual framework (Robson 1981). His most influential works were *Cities in Evolution* (1915) and *Civics as Applied Sociology* (1905). Geddes became an advocate of the community self-survey as a means of studying family and community in their ecological setting. The work was to be done locally by volunteers (not by trained workers from universities) and to be publicised in the local town hall. In

Branford's words the aim of the survey was to 'make us see Eutopia, and, seeing it, to create it' (Branford 1912). The conception of applied social science was both naive and messianic by comparison with that being developed at the same period in, for example, psychology (cf. Sutherland and Sharp 1980).

The specific contribution of Geddes to urban sociology was of doubtful value (Glass 1955). His negative impact upon the advancement of sociology was greater, however, because *The Sociological Review* was the only British journal in the subject before 1950. Geddes was a skilful writer and publicist, and for a time he had Martin White's financial backing. By appropriating the word 'sociology', he increased the suspicion of it among the more conventionally-minded. Moreover, Geddes – by the later period of his life – felt antipathetic to universities, perhaps because of the number of chairs for which he had been rejected. He and Branford were leading figures in the Sociological Society before their deaths in 1932 and 1930 respectively. They created after 1920 in Le Play House a centre for their various activities. After 1930, Le Play House and the Sociological Society merged to form the Institute of Sociology, which published a number of notable monographs during the 1930's and *The Sociological Review* from 1930 to 1952, containing much more real sociology than hitherto. Geddes's influence upon British thought and practice has been greatest in town planning, where his ideas were taken up with considerable seriousness by Patrick Abercrombie and others. Lewis Mumford worked with Geddes for a time and was considerably influenced by him (Mumford 1982:252–84).

Another kind of amateurism was represented by Mass-Observation, discussed by Angus Calder in chapter 7. As with Geddes, the original inspiration seems to have been drawn from biology, but of a rather different kind. Tom Harrisson was a keen ornithologist, and the movement was a kind of social bird-watching, observing externals without an attempt to elicit the meanings attached to action. In *The Pub and the People*, the authors professed to have been influenced in part by the Chicago School of Sociology, but there was little trace of this in their work. For the historian, the Mass-Observation studies may provide interesting contemporary evidence. As social research, the methods used were unsystematic, relied too greatly on externals, and suffered from the instigators' conception of what they were doing as a form of art. There were frequent clashes with academic anthropologists and sociologists, who were generally unsympathetic to the exaggerated claims that Harrisson and Charles Madge made (Stanley 1981). After the war Mass-Observation petered out, being transmuted into a minor market research organisation.

Mass-Observation was perhaps also a small example of the negative influence of Oxford and Cambridge on the development of sociology, discussed by Edward Shils in chapter 10. The originators lacked any training in social science, but were educated gentlemen who thought they could turn their hand to social inquiry. Class perceptions and class distance are evident throughout Mass-Observation work, particularly the Bolton studies. The ethos of undergraduate education at the ancient universities could foster the idea that social observation was a skill that did not require any formal training. In fact, the best amateur social observers of the period were individuals who came from slightly odd backgrounds in different parts of the social spectrum and based their accounts upon first-hand acquaintance with the social worlds studied. In different ways George Orwell in *Down and Out in Paris and London* (1933) and *The Road to Wigan Pier* (1937) (cf. Crick 1980) and Mark Benney in *Charity Main; a coalfield chronicle* (1946) provided penetrating social observation superior to anything being done at the time by sociologists (Benney himself later moved into sociology, directing a voting study in London and collaborating with David Riesman in Chicago (cf. Benney 1966)).

The fourth, fifth and sixth strands were firmly located in universities, though at some distance from each other. Eugenicists had adhered briefly to the Sociological Society after 1903. The eugenics movement, though not university based, had powerful support through the work of the statisticians Galton, Pearson and Fisher, particularly at University College, London. The National Eugenic Laboratory there, with its journal *Biometrika*, became the centre for the statistical study of genetic biology. This was important for social investigation because of its impact upon demography. The Department of Social Biology at L.S.E. under Lancelot Hogben during the 1930's had similar antecedents, and stemmed from concern with a similar set of problems. Hogben's work is discussed below. The studies of social mobility and social selection of the 1950's, as well as the flowering of demographic research after 1945, may be traced back to this tradition.

Quite distinct is the fifth strand, academic social anthropology. This is not the place for a thumbnail sketch of British anthropology (cf. Kuper 1983), but several points are significant for the story of British sociology. Anthropology in general has a longer academic pedigree than most social sciences in Britain, in part because of its association with physical anthropology and human biology. Even social anthropology, going back to Tylor and Frazer, had a longer history than sociology and, more important, a stronger foothold in the university. In contrast to sociology, anthropology gradually became established in the ancient universities, and did not have to battle so hard for recognition. This in turn led to the recruitment of anthropologists from higher status and less marginal backgrounds to those of the sociologists described by Halsey in chapter 9. More integrated into the national elite and closer to its central value system, anthropologists and their subject were more accepted than sociology. Not for nothing is there a *Royal* Anthropological Institute but a *British* Sociological Association.

These social and institutional characteristics were allied to two intellectual tendencies. One was the thoroughgoing commitment to first-hand observation in simple societies. From 1898–9, when Haddon in Cambridge organised the expedition to the Torres Straits whose members included Rivers, Seligman and Myers, serious empirical investigation began to be a necessary *rite de passage* for becoming a social anthropologist. Radcliffe-Brown studied the Andaman Islanders in 1906–8. Fieldwork proper, rather than reliance on informants and colonial administrators, began with Malinowski in the Trobriand Islands in 1914–18. This commitment to research in the field has never been matched by a comparable requirement among British sociologists.

The second tendency, which only became apparent between the wars, was the alliance of first-hand inquiry with a commitment to rigorous general theory. Classical functionalism is no longer fashionable, but what characterises the work of Malinowski and Radcliffe-Brown and their students was a determination to set their findings in a more general framework, and one with considerable sociological content. There were sharp differences between Malinowski and Radcliffe-Brown, but they agreed on the importance of general theory. Radcliffe-Brown, of course, was considerably influenced by Durkheim, treating French sociology more seriously than his (few) British sociological colleagues were wont to do. It is noteworthy that when John Rex published *Key Problems in Sociological Theory* in 1961, an influential text on general theory, Hobhouse and Ginsberg do not appear but Malinowski and Radcliffe-Brown are discussed at length.

Social anthropology thus to some extent took the place of sociology, but transposing it to the colonial sphere. Paradoxically, social scientists flowed overseas while neglecting their home territory. When Mark Benney went to the north-east of England in 1944 to work in the mining industry, he found 'a tribe of Englishmen so distinctive in their way of life that, had they been situated on a remote island in the South Seas, they would have been the subject of a dozen ethnographic monographs' (Benney 1966:155). No British social scientist had hitherto studied them. Frazer in 1906 had defined social anthropology as a brand of sociology that dealt with primitive peoples, and at L.S.E. E.A. Westermarck held a chair in sociology though his main work was anthropological (Malinowski was one of his students). The tendency of anthropology to colonise sociology persisted well into the latter part of the century, even to the extent of appointing a social anthropologist, John Barnes, as the first Professor of Sociology in Cambridge in 1969. The earlier academic establishment and institutionalisation of anthropology, together with the commitment to empirical research, was also decisive in obtaining grant aid at a much earlier date than sociology. The creation of the International African Institute with Rockefeller funding in 1931 led to the provision of graduate studentships abroad for the academic leaders of the next generation. This was followed by the creation of research centres, notably at Makerere in Uganda and on the Northern Rhodesia Copperbelt, which after the war were supported by the Colonial Social Science Research Council. If a true parallel is sought in Britain to the Chicago School, it is arguably the group of anthropologists which Max Gluckman formed at the Rhodes-Livingstone Institute on the Copperbelt, later transposed to Manchester (Brown 1979).

By comparison to the steady maturation of anthropology up to 1945, the history of academic sociology (the sixth strand) is that of a sickly infant. The strength of idealism which was such a marked trait at an earlier period (cf. Collini 1978) persisted. The narrow base which L.S.E. provided meant that everything depended on the incumbent of the chair of sociology established there in 1907. L.T. Hobhouse was a more suitable choice than Patrick Geddes would have been, but he was not a scholar of the stature of Herbert Spencer, Durkheim, Weber or Robert Park. Hobhouse's background, as Collini (1979) has shown, lay in philosophical idealism and radical journalism. His contribution to sociology lay in an evolutionism which saw moral institutions as of central concern; a weak historical functionalism; and a belief that social development was shaped by the growing rationality and self-consciousness of mankind (MacRae 1972:50). He also collaborated with Wheeler and Ginsberg in a major comparative, quantitative institutional study that was a rare example of its kind (Hobhouse, Wheeler and Ginsberg 1915).

The student of early university 'sociology' must wrestle with the question of what, at this period, the term meant. Collini (1978, 1979) implies that it was not what academic sociologists nowadays mean by it, and was none the worse for that. There is a real question, however, about the extent to which Hobhouse's concerns were truly sociological. Donald MacRae, for example, has suggested that 'his vision of rational moral harmony in society while very amiable is very unconvincing and not sociology nor scholarship' (1972:51). A review of Hobhouse's major sociological work, *Social Development* (1924), by the dean of Chicago sociology, Albion Small, in 1924, struck him

> very much as a book on railroading, by the foremost engineer of England, would affect American railroad men, if it turned out to be chiefly an abstract treatise on the relations of transportation to human welfare in general, with such allusions as it contained to railroads in the concrete in terms of Charing Cross and Euston stations as we knew them forty years ago. . . . It does not yet appear that the center of Professor Hobhouse's

interest is in sociology rather than in general philosophy (Small 1924:218, 219).

Hobhouse's lack of influence has also been attributed to the marginal position of L.S.E. in the British academic firmament before his retirement in 1929 (Shils 1980:180–2).

What is clear is that today Hobhouse is almost entirely forgotten as a sociologist, and to some extent this reflects his lack of impact at the time (cf. Hawthorn 1976:111). Talcott Parsons, who studied for a year at the L.S.E. in the 1920's *en route* for Heidelberg and sociology, attended Hobhouse's seminars and learnt little from him (Shils 1980:182, n. 7). Parsons was introduced to Weber by the historian R.H. Tawney and to Durkheim by Malinowski (MacRae 1972:47). Hobhouse's sole protégé of distinction was Morris Ginsberg, who succeeded him to the chair of sociology in 1930, and carried on the philosophical and anti-empiricist tradition of the department (Hawthorn 1976:167–8). Ginsberg's view of sociology was in tune with that of Hobhouse, if more vigorous and more aware of contemporary European developments (Fletcher 1974:6–8). His leadership was no more dynamic than that of Hobhouse, for though an effective teacher, he was of a very shy and retiring disposition. Ginsberg was for a quarter of a century, from 1930 to 1954, the *doyen* of British sociologists and a respected figure (cf. Fletcher 1974). His residual influence appears to have been relatively slight, certainly compared to someone like Malinowski, though this would be disputed (MacRae 1972:51–3).

Academic sociology before 1945 – to all intents and purposes L.S.E. sociology – was thus cast in a very particular mould. The lack of impact of Hobhouse and of Ginsberg upon empirical social inquiry between the wars no doubt partially accounted for its relative impoverishment, but it reflected also an impoverishment in the conception of sociology held by the holders of the L.S.E. chairs.

One way of approaching the recent history of empirical social research in Britain is to pose the question: why, given the strong nineteenth-century tradition, did it take until the second half of the century for empirical inquiry to be securely established? What obstacles were there to institutionalisation? Why until 1945 did academic sociology play such a comparatively minor part? These were questions close to Philip Abrams's interests, and some hints at answers are given by him in chapter 11. Three particular aspects deserve closer attention, although they do not provide an exhaustive answer to the problem. The story of empirical inquiry at L.S.E. between the wars, the fate of sociology at Cambridge, and the ways in which large-scale survey research was established in Britain all provide some clues.

Between the two world wars the empirical study of society flourished in Britain, but in relatively disconnected ways which did not establish a solid base. The social survey tradition, as Raymond Kent shows in chapter 3, continued to flourish. Social anthropology made notable advances. The scientific study of population became fairly firmly established. Sociology, however, retained a rather uncertain position, pulled between philosophy, anthropology, fact-gathering and amateur efforts like Mass-Observation. At the end of the First World War the London School of Economics and Political Science, though it had a number of distinguished staff, was a small and relatively obscure part of London University. Under the Directorship of William Beveridge from 1919 to 1937, it grew in strength and reputation. During the period the number of graduate students increased ninefold, many new buildings were erected, the library was expanded and rehoused, new chairs were created in several subjects and modest research funds were available to support the research of staff. This was due not only to the leadership of Beveridge (cf. Harris 1977:263–83) but to his skill in securing outside philanthropic funding, notably from the Laura Spelman Rockefeller Memorial and later from the Rockefeller Foundation (Bulmer and Bulmer 1981). Yet at this period, despite the expansion, sociology at the School hardly flourished. The staff originally consisted of the two Martin White Professors appointed in 1907, Hobhouse and E.A. Westermarck; the latter's university chair was part-time, and he was a comparative ethnologist with more than a foot in anthropology. Ginsberg joined the L.S.E. staff in 1922, becoming reader in 1924. When he succeeded Hobhouse in 1930, the department consisted of a professor (Ginsberg), a reader (T.H. Marshall) and an assistant. In 1939 there was still only a professor, a reader and two lecturers. Only after World War Two did sociology teaching grow toward its present size; in 1946 there were two professors (Ginsberg and Marshall), two readers (D.V. Glass (in demography) and Edward Shils) and five other teachers; by 1954, three professors and nine other teachers (Caine 1974:30–1). Between the wars, therefore, the extent to which L.S.E. sociology nurtured empirical research depended upon the orientation of Hobhouse and Ginsberg in particular, who did not take a primary interest in the empirical side of sociology.

This is not to say, however, that there were no significant developments at the School. There were, and their very diversity and lack of coherence in part explains the slow development of British empirical research. Some of the incoherence was intellectual, some institutional. At this period the Webbs, and Sidney Webb in particular, still took a very active interest in the affairs of the School. Beveridge was their choice as Director. The Webbs were fond of the word 'sociology' and often referred to themselves as sociologists. Indeed, though their major researches were in the past, they published in 1932 a text *Methods of Social Study* which is still worth reading as an account of their way of working and their thoroughgoing inductivism. This was a very different conception of social inquiry to that of Hobhouse. Donald MacRae has indeed claimed that Hobhouse saved the School and to some extent British sociology from such 'barren philistinism . . . [the Webbs] were radical empiricists of a kind valuable indeed to society and social policy, but absolutely divorced from the central effort of sociology. Their world was one of hard, accurately ascertained, discrete facts' (1972:50).

William Beveridge shared their empirical orientation, having attached himself in his youth to the empirical tradition of social science. When he came to L.S.E. he was convinced that the social sciences were too theoretical, deductive and metaphysical and the way ahead lay in empirical studies of social phenomena. He combined the Webbs's inductivism with a belief in the possibility of framing general social laws, an aim to which his own unfinished research on the history of prices was devoted. As Director, he sought and obtained a substantial grant from the Memorial in New York to develop the study of 'the natural basis of the social sciences'. The resulting grant in 1927 was divided between International Studies, Modern Social Conditions, Social Biology and Anthropology. Hobhouse protested that he had not been consulted, but his was a lone voice (Harris 1977:284–90). Three of the areas developed were of major significance for social inquiry.

The grant for 'modern social conditions' was used to fund the Second Survey of London Life and Labour, envisaged as a replication of Booth's work of forty years before (Smith 1930–5). Sir Hubert Llewellyn Smith, retired Permanent Secretary of the Ministry of Labour, who had participated as a young man in Booth's research and whom Beveridge had worked for earlier in his career, was appointed as director of the survey. Though based at L.S.E., the survey seems to have been largely independent of the academic departments, with the exception of a substantial contribution from A.L. Bowley as Professor of Statistics. In conception the work was a massive inductive catalogue of social conditions in the capital, in many cases following Booth's methods far too closely, though Bowley did introduce random sampling into the design of his part of the project, which also involved 12,000 household interviews. The central problem which the survey tackled was, if not trivial, not of burning consequence to academic social science: 'What has been the change [since Booth] in the numerical relation of poverty to well-being?' (Smith 1930–5:Vol. 1:55). Methodologically, the innovations of Bowley had already been proved elsewhere. The *New Survey of London Life and Labour* was a dramatic proof of the proposition that the cost of social research is in no way related to its scholarly value. The study is nowadays largely forgotten, and left little residue.

The same was not true of Beveridge's innovations in the field of Social Biology, though these were attended at the time by much more controversy. They did however have some lasting impact. By social biology Beveridge meant 'genetics, population, vital statistics, heredity, eugenics and dysgenics' (Harris 1977:287). The University created a chair in the subject, and in 1929 Lancelot Hogben, Professor of Zoology at Cape Town, was appointed. With a distinguished group of researchers, including his demographer wife, Enid Charles, R.R. Kuczynski, Pearl Moshinsky, J.L. Gray, and the young D.V. Glass, the team produced monographs on population control, human reproduction, heredity and statistical method. *Political Arithmetic*, edited by Hogben (1938), presented their main demographic findings on fertility and family structure and the results of their investigations into the relationship between ability, parents' occupation and educational opportunity. 'The study of population', Hogben stated, 'is the only branch of social research with its own logical technique for the detection and co-ordination of *factual* data' (1938:13).

If Hogben had contented himself with such solid work, social biology might have endured at the School. His relations with colleagues were marred, however, by his complaints of inadequate resources for research, allegations by others that social biology received favourable treatment from the Director, and in particular by intellectual fireworks. The controversy which Hogben was capable of engendering is hinted at in references to Malthus as the 'phlogistonist of demography' (1938:29) and the suggestion that the substantial scholarship and empirical commonsense of the Webbs should have produced a more healthy attitude to social research in the university. In the three-way controversies at L.S.E. in the early 1930's between scientific empiricism (represented by Beveridge), deductive theory (represented by Hayek and Robbins), and Marxist political theory (represented by Laski), Hogben aligned himself with Beveridge as a critic both of partisan commitment and of deductive theorising (Hogben 1938:29, 46; 1942). Hogben's fierce criticisms alienated him from most of his colleagues outside his department, and when the recession cut his research grants, he resigned at the end of 1936. He was not replaced, and to Beveridge's chagrin social biology disappeared from the School's curriculum. Some of this was undoubtedly due to Hogben's personality. He was described as 'one of the most controversial figures in scientific and academic life . . . who did not so much conduct research as explode firecrackers' (*The Times* Obituary, 23 August 1975). The particular conception of empirical inquiry modelled on natural science also contributed. Hogben inveighed against the secular Platonism of the universities, wedded to the 'pernicious belief in the all-sufficiency of formal reasoning unchecked by search for new information' and the 'ostentatious insistence upon sheer uselessness' (1942: 126).

> The plain truth is that the academic value of social research in our universities is largely rated on a futility scale. A social inquiry which leads to the conclusion that something has to be done or might be done is said to the 'tendentious' – the Idol of Purity ensures 'innocuous aimlessness' when social inquiry makes contact with the real world (1938:29).

Beveridge on retiring from L.S.E. expressed equally definite views:

> I challenge a tradition of a hundred years of political economy, in which facts have been treated, not as controls of theory, but as illustrations . . . If, in the Social Sciences, we cannot yet run or fly, we ought to be content to walk, or to creep on all fours as infants. If we are not qualified to advance beyond the primitive stage of collection and classification of facts, we had better stay at that stage. For . . . theorising not based on facts and not controlled by facts assuredly does lead nowhere (1937:467–8).

Such views did not commend themselves to scholars of the cast of mind of Ginsberg, Laski or Robbins. Social Biology died with the departure of Hogben and Beveridge. Hogben himself did not continue with social and demographic research, but he had trained a group of younger demographers who carried on the tradition of social inquiry which he began. He thus left an intellectual legacy for empirical social science, given institutional form in 1938 in the Population Investigation Committee (Blacker 1950) which has since had a permanent existence at the School and a voice through its renowned journal *Population Studies*. This complemented government demographic work in the General Register Office. The P.I.C.'s first secretary was D.V. Glass. Its foundation was also due to the fact that Beveridge's successor, Sir Alexander Carr-Saunders, was a student of population, who gave the project an impetus that might otherwise have been lacking. This demographic tradition had its first flowering after World War Two, in the impressive research mounted by social scientists from this background for the Royal Commission on Population, 1944–8 (Royal Commission on Population 1949 and its Research Reports 1949–54, especially Glass and Grebenik 1954) of which Carr-Saunders was a member. The more specifically sociological legacy of Hogben may be traced through David Glass (who became Professor of Sociology in 1948 and Martin White Professor in 1961) and the studies of social mobility and social selection which he, Halsey, Floud and others carried out in the 1950's. Sociology at L.S.E. then, particularly its empirical variety, owed as much to problems derived from eugenics and social biology as it did to the legacy of Hobhouse and Ginsberg.

Several conditions were necessary for the successful establishment at this period of a coherent tradition of social research. They included the intellectual coherence provided by an academic discipline, a commitment to first-hand inquiry, funds to support such inquiry either by graduate students or research assistants, and the training of younger people to carry on the tradition. In sociology under Hobhouse and Ginsberg only the first condition was satisfied; they were not committed to empirical research, and had few graduate students. The *New Survey of London Life and Labour* satisfied only the second and third criteria; it lacked an intellectual rationale and was not a training ground for younger scholars. Social biology satisfied the second, third, and fourth criteria, but its academic location was contingent upon the mercurial Hogben. The younger scholars he trained subsequently gravitated into demography or sociology. Only in anthropology under Malinowski were all four conditions fully satisfied. Between the wars, social anthropology at L.S.E. was the most successful example of organised empirical social research.

Anthropology at L.S.E. was established by C.G. Seligman, who began teaching in 1910 and was appointed to the (part-time) chair in Ethnology in 1913, which he held until retirement in 1934. The subject is particularly associated with the name of Bronislaw Malinowski, who was a research student from 1910, and who became reader in anthropology in 1924. Malinowski suggested the title '*social* anthropology' for his post, and three years later, with funds from Beveridge's Rockefeller research programme, became the first Professor of Anthropology in the university (Firth 1957:1–8; L.S.E. Department of Anthropology 1981). Malinowski's own research in the Trobriands was decisive in establishing first-hand field research as the mode of inquiry used by social anthropologists (cf. Kuper 1983:1–19). At L.S.E., Malinowski successfully built up a 'school' around him. Empirical research was firmly located within the academic discipline of anthropology. It possessed an adumbrated general methodological framework and an outline general theory, that of functionalism in its Malinowskian form (Rex 1961:ch. 3). This differentiated the work of his students from that of others discussed so far, whose orientation was either rationalist (like Hobhouse) or inductivist (which was true even of Hogben and his group). Theory and research were woven together in a way not achieved in sociology, social biology or social investigation at the time. Malinowski's commitment to empirical research was a strong one. It was assumed that graduate students would go out to do fieldwork in small-scale, primitive, societies. Through the Rockefeller-supported International African Institute, funding was provided for graduate work which combined field research with close attention to theoretical problems. And Malinowski, who was a brilliant teacher, created a group of students many of whom became leading figures in the subject subsequently, including Ashley Montagu, Meyer Fortes, E.R. Leach and S.F. Nadel. Raymond Firth and Audrey Richards were closely associated with his work. Malinowski's commitment and impact as a teacher have been acknowledged by his students (cf. Firth 1957:7–11), a characteristic which distinguished him from the other L.S.E. practitioners of sociology and social research with the possible exception of Hogben. Malinowski, too, because of his egocentricity and the fervour he expected of his students, aroused criticism by fellow-anthropologists (cf. Kuper 1983:22–4) but his position at the School was a secure one, and his commitment to empirical research found favour with Beveridge. The teachers of anthropology numbered no more than the sociologists during the 1920's and 1930's, but his efforts showed how much could be done to foster fruitful and theoretically-informed empirical work. This did not feed directly into social research at home (though Malinowski offered friendly advice to Mass-Observation) but it was important indirectly in establishing the relative standing of sociology and anthropology.

The position in all this of teachers of sociology should not be forgotten. Apart from the problem of leadership, the subject was not a particularly highly-regarded one; R.H. Tawney was one of its few non-sociological supporters among the professoriate. Ginsberg, if by no means hostile to empirical research, equally did little to encourage it. In one of his gloomier moments about the state of sociology, he once told Maurice Freedman that he wished he had remained a philosopher (Freedman 1974:270). Two developments in the 1930's, one minor and one major, were noteworthy. Karl Mannheim left Germany in 1933 and came to the School, where he lectured in sociology for ten years, before moving to a chair at the Institute of Education. Intellectually the move to Britain marked a caesura in his work; he turned increasingly to his interests in social planning and applied sociology, and to 'preaching at large the gospel of salvation through sociology' (Floud 1979:281), which left little mark except the Routledge *International Library of Sociology and Social Reconstruction*. Institutionally, he found himself teaching a subject with few postgraduate students, with few facilities for or encouragement of research, no organ of publication, and almost no employment opportunities for those trained in the subject (Shils 1980:189).

More important was T.H. Marshall. Appointed from a Cambridge background in economic history as Assistant Lecturer in Social Science in 1925, he became Reader in Sociology in 1930. He was an important stabilising influence through the next decade; teaching

> with irenic clarity and committed concern. He brought knowledge of wider cultural worlds to students of that age. He did much to heal the break be-

> tween Ginsberg and Mannheim . . . Modern sociology in Britain had its birth through Marshall and Ginsberg in the 1930's. They contributed both to the civility of the subject as well as to its rigour (MacRae 1982:iv).

In 1938 he edited for the Institute of Sociology an interdisciplinary symposium on *Class Conflict and Social Stratification* whose contributors included R.G.D. Allen, Harry Campion, Lionel Robbins, Maurice Dobb and H.A. Mess. Marshall's period of greatest influence was after 1945, partly through his famous inaugural lecture as Professor of Sociology in 1945, 'Sociology at the Crossroads' (Marshall 1977:3–25) and partly through postgraduate supervision. Ralf Dahrendorf was one of his students. Marshall succeeded Ginsberg briefly as Martin White Professor, from 1954 to 1956, before ending his career as head of social science at UNESCO (cf. Marshall 1973; Halsey 1984).

Marshall was important too in providing a bridge between sociology and social policy, to which he devoted increasing attention in later years. From 1945 to 1950, prior to Richard Titmuss's appointment as Professor of Social Administration, he was in charge of the teaching of that subject. The Department of Social Science had been founded in 1912 to teach social work, and included among its early staff C.R. Attlee prior to World War One and Marshall himself between 1925 and 1930 (cf. Russell 1981:7–16). It had an orientation distinct from sociology, including a distrust of philosophical systems. E.J. Urwick, the first head, was sharply critical of Hobhouse and maintained that 'the claim of the general sociologist is invalid at every point' (Abrams 1981b:6). Research in social policy and administration did not develop until after World War Two, under the influence of Marshall and particularly of Richard Titmuss. The subject was less concerned with the philosophical basis of social science and more committed to first-hand investigation than has British academic sociology, even if it lacks theoretical muscle (cf. Pinker 1971). It is also of interest that it was from this department and from Titmuss that Michael Young received encouragement when he embarked upon his venture in London community studies (chapter 8).

The groundwork for the flowering of L.S.E. sociology after 1945 was thus laid principally by Marshall and Glass. Another important influence was Edward Shils, bringing news of American developments and inspiring the growing number of students 'with a belief in their endeavours and the desirability of sustained empirical inquiry . . . [T]o all his students sociology became not only a discipline, but a commitment, and from him many learned a quirky tolerance and a resigned moralism' (MacRae 1972:53). Halsey's account is perhaps a retrospective view through slightly rose-tinted spectacles. All who participated, however, attest to the post-war renaissance of L.S.E. sociology which he describes, and there can be no doubt of its formative influence upon the discipline.

This influence was all the stronger because of the continuing indifference of Oxford and Cambridge to the study of the subject. The fate of sociology at the ancient universities is important both in its own right and in any memorial to Philip Abrams, who later played such an important role in its introduction to Cambridge. Pessimistically surveying the condition of sociology in England in the late 1920's, the American sociologist Harry Elmer Barnes (1927:45–6) singled out the ideology of the ancient universities as a particular cause of the backwardness of the discipline. A decade later, Lancelot Hogben was inveighing against the influence of humanist teaching in the older universities. 'A course in Greats (ancient or modern) accompanied by practical exploits in the Union debating society provide the chief method of preparing students for research and teaching in economics and sociology. The results might be anticipated . . .' (Hogben 1942:126).

Victorian Cambridge had been guided in its attitude to sociology by Henry Sidgwick. In 1885, he told the British Association that sociology was 'in a very rudimentary condition' and that the task of establishing a genuinely scientific evolutionary sociology must take place at some other university (Sidgwick 1904:198, 257). The university was not without traces of sociology – Sir Henry Maine began and ended his career there, Maitland wrote a sociologically-informed history of English law, Haddon and Rivers mounted anthropological expeditions – but institutionally sociology remained an unacceptable subject. This was apparent in 1925, when the Laura Spelman Rockefeller Memorial, through its British correspondent J.R.M. Butler of Trinity, offered to endow chairs at Cambridge in Political Science and in Sociology (Bulmer 1981). After due deliberation the endowment of the Chair in Political Science was accepted, because it consolidated existing teaching, particularly in the History Faculty (Collini 1983:339–77). The political philosopher Ernest Barker was appointed in 1927, which did not please the Memorial's Director Beardsley Ruml, who had hoped for a move to establish empirical political science, and get away from the 'formal, deductive, ex-cathedra, presentation of the subject'. The offer of a Chair in Sociology was treated more equivocally. In his reply to the Memorial, both the Vice-Chancellor and the accompanying Memorandum were less enthusiastic. The Memorandum simply stated:

> At present the University does not possess any Professorship, Readership, or Lectureship in Sociology.
>
> As long ago as 1899 Professor Henry Sidgwick, in a statement of the needs of the University in his department, concluded with the words:
>
> 'I have said nothing of Anthropology, Ethnology, or Sociology, partly

> because they are not at present included in any branch of our curriculum, partly because their boundaries, relations and methods are still rather indeterminate. But the scientific study of social man, however defined and denominated, is of growing importance; and I expect that the absence of any representation of it in our staff of Professors and Readers will before long be regarded as a serious and palpable deficiency.'
>
> Since this statement was made a Readership has been established in Ethnology; courses of lectures are also given at present in Social Anthropology and in Social Psychology; but there is still no provision for dealing with the field of Sociology as a whole. Nor is it an examination-subject in any Tripos; although the proposals of the Moral Science Board contemplate its inclusion in that Tripos. The need for its representation on the teaching staff of the University has certainly not become less since 1899 (quoted in Bulmer 1981:158).

As a reply to an informal offer to endow a chair in the subject, this amounted to a polite negative. In his letter, the Vice-Chancellor was compelled to face the realities of the situation within the University:

> The Council think that if the Memorial were to make the munificent offer of a professorship of Sociology, its place in the studies and examinations of the University would be assured and that the provision of any additional teaching required would be forthcoming . . . The Council is necessarily in a difficult position in writing on the subject. Under the constitution of the University the Council has power of initiative only, while decisions rest with the Senate, comprising the whole body of teachers, some hundreds in all (quoted in Bulmer 1981:158).

The implication was clear that Senate was not thought likely to be willing to countenance the establishment of a chair in the subject.

In the event, the Memorial did not immediately offer to endow a chair. Ruml recognised that 'one of the most conservative of universities', as he put it, was not particularly encouraging or definite in its plans for sociology and so the matter lapsed. The specific reasons for the missed opportunity are fairly clear. Sociology was not taught in any Tripos, and did not enjoy high esteem in the academic community. Its general intellectual standing (as Butler had reported to Ruml in 1923) was doubtful, being particularly harmed by identification with extra-academic figures such as Geddes and Branford, with the activities of the Sociological Society, and with the awful variety of material published in *The Sociological Review* before 1930. Though it had a respectable academic foothold at L.S.E., British sociology in the 1920's (to the extent that it existed) was a weak and divided subject with little appeal to the ancient universities. This, of course, was precisely the situation which Beardsley Ruml, through his strategy for the development of the basic social sciences, was trying to remedy and surmount. Cambridge in the 1920's, however, was not responsive to the Memorial's initiative.

Some of the more general reasons for resistance to sociology at the ancient universities are discussed in chapter 10 by Edward Shils, who had the opportunity through teaching at Cambridge in the 1950's and 1960's to observe the situation at first hand. The power of the antipathy to sociology is shown by the fact that it was nearly half a century after the Memorial's offer before a chair in the subject was established. Moves were made in that direction earlier, but nothing came of them or they tended to be counter-productive. During the 1930's a committee was established to look into the possibility of expanding the teaching of sociology, without result. After the Clapham Report in 1946, the government injected more resources to universities for social science. As a result, around 1948 the University of Cambridge was provided, without asking, with additional funds for this purpose. This seems to have been interpreted as, among other things, money to establish a Chair of Sociology, but either the university failed to find a suitable person, or it could not agree upon the type of person it wanted, for no appointment was made. According to one account T.H. Marshall was informally offered the chair and declined it. Another version has it that his election to the chair was blocked by the economists as part of faculty politics (Johnson 1978:154–5). Gregory Bateson was also apparently approached unsuccessfully.

The money was, however, diverted into a scheme for distinguished Visiting Professors in Social Theory, which was instituted early in the 1950's. The first of these was Talcott Parsons, from Harvard, in 1953–4. While in Cambridge, he delivered by invitation the Marshall lectures, in which he returned to economic theory (which he had lost touch with since the 1930's) and gave what later appeared as the first three chapters of *Economy and Society* (1956). Parsons argued for the continuity of economic theory and social theory in general, maintaining that the former was but a special case of the latter. Attended mainly by economists, the lectures were generally considered a failure (cf. Johnson 1978:155) His approach was too remote from the interests of economists, and only a few anthropologists were more sympathetic (Smelser 1981:145–6). He was followed by the social anthropologist Lloyd Warner from Chicago in 1954–5, and George Homans, also from Harvard, in 1955–6. Homans recounted how his Cambridge friends said to him: 'You used to be a historian. What did you get into *that* [sociology] for?' He observed wryly that Cambridge recognised the legitimacy of social history, social anthropology and ethnology ('What country has more bird-watchers per square mile?') but balked at admitting sociology to the academic Pantheon (Homans 1956: 232–33).

The visiting professors did not lead to the immediate introduction of the subject. Cynics suggested that Parsons had put the cause back ten years, and in a later article Homans pointed out that the reading of the opponents and proponents of the subject in Cambridge was too limited. It extended to figures like Parsons and David Riesman, practising formal social theory or literary sociology but did not encompass a really scientific approach (Homans 1959:461). The argument about the merits of the subject continued in the pages of *The Cambridge Review* and *Cambridge Opinion* in the late 1950's, with Peter Laslett and Maurice Cowling arguing the case for and against the inclusion of some sociology in the History Tripos and Robin Marris suggesting it might find a home in Economics and Politics. Jack Goody, however, pointed out that, though Anthropology also had a claim, the most satisfactory solution might be to allow sociology to be taught in its own right, administered by a committee to organise lectures on the model provided by other 'new' subjects such as the History of Science and Meteorology (1959:311–12).

A modest beginning was made through the introduction of two papers into Part II of the Economics Tripos, with some associated appointments. Michael Young held a university lectureship from 1960 to 1963, and remained a fellow of Churchill until 1966. David Lockwood was appointed to a university lectureship in 1961, and Philip Abrams to an assistant lectureship in 1962. Meanwhile W.G. Runciman held a research fellowship at Trinity and John Goldthorpe was appointed a fellow of King's. Sociological perspectives were also opened up by the teaching of industrial sociology by a group in the Engineering Department and by the existence of the Institute of Criminology.

The proponents of sociology, however, aspired to see the subject established in its own right. This possibility was advanced significantly by the report of the Boys-Smith Committee on the Organisation of the Social Sciences which reported at the beginning of 1968, recommending a new Tripos which would include sociology (cf. Hadden 1968). Philip Abrams was actively involved in developments at this period, being co-author of a response to Boys-Smith which emphasised the need to maintain contacts with economists, historians and philosophers, while establishing a separate Part II Tripos in Social and Political Sciences (Abrams *et al.* 1968). Meanwhile the General Board of the Faculties decided to establish a Chair in Sociology, to which the social anthropologist John Barnes was appointed. The Social and Political Sciences Committee came into existence in 1968, and its chairman until he moved to Durham University in 1971 was Philip Abrams. He played an influential part in the moves which culminated early in 1969 in the formal proposal to the Regent House to institute a Part 2 Tripos in Social and Political Sciences, which would include substantial teaching of sociology. This proposal, after considerable public debate, with the issuing of flysheets and exchanges in the correspondence columns of

The Times and *The Guardian*, was narrowly approved. It attracted one of the largest Regent House votes for many years. Though the Tripos was in fact considerably broader than just sociology, partly in order to accommodate the interests of those already teaching social sciences (other than economics and psychology), many of those who voted *non placet* were not opposed to the social sciences as such but to sociology (Barnes 1970). The successful outcome of this campaign owed a good deal to the skill of Philip Abrams in marshalling the forces of those in favour of innovation. The Regent House vote was followed by the filling of three new lectureships (one of them in sociology) and the decision by the General Board to start teaching the new Tripos in October 1969. The first preliminary examinations were sat in 1970 and the first Social and Political Sciences Tripos in 1971. So sociology was to some extent legitimated in the University of Cambridge, against considerable opposition. The Chair in Sociology was established for one tenure only, and when the holder retired in 1982 it simply disappeared. A proposal to re-establish the chair, again for one tenure only, was approved by the General Board in November 1983 (*Cambridge University Reporter*, 7 December 1983, pp. 199–200). It cannot be said that even now Cambridge has fully reconciled itself to the existence of the subject. It was still necessary, in his inaugural lecture, for John Barnes to acknowledge the fact that 'there are many members of the university, junior as well as senior, who do not regard sociology as a proper academic subject' (Barnes 1970:1).

This continuing scepticism has been paralleled at Oxford, where Donald MacRae was briefly a university lecturer from 1949 to 1954, and the first full university lectureship in the subject was established in 1955. Optional papers were introduced in the Philosophy, Politics and Economics degree in 1962, but there is still no honours school and no chair in sociology. There are, however, a number of sociologists holding college appointments and a substantial centre of postgraduate work at Nuffield College. The Department of Social and Administrative Studies, whose professorial head is the sociologist A.H. Halsey, includes one or two sociologists on its staff. The total number of Oxford sociologists is now greater than in Cambridge (Heath and Edmondson 1981). How far the development of sociology and empirical social research has been retarded by their slow acceptance at Oxbridge is difficult to determine. What is certain, as Shils points out, is that it has contributed to the marginality of the subject in Britain, both socially and to some extent intellectually.

The post-war growth of sociological research broke down the isolation from empirical social inquiry which Hobhouse and Ginsberg had maintained. Sociology and social research did not, however, become synonymous. For new developments, particularly the growth of large-scale survey research, took place to a considerable extent outside the universities and apart from sociology. The modern social survey bears only a cousinly resemblance to the inter-war surveys, being characterised by more rigorous standards of research design, sampling, questionnaire construction, fieldwork and coding (cf. Marsh 1982:33–6). The organisation required to conduct it is large and relatively bureaucratic, with an internal division of labour and close adherence to time and resource constraints. Such enterprises do not fit easily into an academic teaching institution organised departmentally. Moreover, one does not find in British universities the equivalent of the large American academic survey research institute such as National Opinion Research Center at Chicago, the Institute of Social Research at Michigan or the Columbia Bureau, with sociologists actively involved in the programmes of each. The Government Social Survey, whose growth is traced by Frank Whitehead in chapter 5, developed almost entirely apart from academic social science. Gerald Hoinville's account of methodological research on surveys, in chapter 6, also shows a surprising lack of academic involvement, apart from a group of statisticians at L.S.E. around Maurice Kendall in the early 1950's. Sociologists are almost totally absent. An American observer in the early 1960's was surprised to find so few sociologists in Britain associated with large-scale survey research, either in teaching or research (Selvin 1965). Mark Abrams, Henry Durant and Louis Moss were students at L.S.E. during the 1930's, but in their subsequent careers in survey research they had no formal academic affiliations.

The reasons for this distance between sociology and survey research are complex, and beyond a simple summary. They have a good deal to do with the philosophical origins of British sociology and some antipathy among sociologists at its leading centre, L.S.E., to large-scale quantitative research. The consequent gap between sociology and statistics has been a wide one, which few have successfully bridged. There are no British equivalents to W.F. Ogburn, Paul Lazarsfeld or Samuel Stouffer, who combined the sociological imagination with considerable statistical or mathematical competence (cf. Bernert 1983). The reasons also have to do with the institutional obstacles to the university establishment of survey research, which have been powerful. The nearest one came to this was Dr W.A. Belson's Survey Research Centre at L.S.E. in the 1960's, which had slight contact with academic departments. The new Social and Community Planning Research–City University Survey Methods Centre, set up by the Social Science Research Council, is more promising, but it is not located at a university with a leading reputation in social science research. How to promote collaboration between survey researchers and academic social scientists is, as the S.S.R.C. Survey Unit found between 1970 and 1976, problematic (cf. M. Abrams 1979. For a more general discussion see McKennell, Bulmer and Bynner, 1982).

The reasons for the growth of independent research institutes are also worth pondering. Peter Willmott's case study in chapter 8 of the Institute of Community Studies shows that while individual academics such as Edward Shils and Richard Titmuss encouraged Michael Young at its inception, institutionally an independent existence, despite its financial problems, was the most satisfactory way of fostering an extensive research programme. One would need to review the history of other bodies such as Political and Economic Planning (now part of Policy Studies Institute) or the Tavistock Institute of Human Relations to what were the common elements, if any, in their histories. It does seem, however, that the more extensive the scale on which empirical social research is conducted, the more likely it is that it will be conducted outside a university environment (Bulmer 1983). Rare British exceptions, such as research lectureships in sociology at Liverpool University, only strengthen this conclusion.

This survey of some aspects of the history of twentieth-century British sociology does not aim to take the story much beyond 1950. (It did so in the case of Cambridge because of Philip Abrams's active involvement there.) In part this is because the period is already partially covered in another collection (Abrams 1981a). In part it is because perspective is more difficult to achieve the nearer one comes to the present. As soon as one approaches the present day, it would be necessary to broaden the canvas and consider in more detail what Halsey hints at, the movement of his generation of young L.S.E. sociologists in the 1950's to staff the growing departments of sociology in provincial universities, such as Liverpool, Birmingham, Leicester, Leeds, Manchester. Later still the development of the subject at Edinburgh, Aberdeen, Durham, Bristol and then Essex, Sussex, Warwick, and elsewhere would need to be charted. The volume of sociological research has increased correspondingly as the teaching has expanded in universities. If one did come nearer to the present, the growth of empirical social research outside sociology, in social administration, industrial relations, criminology, education, medicine and other fields would need to be stressed. The boundaries of social research, and indeed of sociology, are less sharp and clear than they were. A growing interest in theory, crystallising in the formation of a Teacher's Section of the British Sociological Association around 1960, would need to be studied. The increasing radicalisation of sociologists, and the interest in different approaches to the subject, whether Marxist, phenomenological or critical, would need to be considered (cf. Rex 1983). The expansion and contraction of employment opportunities, and the place of sociology in the school curriculum, would require attention. Above all, perhaps, the rapid expansion of the subject in the period between 1964 and the late 1970's would need to be analysed. Sociology in Britain has a long past and a short history. There is a sense in which much of the material in this book is about the prehistory of sociology.

> It is important to remind ourselves just how recent, rapid and extensive the real expansion and establishment of sociology as an academic discipline in this country has been. Many of the complaints made about the turbulence, incoherence, mystification and of course uselessness of the subject lose their force when one remembers that sociology, as a nationally established discipline, is still in its first twenty years (Abrams 1981b:9).

Most large-scale, non-academic, social surveys are conducted to be of direct or indirect use to policy-makers or those seeking to influence the policy-making process. The consumers of research include politicians and political parties, government and the civil service, quangos, local government, commercial firms, pressure groups, voluntary associations and the 'educated public'. For much of its history, those conducting social research in Britain have hoped that their work will in one way or another be 'useful'. It is therefore particularly appropriate to conclude this collection of essays with four dealing with the use of sociology and social research. All four papers were given at the York Symposium, reflecting a continuing impulse to examine the social significance and justification of sociology in the face of public scepticism, not least from government ministers.

Philip Abrams in chapter 11 provides a masterly historical overview of the uses of British sociology, drawn from an unfinished project on the uses of British sociology after 1914. Catherine Marsh in chapter 12 focuses specifically upon the social survey to chart its changing social significance over a century and more. Peter Townsend writes in chapter 13 as a leading representative of the social administration tradition viewed sociologically, which particularly through the influence of Richard Titmuss and his colleagues had a marked influence upon public policy in the 1960's and 1970's (cf. Banting 1979). He emphasises the need for awareness of the radical potential of survey research, and of the ways in which it can be manipulated by government. Both he and Lorraine Barić on social indicators in chapter 14, writing in the climate of cuts in government statistical services, emphasise the need for sociology to provide an independent and critical view of socially 'useful' investigation. Research is conducted in a political context, as Philip Abrams emphasised at the York meeting.

> In the social sciences at least knowledge is *not* power. Sociological knowledge is relevant to policy and is deployed within the arena of politics. But it cannot hope to be either politically neutral or politically authoritative. Its unavoidable and proper form is that of the empirically informed and reasoned argument – an injection of carefully gathered and interpreted

> evidence, settling no political issues, fuelling them rather, but also constantly shifting the process of political debate as a whole towards ground on which mystification and spurious authority can less easily take root. Given what we now know, thanks to the intellectual turmoil of the last twenty years, about the nature of the social, that seems to me to be both a properly scientific task for sociology and its only possible task. The performance of sociology since 1960 has dashed many of the expectations of that period about sociology irrevocably but constructively. It remains to be seen whether the ground-clearing sociologists thus achieved will be recognised by others. It remains, that is to say, for others to lose their illusions about sociology just as sociologists have done – for them, too, to come to see social inquiry and analysis as an argumentative force within society, not authoritatively pre-empting politics but making politics more strenuous, more complicated, more sensitive to uncertainties, more finely informed of subtleties and ambiguities, more burdened with arguments against simplicity, but above all more political not less, more a matter of informed, reasoned and responsible choice within a more inclusive political community. Government longs for certainty; but in social analysis certainty is not to be had; sociology is an active resource for politics not a passive resource for government; a resource for better judgements in the face of uncertainty (Abrams 1981b:14–15).

Such a view of the social role of sociology would not command universal assent, as some of the types of use of research identified in Abrams's chapter indicate. A more dispassionate critic might also argue that Townsend's chapter, for example, is premised upon certain strong political commitments which in themselves are contentious rather than proven. Such debate about the purposes of sociology and of social research is, however, necessary and valuable. Without this debate, and without the wider social significance of social inquiry, there would not be the span of a hundred and fifty year history to review and ponder.

REFERENCES

Abrams, M. (1979) 'Social surveys, social theory and social policy', *Quantitative Sociology Newsletter* 21:15–24.

Abrams, P. (1968) *The Origins of British Sociology 1834–1914* (Chicago: University of Chicago Press).

Abrams, P., Cowling, M., and Shils, E. (1968) 'The social and political sciences – and how many more?', *The Cambridge Review* 89A, no. 2163, February 2: 230–2.

Abrams, P. *et al* (eds.) (1981a) *Practice and Progress: British Sociology 1950–1980* (London: Allen & Unwin).

Abrams, P. (1981b) 'Sociology – could there be another 150 years?', Contribution to Social Science Symposium no. 9, York meeting, 2nd September (London: British Association for the Advancement of Science, mimeo).

Alderson, M. (1983) 'William Farr 1807–1883: his contribution to present day vital and health statistics', *Population Trends* 31:5–8.

Annan, N. (1959) *The Curious Strength of Positivism in English Social Thought* (London: Oxford University Press).

Banks, J.A. (1967) 'The British Sociological Association – the first fifteen years', *Sociology* 1:1–9.

Banting, K. (1979) *Poverty, Politics and Policy* (London: Macmillan).

Barnes, H.E. (1927) 'The fate of sociology in England' in *The Progress of Sociology: Papers and Proceedings of the Twenty-first Annual Meeting of the American Sociological Society at St. Louis, December 1926* (Chicago: University of Chicago Press, 1927), pp. 26–46.

Barnes, J.A. (1970) *Sociology in Cambridge: an inaugural lecture* (Cambridge: Cambridge University Press).

Benney, M. (1946) *Charity Main: a coalfield chronicle* (London: Allen & Unwin).

Benney, M. (1966) *Almost a Gentleman* (London: Peter Davies).

Bernert, C. (1983) 'The career of causal analysis in American sociology', *British Journal of Sociology* 34(2):230–54.

Besnard, P. (1983) *The Sociological Domain: the Durkheimians and the founding of French sociology* (Cambridge: Cambridge University Press).

Beveridge, Sir W. (1937) 'The place of the social sciences in human knowledge: a farewell address given at the L.S.E., June 1937', *Politica* II, no. 9 (September): 459–79.

Blacker, C.P. (1950) *Eugenics in Retrospect and Prospect* (Occasional Papers on Eugenics, no. 1, London).

Boardman, P. (1978) *The Worlds of Patrick Geddes: biologist, town planner, re-educator, peace warrior* (London: Routledge).

Bowley, A.L. (1906) 'Address to the Economic Science and Statistics Section of the British Association for the Advancement of Science', *Journal of the Royal Statistical Society A* 69:548–57.

Bowley, A.L. (1915) *The Nature and Purpose of the Measurement of Social Phenomena* (London: P.S. King).

Bowley, A.L. and Burnett-Hurst, A.R. (1915) *Livelihood and Poverty: a study of economic conditions of working-class households in Northampton, Warrington, Stanley and Reading* (London: Bell).

Bowley, A.L. and Hogg, M.H. (1925) *Has Poverty Diminished?* (London: P.S. King).

Branford, V. (1912) 'The sociological survey', *The Sociological Review* 5(2): 105–14.

Brown, R. (1979) 'Passages in the life of a white anthropologist: Max Gluckman in Northern Rhodesia', *Journal of African History* 20:525–41.

Bulmer, M. (1981) 'Sociology and political science at Cambridge in the 1920's: an opportunity missed and an opportunity taken', *The Cambridge Review* CII, 2262 (29 April):156–9.

Bulmer, M. (1982) *The Uses of Social Research: social investigation in public policy-making* (London: Allen & Unwin).

Bulmer, M. (1983) 'The social sciences', in J.W. Chapman (ed.), *The Western University on Trial* (Berkeley: University of California Press), pp. 102–17.
Bulmer, M. (1984) *The Chicago School of Sociology; institutionalisation, diversity and the rise of sociological research* (Chicago: University of Chicago Press).
Bulmer, M. and Bulmer, J. (1981) 'Philanthropy and social science in the 1920's: Beardsley Ruml and the Laura Spelman Rockefeller Memorial, 1922–29'. *Minerva* 19(3) (Autumn):347–407.
Caine, S. (1974) 'Ginsberg at the L.S.E.', in Fletcher (1974), pp. 29–32.
Collini, S. (1978) 'Sociology and idealism in Britain, 1880–1920', *Archives européens de sociologie* 19:3–50.
Collini, S. (1979) *Liberalism and Sociology: L.T. Hobhouse and political argument in England 1880–1914* (Cambridge: Cambridge University Press).
Collini, S., Winch, D. and Burrow, J.W. (1983) *That Noble Science of Politics* (Cambridge: Cambridge University Press).
Crick, B. (1980) *George Orwell: a life* (London: Secker & Warburg).
Cullen, M.J. (1976) *The Statistical Movement in Early Victorian Britain: the foundations of empirical social research* (Hassocks, Sussex: Harvester).
Duncan, J.W. and Shelton, W.C. (1978) *Revolution in United States Government Statistics 1926–1976* (Washington D.C.: U.S. Government Printing Office of Federal Statistical Policy and Standards, U.S. Department of Commerce).
Eldridge, J. (1980) *Recent British Sociology* (London: Macmillan).
Eyler, J.M. (1979) *Victorian Social Medicine: the ideas and methods of William Farr* (Baltimore, Maryland: Johns Hopkins University Press).
Faris, R.E.L. (1967) *Chicago Sociology, 1920–1932* (San Francisco: Chandler).
Finer, S.E. (1952) *The Life and Times of Sir Edwin Chadwick* (London: Methuen).
Firth, R. (ed.) (1957) *Man and Culture: an evaluation of the work of Bronislaw Malinowski* (London: Routledge).
Fletcher, R. (ed.) (1974) *The Science of Society and the Unity of Mankind: a memorial volume for Morris Ginsberg* (London: Heinemann).
Floud, J. (1979) 'Karl Mannheim', in T. Raison (ed.) (1979), pp. 272–83.
Freedman, M. (1974) 'Morris Ginsberg: Personal Recollections' in Fletcher (1974), pp. 269–71.
Geddes, P. (1905) *Civics as Applied Sociology* (London: Sociological Society Sociological Papers). Reprinted in H.E. Meller (ed.), *The Ideal City* (Leicester: Leicester University Press, 1979).
Geddes, P. (1915) *Cities in Evolution: an introduction to the town planning movement and to the study of civics* (London: Williams & Norgate).
Glass, D.V. and Grebenik, E. (1954) *The trend and pattern of fertility in Great Britain: a report on the family census of 1946* (Royal Commission of Population Papers no. 6: London: H.M.S.O.).
Glass, R. (1955) 'Urban sociology in Great Britain: a trend report', *Current Sociology* 4(4):5–76.
Goldman, L. (1983) 'The origins of British "social science": political economy, natural science and statistics, 1830–1835', *The Historical Journal* 26(3), pp. 587–616.
Goody, J. (1959) 'Social science and the crypto-establishment', *The Cambridge Review* 80, February 7:309–13.

Hadden, T. (1968) 'Social science: the creation of a discipline', *The Cambridge Review* 89A, no. 2161, January 19:183–5.
Halliday, R.J. (1968) 'The Sociological Movement, the Sociological Society, and the genesis of academic sociology in Britain', *The Sociological Review* 16(4):377–98.
Halsey, A.H. (1984) 'T.H. Marshall: past and present, 1893–1981', *Sociology* 18:1–18.
Hansen, M.H. and Madow, W.G. (1976) 'Some important events in the historical development of sample surveys', in D.B. Owen (ed.), *On the History of Statistics and Probability* (New York: Marcel Dekker), pp. 75–102.
Harris, J. (1977) *William Beveridge: a biography* (Oxford: Clarendon Press).
Hawthorn, G. (1976) *Enlightenment and Despair: a history of sociology* (Cambridge: Cambridge University Press).
Heath, A. and Edmondson, R. (1981) 'Oxbridge Sociology: the development of centres of excellence?' in P. Abrams (1981a), pp. 39–52.
Hobhouse, L.T. (1924) *Social Development: its nature and conditions* (vol. 4 of *Principles of Sociology*) (London: Allen & Unwin).
Hobhouse, L.T., Wheeler, G.C. and Ginsberg, M. (1915), *The Material Culture and Social Institutions of the Simpler Peoples: an essay in correlation* (London: London School of Economics Monographs on Sociology no. 3).
Hogben, L. (ed.) (1938) *Political Arithmetic* (London: Allen & Unwin).
Hogben, L. (1942) 'The contemporary challenge to freedom of thought', in R.N. Anshen (ed.), *Freedom: its meaning* (London: Allen & Unwin), pp. 120–30.
Homans, G. (1956) 'Giving a dog a bad name', *The Listener* 56 (August 16), pp. 232–33; reprinted in G. Homans, *Sentiments and Activities: essays in social science* (London: Routledge, 1962), pp. 113–19.
Homans, G. (1959) 'Sociology at Cambridge: a sociologist's view', *The Cambridge Review* 80, May 2:461–3.
Johnson, H.G. (1978) 'The Shadow of Keynes', in E.S. Johnson and H.G. Johnson, *The Shadow of Keynes: understanding Keynes, Cambridge and Keynesian economics* (Oxford: Basil Blackwell), pp. 152–66.
Jones, D.C. (1948) *Social Surveys* (London: Hutchinson).
Kent, R. (1981) *A History of British Empirical Sociology* (Farnborough, Hants.: Gower).
Kitchen, P. (1975) *A Most Unsettling Person: an introduction to the ideas and life of Patrick Geddes* (London: Gollancz).
Krausz, E. (1969) *Sociology in Britain: a survey of research* (London: Batsford).
Kruskal, W. and Mosteller, F. (1980) 'Representative sampling IV: the history of the concept in statistics 1895–1939', *International Statistical Review* 48: 169–95.
Kuper, A. (1983) *Anthropology and Anthropologists: the modern British school* (2nd edition, London: Routledge).
Leete, R. and Fox, J. (1977) 'Registrar General's Social Class: origins and use', *Population Trends* 8:1–7.
Lewes, F. (1983) 'William Farr and cholera', *Population Trends* 31:8–12.
London School of Economics (1981) *Department of Anthropology* (London: L.S.E.).
McDowall, M. (1983) 'William Farr: his work in the field of occupational mortality', *Population Trends* 31:12–14.

McKennell, A.C., Bulmer, M. and Bynner, J. (1982) *Linking Academic Social Science with Survey Research: a proposal* (Southampton: University of Southampton Faculty of Social Science, mimeo).
MacKenzie, D.A. (1981) *Statistics in Britain 1865–1930: the social construction of scientific knowledge* (Edinburgh: Edinburgh University Press).
MacRae, D.G. (1972) 'The basis of social cohesion', in W.A. Robson (ed.), *Man and the Social Sciences* (London: Allen & Unwin), pp. 39–59.
MacRae, D.G. (1982) 'Tom Marshall, 1893–1981: a personal memoir', *British Journal of Sociology* 33(3) (September): iii–vi.
Marsh, C. (1982) *The Survey Method: the contribution of surveys to sociological explanation* (London: Allen & Unwin).
Marshall, T.H. (ed.) (1938) *Class Conflict and Social Stratification* (London: Le Play House Press).
Marshall, T.H. (1973) 'A British sociological career', *British Journal of Sociology* 24(4):399–408.
Marshall, T.H. (1977) *Class, Citizenship and Social Development* (Chicago: University of Chicago Press).
Mass-Observation (1970) *The Pub and the People: A Worktown Study* (revised edition, London: Seven Dials) (first published 1943).
Maunder, W.F. (1972) *Sir Arthur Lyon Bowley 1869–1957* (Inaugural lecture, Exeter: University of Exeter, 1972).
Moser, C.A. and Kalton, G. (1971) *Survey Methods in Social Investigation* (London: Heinemann).
Mumford, L. (1982) *Sketches from life: the autobiography of Lewis Mumford – the early years* (New York: Dial Press).
O'Muircheartaigh, C. and Wong, S.T. (1981) 'The impact of sampling theory on survey sampling practice: a review', *Bulletin of the International Statistical Institute* 40(1):465–93.
Orwell, G. (1933) *Down and Out in Paris and London* (London: Gollancz).
Orwell, G. (1937) *The Road to Wigan Pier: on industrial England and its political future* (London: Gollancz).
Parsons, T. and Smelser, N.J. (1956) *Economy and Society* (Glencoe, Ill.: Free Press).
Pinker, R. (1971) *Social Theory and Social Policy* (London: Heinemann).
Raison, T. (ed.) (1979) *The Founding Fathers of Social Science* (London: Scolar Press).
Rex, J. (1961) *Key Problems in Sociological Theory* (London: Routledge).
Rex, J. (1983) 'British Sociology 1960–1980: an essay', *Social Forces* 61(4):999–1009.
Robson, B.T. (1981) 'Geography and social science: the role of Patrick Geddes', in D.R. Stoddart (ed.), *Geography, Ideology and Social Concern* (Oxford: Blackwell), pp. 186–207.
Royal Commission on Population (1949) *Report* Cmd. 7695 (London: H.M.S.O.).
Royal Commission on Population (1949–54) *Research Papers 1 to 6* (London: H.M.S.O.).
Rumney, J. (1945) 'British Sociology', in G. Gurvitch and W.G. Moore (eds.), *Twentieth Century Sociology* (New York: Philosophical Library), pp. 562–85.
Russell, K. *et al.* (1981) *Changing Course: a follow-up of students taking the L.S.E. Certificate and Diploma in Social Administration 1949–73* (London: L.S.E.).

Selvin, H.C. (1965) 'Training for social research: the recent American experience', in J. Gould (ed.), *Penguin Survey of the Social Sciences 1965* (Harmondsworth: Penguin), pp. 73–95.
Shils, E. (1980) *The Calling of Sociology and other essays on the Pursuit of Learning* (Chicago: University of Chicago Press).
Sidgwick, H. (1904) *Miscellaneous Essays and Addresses* (London: Macmillan).
Silver, C.B. (1982) *Frederic Le Play on Family, Work and Social Change* (Chicago: University of Chicago Press).
Small, A.W. (1924) 'Review of L.T. Hobhouse, *Social Development*', *American Journal of Sociology* 30(2):216–20.
Smelser, N.J. (1981) 'On collaborating with Talcott Parsons', *Sociological Inquiry* 51 (3–4):143–54.
Smith, Sir H.L. (ed.) (1930–5) *The New Survey of London Life and Labour*. 9 vols (London: P.S. King).
Soffer, R.N. (1978) *Ethics and Society in England: the revolution in the social sciences 1870–1914*. (Berkeley: University of California Press).
Sprott, W.J.H. (1957) 'Sociology in Britain: perspectives', in H. Becker and A. Boskoff (eds.), *Modern Sociological Theory in Continuity and Change* (New York: Dryden Press), pp. 596–610.
Stanley, N.S. (1981) 'The Extra Dimension: a study and assessment of the methods employed by Mass Observation in its first period, 1937–40', Unpublished Ph.D. (C.N.A.A.), Birmingham Polytechnic.
Stephan, F.F. (1948) 'History of the uses of modern sampling procedures', *Journal of the American Statistical Association* 43:12–39
Stevenson, J. (1977) *Social Conditions in Britain between the Wars*. (Harmondsworth: Penguin).
Sutherland, G. and Sharp, S. (1980) ' "The fust official psychologist in the wurrld": aspects of the professionalisation of psychology in early twentieth century Britain', *History of Science* 18:818–208.
Teer, F. and Spence, J.D. (1973) *Political Opinion Polls*. (London: Hutchinson).
Tiryakian, E.A. (1979) 'The significance of schools in the development of sociology', in W.E. Snizek *et al.* (eds.), *Contemporary Issues in Theory and Research* (Westport, Conn.: Greenwood), pp. 211–33.
Webb, S. and Webb, B. (1932) *Methods of Social Study* (London: Longman).
Wells, A.F. (1935) *The Local Social Survey in Great Britain* (London: Allen & Unwin).

HISTORY

2 Social monitors: population censuses as social surveys

C. HAKIM

The population census is nowadays a taken for granted element of national social statistics. But the 1801 Census was undertaken only after a debate that had run for fifty years. The controversy consisted primarily of a debate on whether the population of England and Wales was declining or increasing, but ran into a debate on the political dangers of conducting, and publishing, such a detailed account of the whole population (Glass, 1973). Despite precedents elsewhere in Europe, the first bill to propose a census was unsuccessful in 1753, and it was not until 1800 that Parliament authorised such a major survey. The 1801 Census was the first national survey of the socio-economic characteristics of the population and preceded the surveys of Booth and Rowntree by almost a century.

The development of the British census

The earliest censuses (1801–31) took the form of simple headcounts, with the census enumerator responsible for recording the number of people and families at each address by sex and family occupation. Self-completion forms were first issued to households in 1841, so this is regarded as the first modern census in allowing for individual enumeration. The purpose of the census as a survey of social and economic conditions was stated on the 1851 Census form: 'The Return is required to enable the Secretary of State to complete the Census; which is to show the number of the population – their arrangement by ages and families in different ranks, professions, employments and trades – their distribution over the country in villages, towns and cities – their increase and progress in the last ten years' (Hakim, 1982a, p. 37).

For the next century until 1951 the census remained virtually the only national survey of social conditions. The range of data collected was broadened, reflecting the widening responsibilities of government in housing, education, public health, transport, employment and regional development – until 1971, when the topic content of the census was at its broadest, and was further extended by two voluntary census-linked follow-up surveys. This progressive expansion of topics covered by a compulsory census was questioned in the 1970s, when it was argued that regular national sample surveys developed in the 1970s might more appropriately supply some of the data collected through the census. The policy of household surveys providing both complementary and alternative data sources to the census became more explicit and formalised in the 1980s, with the 1981 Census meeting only those information needs that could not be met by national surveys – and the primary purpose of the census became recognised as supplying the need for comprehensive 'benchmark' data that provides the framework for the more regular but smaller interview surveys – such as the annual General Household Survey and the biennial Labour Force Survey. Thus over a period of over one and a half centuries, the census was first established as the most important survey of social and economic conditions, then, more recently, extended and complemented by more frequent voluntary surveys addressed to small but nationally representative samples of the population.

The distinctive strengths of the census as a source of social statistics are the continuity of statistics from census to census, which allows long term changes to be measured; the possibilities of interrelating various characteristics of the population; the details given by the census about small populations, either in local areas or in minorities scattered throughout the country; the comparability of the statistics across the whole country; and the completeness of coverage because the census is compulsory, while all other surveys are voluntary (Redfern, 1981).

Until 1951 in Britain and most other countries, the census was always a 100 per cent enumeration of the population. Since the 1950s sampling has featured increasingly in census work in most countries. For example the mid-term census taken in 1966 was a Ten Per Cent Sample Census, with only ten per cent of all identified households being required to fill in a form. In 1981 (as in 1971) there was a complete enumeration, with all households required to complete the census form, but some of the more complex information (for example on occupation and industry) is only processed for a 10 per cent sample of the forms. In other countries, more extensive use is made of sampling, with more extensive information being collected from between 5 and 25 per cent of the population while the remainder complete shorter versions of the census form. The use of sampling in the census illustrates further the close connections between censuses and social surveys and highlights the fact that it is the compulsory nature of the census that distinguishes it from sample surveys.

Although the amount of information collected by the census has expanded gradually over the past century, it is notable that the British census is today a much more restricted exercise than that carried out in other industrialised countries. Between 1931 and 1971, the number of questions in the British census increased from 12 to 30, but was then reduced to only 21 in the 1981 Census. By way of contrast, the 1980/81 censuses of Australia, Canada and the United States contained twice or three times as many questions (35, 42 and 60 questions respectively). Thus other countries make much fuller use of the census as a survey of the conditions of life of the population. In some cases more detailed information is collected on those topics that are covered by the British census; in some cases information is collected on additional topics not covered in Britain. Topics covered by censuses elsewhere, but not in Britain, include race and ethnic group; nationality; parents' countries of birth; languages spoken; religion; disability; duration of residence; main source of livelihood; income; duration of unemployment; secondary occupation; literacy; dependency relationships; marital and fertility history; ownership of durable consumer goods; heating and fuel for the home; availability of telephone; type of housing; housing costs (rental or mortgage costs and costs of services); holidays taken; and child care services used (Redfern, 1981; Hakim, 1982a, pp. 36–7).

The main reason given to explain the limited scope of the census in Britain as compared with other countries is a greater concern with privacy, or that a wider variety of personal information is regarded as private or sensitive. For example it is established practice to ask detailed questions on each person's income in North American censuses, but no question on income has ever been asked in British censuses. An income question was tested in the 1960s, but the question was judged to be too sensitive for inclusion in a compulsory census. Instead, a voluntary follow-up survey on income was carried out after the 1971 Census. This was carried out as a postal survey in June 1972, based on a 1 per cent sample of the population aged 15 and over, but obtained a poor response rate of about 50 per cent (Banfield, 1978; OPCS, 1978). Similarly questions on ethnic origin were tested in the 1970s with a view to inclusion in the 1981 Census. In the event, such a question was judged too sensitive for the census and was excluded. The question that had proved most successful in trials and census tests was included in other voluntary surveys, including the 1979 and 1981 Labour Force Surveys (Sillitoe, 1978; Bulmer, 1980). However a greater sensitivity to privacy cannot wholly explain the limited scope of the British census as compared with other industrialised countries. There is little evidence that France, Canada and the United States for example have been less concerned with the issue of privacy than is the case in Britain (Bulmer, 1979).

Whatever the explanation, it remains the case that the British census provides more meagre and limited statistical information on the social and economic conditions of the population than censuses in other industrialised countries. Putting aside the question on income, it appears that the British census provides more limited data on the non-economic topics – the social or quality of life topics – and is hence a more restricted source of social statistics than censuses elsewhere.

The use of census statistics

This may explain in part why census statistics are relatively little used by sociologists in Britain as compared with the level of usage by economists in Britain or when compared with the level of usage by sociologists in North America for example. Of course the main purpose of the census is to serve the information needs of central and local government, but both within these institutional settings and in the universities, economists appear to make greater use of the census results than do sociologists.

The best-known data from the decennial censuses are the statistics published in weighty tomes after each census. But there are in fact three types of data available from the census:

(a) the original census returns deposited at the Public Records Office after 100 years, currently the census enumerators' books for 1841–81 which are readily accessible on microfilm;
(b) the census commentaries and social reports contained in the published census reports for 1801–1951;
(c) the census statistics presented in the published reports for 1801–1981 and in non-printed formats (such as microfilm) for 1961–81.

The most extensive use at any one time is of the statistical results (both in published and in non-printed formats) from the most recent census. These have been described elsewhere in some detail (Hakim, 1982a). But equally important are those uses of census data that identify changing trends over the past two centuries, those that exploit the census' potential as an ongoing historical record of social trends and social change.

Precisely because the census has been carried out every decade since 1801 (with the exception of 1941), it provides a large fund of social statistics and of commentary on social trends which can be tapped to study the historical antecedents and development of aspects of society which have only recently become topical issues. Techniques of statistical analysis and data processing methods that have only been developed in the last few decades can be applied retrospectively to analyse afresh this vast body of data which is uniquely available on a continuous basis for a period of 180 years. It has been found repeatedly that the application of modern data analysis techniques to historical census data can overthrow accepted views and interpretations of the recent past, so that this type of census usage is where the liveliest debates are seen. A few examples illustrate how census data has thrown new light on current issues.

There has been a general consensus that women have entered the labour force in increasing numbers in recent decades. Studies based on census statistics have documented the rise in women's work rates generally and those for married women more specifically.[1] By the 1970s, over half of all married women were going out to work, making the two-earner family the most common or typical pattern and replacing the dominant pattern of the family with a single (male) breadwinner. The phenomenon of working wives and mothers has been typically seen as a new pattern in family life and in the workforce generally, raising issues about child-care provision, equal opportunities and sex discrimination. It appears however that this picture is partial and misleading. Economic activity rates for men and women were not routinely compiled and published in census reports until the twentieth century, so that the work rates for the period 1901–71 are the ones most commonly quoted. Over this century, the work rates have risen dramatically, from 10 per cent of all married women in 1901 to 49 per cent in 1971 (Table 2.2). But when economic activity rates are calculated for the nineteenth century as well, a rather different picture emerges. A comparison of Tables 2.1 and 2.2 shows that the work rate for women (excluding those in unpaid domestic work) was as high in 1861 as it was in 1971: 43 per cent in both cases. Similarly the work rate for married women engaged in work other than unpaid domestic work was as high in 1851 as in 1951. The census report for 1851 notes that a quarter of all wives and two-thirds of all widows had a specific occupation other than domestic work in the home; the rate declined to only one in ten married women in the period 1901–1931, then rose again to one quarter (26 per cent) of all married women aged 15–59 in 1951. Thus, casting the analysis backwards into the nineteenth century shows that the 'rise' of women's propensity to work is a twentieth-century myth. Rather, women were typically involved in work in the mid-nineteenth century (either in collaboration with their husband's or family's business or in their own independent occupation); they were then virtually excluded from the labour force and confined to domestic activity in the home in the early part of this century; they have now resumed their role in the labour force in the second half of the twentieth century. This places women's current work activities in a new light. It suggests that we should be asking why and how it was that women were excluded from gainful work in the early part of this century instead of seeking to explain the recent rise in women's work rates (Hakim, 1980).

Table 2.1. *Economic activity* rates 1801–1891, England and Wales*

1801	40%	of all persons
1811	81%	of all households
1821	81%	of all households
1831	71%	of all households

	Men aged 20+	Women aged 20+
1831	94	—
1841	89	23
1851	98.6 (98.2)	96 (42)
1861	99.2 (99)	98 (43)
1871	99.6 (99.6)	98 (42)
1881	95	32
1891	94	32

* The *economically active*, or 'occupied', include those with a specified occupation and those with an unspecified occupation, but exclude persons of rank or property with no occupation specified (Order 17 in 1861) and paupers, prisoners, vagrants, etc. with no occupation specified (Order 18 in 1861). The retired and pensioners separately identified in 1881 and 1891 among the 'unoccupied' are also excluded.

Figures in brackets give economic activity rates as defined above, but excluding people who were engaged in unpaid household work (Order 4 in 1861). These figures are thus given only for those censuses when unpaid household work was listed as an occupation.

Sources: Census reports for Great Britain 1801–1851 and for England and Wales 1861–1891. Figures for England and Wales. Tables 2.1 and 2.2 are taken from C. Hakim, 'Census reports as documentary evidence', *Sociological Review*, vol. 28, no. 3, 1980, p. 559.

The fact that women have re-entered the labour force in large numbers within this century has given rise to another myth: that the 'traditional' distinctions between men and women's work have been eroded in consequence and that, with women taking up jobs that were previously male strongholds, the occupational segregation of the sexes in the labour force had declined markedly. A study based on recently developed measures of job segregation, which were applied to census statistics for the last seventy years, shows however that there has been little or no change since the turn of the century in the position of women in the workforce. Small inroads were made by women into typically male occupations; but overall women have largely remained confined to the typically-female jobs. Furthermore, the last seventy years has seen a trend towards women being increasingly concen-

Table 2.2. *Economic activity rates 1901–1971: proportion (%) of people in specified age groups who were 'occupied' (1901–1951) or 'economically active' (1961–1971)*

	Men of working age*	Women of working age*	Men 15–64	Women 15–59	Married Women 15–59
1901	84	32	96	38	10
1911	84	32	96	38	10
1921	87	32	94	38	10
1931	91	34	96	38	11
1941	—	—	—	—	—
1951	88	35	96	43	26
1961	86	38	95	47	35
1971	81	43	92	55	49

* 1901–11 persons aged 10 or over
1921 persons aged 12 or over
1931 persons aged 14 or over
1951–71 persons aged 15 or over
Source: Population census reports for England and Wales 1901–1971.

trated in the lowest grades of white-collar and blue-collar work and very much under-represented in the higher grades of white-collar and blue-collar work. Thus, there is little evidence of a consistent trend over the century towards greater integration of the sexes in the work sphere, as previously assumed. This study suggested that sex discrimination and equal opportunities legislation carries the burden of reversing a trend towards greater job segregation and not simply supporting an existing trend towards the desegregation of occupations (Hakim, 1979, 1981).

Census statistics and the social commentaries in the reports are also used simply to document more fully the nature and direction of social change over the past two centuries. For example they have been used to study the changing pattern of social structure in the nineteenth and twentieth centuries; the processes of urbanisation and industrialisation; patterns of family life; or the gradual professionalisation of occupations such as nursing (Lawton, 1978; Davies, 1980). But the value of the historical record contained in the census is perhaps most fully exploited by those researchers who turn to the original records deposited at the Public Records Office and analyse them afresh with the modern techniques and methods of data analysis now applied to sample surveys. This usually means entering the results for the first time onto computers, which opens up the possibility of more extensive and detailed analyses than were carried out in the nineteenth century, when the census results were compiled manually (using five-bar gates, it is said).

Professor Michael Anderson's research team at Edinburgh University has already computerised a 2 per cent national sample of the 1851 census records, thus opening up new avenues for census analysis. But smaller scale work has been done using the records for particular towns or areas, to study social structure and social change in periods when surveys were still a rarity. For example, John Foster used census records for 1841, 1851 and 1861 (as well as other sources) to study the incidence of poverty, patterns of marriage and neighbouring, the keeping of servants, the extent of families sharing accommodation, migration patterns and the occupational and industrial mix of three English towns (Foster, 1974; see also Anderson, 1971; Armstrong, 1974).

The census as a record of the development of social science

The census is used as a source of documentary evidence and statistics on social change in Britain, but it also provides a record of the development of social science itself. As the longest-standing social survey, the development of social science is reflected and illustrated in the methods and techniques used in taking the census, in analysing the returns and reporting on results. If each census is a snapshot of the nation at a particular point in time, the series of nineteen censuses over the period 1801–1981 document the development of national photography.[2] The census can also tell us something about what was considered worth photographing and recording, how and why the camera was angled, how and why the picture was framed in a certain way. It can only be a partial document of course. The methods used in taking and analysing the census are to some extent peculiar to it, because of its very size and because of its compulsory nature. Also, as noted above, some topics may be so topical that they become too hot to handle. While the position of ethnic minority groups in general, and immigrants from the Commonwealth countries in particular, became a subject of some debate and public interest in the second half of the twentieth century, the heated nature of the debate led eventually to the *exclusion* of relevant questions from the 1981 Census. Similarly, as Lawton has observed, the turmoil of change in mid-Victorian times produced pressures to collect additional information in the censuses of 1861, 1871 and 1881, but all these proposals were eventually rejected (Lawton, 1978, pp. 18–19). But it is instructive to look at the census from this perspective also.

In terms of methodology, the census is often at the forefront of developments. The possibility of using Hollerith punched cards to store and process census data had been first discussed by the Departmental Committee on the Census in 1890, and it was adopted for the 1911 Census, well before punched-card processing was used in other social surveys (Lawton, 1978, p. 20). Computer-based processing and analysis of the census results was introduced in 1961, again well before the use of computers became widely established in university social science departments.[3] The use of sampling was introduced with the 1951 Census, when a 1 per cent sample was taken from the records in order to produce early results, and has since been extended, as noted above. Because the census is a costly exercise, there is an incentive to adopt new methods and techniques if these will help contain or reduce costs, or if they ensure that better use can be made of the resulting data. The introduction of automated data processing for the census allowed a very dramatic increase in the statistical output from the 1961 and 1971 Censuses, and as a result the use made of census results was 'democratised', with regular usage extending beyond central government departments to include a very much larger number and wider variety of users outside central government: local authorities; area health, water and other authorities; nationalised industries; market research and other commercial concerns in the private sector; local community and pressure groups; the academic community and independent research institutes, among others.[4]

In terms of the topics covered by the census, there appears to be a gradual move away from a broad social science perspective in the 1850s towards an increasingly narrow economic perspective which was already apparent at the turn of the century. This trend may reflect the increasing specialisation (or, on another view, fragmentation) of the social sciences into the separate disciplines of economics, sociology, geography, psychology and so forth and, concomitantly, the earlier rise and dominance of economics in public affairs.

As noted earlier, the census provides very limited statistics on social topics and on living standards, certainly more limited than the range of social data covered by censuses elsewhere. The fact that such data is available from the more frequent sample surveys (such as the General Household Survey) is not an adequate explanation, since these surveys are too small to provide regional data, and too small also to provide detailed statistics on social or ethnic minority groups (such as one-parent families or persons of New Commonwealth descent). The fact that out-of-date census social statistics have to be used in the calculation of the Rate Support Grant 'special needs' assessment during the inter-censal period attests to the need for more up-to-date information on social topics.

The dominance of the economists' perspective is also reflected in the changing definitions of work, employment and occupation applied in consecutive censuses. The very earliest censuses (1811–31) collected information on each family's occupation or work, as it was assumed that all members of the family (or household as it would now be termed) contributed to the family enterprise in agriculture, trade, manufacture or handicraft. As the concept of a personal occupation became established, the census began to collect data on the occupations of individuals in each family or household. But apart from persons of rank or property, paupers, prisoners and vagrants with no occupation specified, all adults were taken to be occupied in some activity or other and this activity was recorded as their occupation. Domestic work in the home, both paid and unpaid, was included in the list of occupations in the 1851, 1861 and 1871 censuses, and each census report reaffirmed the importance and value of the economic functions of women (and men) in the household, 'the most useful of all occupations'. After this the census began to distinguish between paid and unpaid work and gradually excluded the latter, although the treatment of unpaid family workers in a family enterprise wavered somewhat in practice. By 1961 the term 'economically active' had replaced the term 'occupied', and the definition was explicitly concerned only with work for pay or profit. Thus over the period of about a century the census moved away from a broad concern with establishing the main activity of each adult in the population towards a much narrower concern with measuring the size of the labour force as defined by economists or, more precisely, the size of the labour force engaged in the market economy, which is the sole interest of economists.[5]

The change in perspective is highlighted by contrasting the classification of occupations used in the 1861 Census with that used in the 1961 Census. The 1861 Census used a classification of occupations with seven broad classes: professional; domestic; commercial; agricultural; industrial; indefinite; and non-productive. Apart from the last group, all the occupational classes covered *productive work*. The last group, of non-productive occupations, comprised children, the sick and infirm, gypsies, vagrants, paupers and other persons supported by the community, and persons of rank or property with no specified occupation (Davies, 1980, pp. 587–8). The 1961 Census was concerned only with identifying persons engaged in *gainful work*, so that all other types of work were excluded, such as voluntary work, unpaid domestic work, nursing, teaching and other work carried out for family and relatives. Thus between 1861 and 1961 the focus of interest moved from a broad concern with productive work to a narrow concern with gainful employment. As a result the census now provides little or no information on persons who are not economically active: full-time students, the permanently sick and the retired are separately identified but there is no information on the main activity of the largest catch-all group of 'other economically inactive'.

The predominance of the economists' perspective is reflected in other data sources as well as the census. For example the development of British unemployment statistics based on the official register has been guided by the information needs of administrators for managing the work of local offices, and the needs of economists for managing the economy. Sociologists have played almost no part in the development of official unemployment statistics, and as a result they provide extremely limited information on the social distribution, impact and social costs of unemployment.[6]

The predominance of the economists' perspective in the census (and other data sources) carries disbenefits, as well as the advantages arising from the greater accuracy and quality of the statistics that are used within the disciplinary framework of economics. The main disadvantage would be that the value of the census as a broad historical record of social as well as economic change is reduced, leading to a greater need for and reliance on contemporary ad hoc social surveys than might otherwise have been the case. The more limited census coverage of social topics and living standards might also explain the more limited use of census statistics outside the discipline of economics (especially in sociology).

Conclusions

There is a tendency to regard the population census as a demographic data base but the census can more appropriately be used as the longest-standing socio-economic survey of the population. The most extensive use of the census relates to the statistical results of the most recent census. But the application of modern data analysis techniques to historical census data has also been developed to exploit more fully this vast body of data covering 180 years. Such re-analyses of census statistics have sometimes overthrown accepted views of recent social change. For example it has been shown that the current pattern of women's participation in the labour force is not a new phenomenon but was observed also in the mid-nineteenth century. This raises the question of why women were effectively excluded from the labour force around the turn of the century, and whether the processes that led to this exclusion also produced the pattern of job segregation which has persisted almost unchanged since the turn of the century.

Because it has been running for such a long time, the census can also be used as a record of the development of social science itself. For example the development of sampling, of questionnaire design, and of automated data processing are all reflected in the techniques and methods used in taking each census over the past two centuries. The use of computer processing has had particularly dramatic (and arguably democratic) effects – greatly extending the uses made of census statistics outside central government. The specialisation of social science into the separate disciplines of economics, sociology, geography and so on, and the early rise and predominance of economics are also reflected in the topics covered by the census, and in the labour economics perspective which has come to dominate census information on work activities. This narrowing of the framework within which the census is taken necessarily constrains and limits the value of the census as a historical record and the current uses of census statistics. Unless it is possible to return to the broader social science perspective that informed the nineteenth-century censuses, there will be greater need for the broader based social statistics that are currently available only from regular and ad hoc household surveys, such as the General Household Survey, which both extend and complement the data provided by decennial censuses.

NOTES

1 The work rate, or more precisely the economic activity rate, is the proportion of all women of working age (currently 16 to 59 years) who are in paid employment.

2 Since no census was taken in 1941, there were only eighteen decennial censuses over the period 1801–1981, but there was in addition the mid-term 1966 Ten Per Cent Sample Census, making a total of nineteen.

3 Even in the 1980s, many social science students do not gain any experience of computer-based data processing as part of their professional training.

4 The statistical output from the census rose from 8 thousand pages of tables for 1951 to 100 thousand pages from the 1961 Census and 1.6 million pages of tables from the 1971 Census. By the 1970s, the number of orders for census statistics from persons or organisations outside central government had reached 8 thousand, eight times greater than the number of orders from government departments (Hakim, 1978, pp. 1–9).

5 It is notable that the United Nations recommendations on census methods have recently widened the concept of economic activity to include work outside the market economy so as to ensure its usefulness in mixed as well as market economies (Hakim, 1980, p. 579).

6 As recent reviews of unemployment statistics illustrate, the official statistics are geared primarily to serving as an economic indicator for the evaluation of economic performance, with the emphasis on seasonal adjustment and other smoothing techniques in order to highlight the size and direction of trends (Department of Employment, 1980; Garside, 1980). As a result separate specially-designed surveys have to be carried out to assess the social impact of unemployment (Hakim, 1982b, pp. 435–42).

BIBLIOGRAPHY

Anderson, M. (1971) *Family Structure in Nineteenth Century Lancashire*, Cambridge: Cambridge University Press.

Armstrong, W.A. (1974) *Stability and Change in an English County Town: A Social Study of York 1801–51*, Cambridge: Cambridge University Press.

Banfield, F. (1978) '1971 Census Voluntary Survey on Income', *Population Trends*, no. 12, pp. 18–21.

Bulmer, M. (ed.) (1979) *Censuses, Surveys and Privacy*, London: Macmillan.

Bulmer, M. (1980) 'On the feasibility of identifying "race" and "ethnicity" in censuses and surveys', *New Community*, vol. 8, nos. 1–2, pp. 3–16.

Davies, C. (1980) 'Making sense of the census in Britain and the USA: the changing occupational classification of the position of nurses', *Sociological Review*, vol. 28, no. 3, pp. 581–609.

Department of Employment (1980) 'A review of unemployment and vacancy statistics', *Department of Employment Gazette*, vol. 88, no. 5, pp. 497–508.

Foster, J. (1974) *Class Struggle and the Industrial Revolution*, London: Weidenfeld and Nicolson.

Garside, W.R. (1980) *The Measurement of Unemployment*, Oxford: Basil Blackwell.

Glass, D.V. (1973) *Numbering the People: The eighteenth-century population controversy and the development of census and vital statistics in Britain*, Farnborough, Hants: Saxon House.

Hakim, C. (1978) *Data Dissemination for the Population Census*, Occasional Paper No. 11, London: Office of Population Censuses and Surveys.

Hakim, C. (1979) *Occupational Segregation: A comparative study of the degree and pattern of the differentiation between men and women's work in Britain, the United States and other countries*, Research paper No. 9, London: Department of Employment.

Hakim, C. (1980) 'Census reports as documentary evidence: the census commentaries 1801–1951', *Sociological Review*, vol. 28, no. 3, pp. 551–80.

Hakim, C. (1981) 'Job segregation: trends in the 1970s', *Department of Employment Gazette*, vol. 89, no. 12, pp. 521–9.

Hakim, C. (1982a) *Secondary Analysis in Social Research: A guide to data sources and methods with examples*, London: Allen & Unwin.

Hakim, C. (1982b) 'The social consequences of high unemployment', *Journal of Social Policy*, vol. 11, part 4, pp. 433–67.

Lawton, R. (ed.) (1978), *The Census and Social Structure*, London: Frank Cass.

Office of Population Censuses and Surveys (1978) *1971 Census Income Follow-up Survey*, Studies on Medical and Population Subjects no. 38, HMSO.

Redfern, P. (1981) 'Census 1981 – an historical and international perspective', *Population Trends*, no. 23, pp. 3–15.

Sillitoe, K. (1978) 'Ethnic origin: the search for a question', *Population Trends*, no. 13, pp. 25–30.

3 The emergence of the sociological survey, 1887–1939

RAYMOND KENT

This chapter focuses on a particular kind of social survey: the sociological survey. Such surveys go beyond exercises in social fact-gathering, and attempt to explain the major findings either by relating them one to another in ways that reveal causal connections between them, or by making reference to general features of society of which they may reasonably be claimed to be a product or to which they may be related. Those individuals who conducted sociological surveys in the period before 1939 were not for the most part, however, consciously trying to develop or to test sociological theory. Their motives lay elsewhere, but the end result of their endeavours was often the formulation of ideas and theories – usually in an implicit manner – whose significance went beyond the immediate findings.

The period chosen was one that saw the development of a conception of the sociological survey which was remarkable for its continuity, and yet which at the same time connected poorly, if at all, with the development of academic sociology in the universities. It begins with the surveys of Charles Booth, whose first findings were published in 1887 at a time when the Victorian boom years were coming to an end. The problem of poverty amongst the working classes was becoming more acute, but there were fierce arguments about its nature and extent. Booth was a liberal, a humanitarian and of Protestant faith, all of which served to put the individual at the centre of the stage. This may help to explain why he focused not so much on the nature and character of poverty as such, as on the poor themselves – their morals, character and behaviour. Although Booth verbalised his central problem as the existence of 'poverty in the midst of plenty' his main concern was about showing how many individuals failed to meet and fulfil the values of the Protestant ethic – and why.

When Booth embarked on his survey he was 46 years of age with a successful family shipping business based in Liverpool. During an earlier period of electioneering for the Liberals in Liverpool in 1865 he had come across poverty and squalor which was of a degree that convinced him that it was an evil for which no possible justification could be advanced. In his youth Booth had thought that the issue was an ethical one which could be approached through political action. His political activities, however, were little short of disastrous. After a nervous breakdown, occasioned, so the Simeys (1960) argue, by the tension and stress of not being able to accept his family religion when it attempted to justify the existing state of affairs, Booth in his mature years came to the conclusion that the application of the scientific method to the investigation of poverty would be the only way in which the controversies surrounding its extent, degree and causes could be resolved.

Booth did not see himself as being in the business of testing theory. In discussions on the problem of poverty with young intellectuals, he had, to his mind, encountered too many who were so possessed by enthusiasm for some great theory or system of society that they were prepared to force every known fact to fit into it. What Booth wanted instead was what he called a 'large statistical framework which is built to receive accumulations of facts out of which is at last evolved the theory and the basis for more intelligent action' (Simey and Simey, 1960:77). Such a framework would give a detached and impartial presentation of the situation as it actually was. It would go beyond existing sources of statistics by making use of all the available methods of collecting information and playing each off against the other in a process of cross-verification.

Seebohm Rowntree was just leaving school at the age of 16 when Booth presented the results of his Tower Hamlets study to the Royal Statistical Society in 1887. He went to Manchester University, but did not take a degree. His main interest was in chemistry – a subject which he quickly put to use when he joined the family business (a cocoa works in York). His family had for generations been Quakers with a natural concern for the twin evils of poverty and intemperance. Booth's experiences of poverty and squalor in Liverpool had their counterpart when Rowntree visited the slums of Newcastle in 1895. He was convinced that only scientific study of the problem would result in its resolution, and when in 1897 he came across Booth's 'statistical' technique, he resolved to do a similar study in York.

Rowntree was not so suspicious of socialism – or, rather, what he saw as 'socialism' – as Booth; but he did not embrace it either. Indeed, he steadfastly refused to become involved in any 'doctrinaire' arguments. He stood aloof when his most active helpers in his social investigations – May Kendall and Bruno Lasker – helped to found a York branch of the Fabian Society. He read few books on socialism and showed a distaste for any reliance on *a priori* reasoning. His purpose, he claimed in the book which contained the results of his investigations, was not to prove any preconceived theory, but 'to ascertain actual facts' (Rowntree, 1901:300). The experience of conducting a poverty survey in York led Rowntree to the conclusion that self-reliance and individualism were not adequate answers to the problem of poverty; wise legislation was also needed (Briggs, 1961:35). He became a vigorous advocate of state-sponsored social security – something that Booth would never have contemplated. Rowntree was in fact much less guarded than most of the other social investigators in putting forward solutions to family poverty and circulating new ideas about the way in which it could be reconciled with the economic needs of industry.

Most of those who followed Booth and Rowntree in making surveys of poverty tended to be either academics or at least more academically inclined. Arthur Bowley, who introduced probability sampling into the survey research process, was a graduate in mathematics from Trinity College, Cambridge. He was a contemporary of Rowntree's (being just two years younger), but became interested in economic and social problems not through the immediate experience of walking the slums of major cities, but through the inspiration of Alfred Marshall, the Cambridge economist.

Bowley became preoccupied with the relationship between the movements of wages and prices – the subject of his first paper to the Royal Statistical Society in 1895. It was on Marshall's recommendation that Bowley was invited to join the small and primarily part-time staff of the London School of Economics when it began its first session in the same year. Bowley was never a socialist, but he was a good liberal and was clearly in favour of free trade and limited government intervention. Unlike Rowntree, Bowley did not see it as part of his brief to make either general or specific recommendations about the alleviation of the poverty he found. Bowley and Hogg (1925:25) in their replication of the earlier five-towns study by Bowley and Burnett-Hurst, declared: 'It is not part of our plan to discuss remedies, but only to provide the detailed numerical setting out of the problem'. Other academics were perhaps a little less purist about the nature of their task, but even they felt constrained to make only guarded comments in an area fraught with political implications.

Sir Hubert Llewellyn Smith, who was Director and Chairman of the Consultative Committee that undertook the *New Survey of London Life and Labour* in 1928, was again a contemporary of Rowntree's. He was educated at Corpus Christi College, Oxford, where he graduated in 1886 with a first class mathematics degree. He became a lecturer in political economy for the Oxford Toynbee Trust. It was then that he became a member of Charles Booth's team of investigators. Thereafter he became a member of a number of government and quasi-government bodies and joined the Board of Trade in 1893. He eventually became permanent secretary in the

Ministry of Labour, but it was not until he had retired from that post at the age of 64 that he undertook the chairmanship of the New London Survey. This, however, was not just a replication. It was concerned with the changes that had taken place since Booth's time and was the only social survey of the period that provided extensive historical comparisons of urban conditions. It was also novel in the sense that it combined the original Booth type inquiry with Bowley's sampling methods to give specific cross-checks between the two.

Booth, Rowntree, Bowley and Llewellyn Smith were the pioneers of the sociological survey. There were many followers of the tradition that they had established. From 1928 onwards there was a more or less continuous series of surveys directed by different individuals: Henry Mess on Tyneside, A.D.K. Owen in Sheffield, Richard Evans in Hull, Percy Ford in Southampton, Terence Young in Becontree and Dagenham, Herbert Tout in Bristol, R.M. Taylor in Plymouth and Caradog Jones in Merseyside. Not all of these involved primary data collection. Some, like Mess's *Industrial Tyneside*, were confined to an analysis of existing materials collected by official and voluntary bodies. In others, available material was supplemented by *ad hoc* investigations. Some concerned particularly depressed areas; others newly developed ones. Some pursued particular aspects of social life such as housing or unemployment. Only the studies by Ford, Tout, Taylor and Caradog Jones were strictly along the lines of the poverty survey as initiated by the pioneers.

All these men were middle class, 'bourgeois' liberals or Liberals who accepted capitalist industrial development as the best way for society to progress. They all had to come to terms, however, with the need for some form of government intervention if the lot of the working classes was to be significantly improved; but that did not necessarily mean intervention in industry except over matters concerning safety, the employment of women and children and the hours of work. The ideal of laissez-faire was still very much in evidence in 1939, and they all hesitated to suggest interference with the mechanisms of the free market economy.

What 'social reform' meant to Booth and those who followed him has all too often been forgotten. Historians have looked forward in the Whig fashion (Butterfield, 1963) to the creation of the welfare state and focused their attention on proposals for state-provided education, pensions, relief of poverty, subsidised housing, national insurance schemes and so on. They have ignored parallel proposals to segregate the casual poor into 'labour colonies' (there has been some debate over whether Booth's suggestion about labour colonies was based on a scientific or on a moral basis – Brown (1968 and 1971) and Lumis (1971)); to establish detention centres for 'loafers'; to separate pauper children from 'degenerate' parents; or to ship the 'social residuum' overseas. Yet, to Booth and his contemporaries, both sets of proposals were part of a single debate over the threat to individualism and self-help posed by the growing popularity of socialism and trade unionism. Both sets of ideas were usually seen as an integral part of proposals for limited state intervention which would forestall demands for a full-blown socialist society that would abolish private property. Such proposals would, furthermore, need to be accompanied by various forms of social control – effective policing, a thoroughly deterrent prison system, curbs on trade union activity, and measures to counter indiscriminate charity giving by controlling financial relief that was being given to 'able-bodied' workers. Pauperism was to be discouraged by means of a more vigorous application of the workhouse test (see Stedman-Jones, 1971).

Poverty and its causes

One difficulty that all the social investigators had to face was that while in general terms it was clear what 'poverty' was, any attempt to so define it that the numbers in that condition could be counted in a systematic manner resulted in arbitrary decisions about what *were* the necessities of life, about how far these could be conditioned by 'cultural' factors, and about the extent to which allowances were to be made for the freedom to spend money in ways that did not fit with middle class standards of virtuous living. The end result was that the numbers 'in poverty' could vary enormously depending upon where the poverty 'line' was drawn and how it was applied.

Booth is usually credited with having 'discovered' that over 30 per cent of the people of London lived in poverty and that he was 'surprised' by his own findings on the extent of the problem. Booth's 30 per cent, however, was in fact the aggregate of three different categories. Only 7.5 per cent were 'in want', that is, ill-nourished and poorly clad. These were the 'very poor'. Most of the rest (27 per cent) were poor, but not in want. Their earnings were small or intermittent. They had no surplus, and their lives 'lacked comfort'. The other group was 'the lowest class of occasional labourers, loafers, and semi-criminals'. These were the people that more sensationalist writers of the day felt were a threat to civilised society – yet Booth showed that they were less than 1 per cent of the population; they were 'a disgrace, but not a danger' averred Booth. Booth himself felt that his results showed that conditions were 'better than was commonly imagined' and, indeed, constituted grounds for optimism.

Historians have seized on the 30 per cent figure, but it was not one that Booth himself emphasised in his 17 volumes of findings. He might just as easily be credited with having discovered that 'only 7.5 per cent' of the people of London were in want or distress. Booth's own definition of poverty suggested that he was using an income standard. In giving 'illustration' to the kind of income he had in mind 'such as 18/- to 21/- per week for a moderate family' (which he later changed to '21/- to 22/- per week for a small family') when referring to 'the poor', he has been seen by historians as having established a 'poverty line' at 21/- per week (see Booth, 1902–3, Poverty Series, Vol. 1:33 and Vol. 5:324). His categorisations into the well-known classes A to H, however, involved an arbitrary combination of moral character, regularity of earnings and social status. Streets, of course, could not be classified in the same way and instead he used an 'appearance of the home' criterion. Booth developed yet other classifications for schoolchildren, for overcrowding, for trades and for earnings. Each determined the 'facts' of poverty in a different way. He tried to show that the different systems produced broadly comparable results; but when they did not he conveniently forgot about the cross-check or adjusted the dividing lines between the categories (for a critical commentary on the work of Booth (and Rowntree), see Williams, 1981).

Whereas Booth's justification for his 'poverty line' had thus been based on complementary classification, for Rowntree it was justified by reference to a technical calculus. He calculated on the basis of new developments in nutritional science the actual costs at current prices (and rent levels) of maintaining families of varying compositions in a state of physical efficiency and compared this with estimates of actual wages. He found just under 10 per cent of the population of York living in families whose incomes did not meet this level.

Booth, in his analyses of poverty, never really solved the problem of what to do with families whose poverty was a result of 'mismanagement' of incomes (which usually meant spending a lot on alcohol). Were they to be counted as being 'in poverty' even if their incomes, had they been more wisely spent, would be adequate for food, clothing and shelter? Booth appeared to change his mind on this issue several times during the course of the inquiry. Historical accounts have generally suggested that Rowntree *did* solve the problem by making a distinction between 'primary' and 'secondary' poverty. The first referred to families 'whose total earnings are insufficient to obtain the minimum necessaries for the maintenance of merely physical efficiency' and the second to families 'whose total earnings would be sufficient for the maintenance of physical efficiency were it not that some portion of them is absorbed by other expenditure, either useful or wasteful'. Rowntree, however, did not measure secondary poverty directly; it was found by subtracting the number found to be in primary poverty from a measure of total poverty. The latter was derived from the visits of a hired investigator to every house in York. Two criteria were used: the 'appearance' of 'want or squalor', and 'information given' (often from neighbours) concerning whether either parent was 'a heavy drinker'. Secondary poverty was thus only a shadow of primary poverty, and it reflected more Rowntree's Quaker origins than it did any attempt to investigate seriously the nature and causes of income 'mismanagement'.

In the inter-war period the measurement of poverty continued to be a central preoccupation of social investigators, but added to their concerns were the changes that had taken place in its nature, incidence and causes since the work of the late Victorian and early Edwardian pioneers of social inquiry. All applied some form of poverty line, mostly refinements of Rowntree's attempts to establish what he himself later preferred to call a 'human needs' standard. Their application revealed that there was a considerable portion of the population still in severe poverty. Thus Bowley and Hogg found 11 per cent of working-class families below the poverty line in the five Midlands towns in 1924; Llewellyn Smith found 10 per cent in London in 1928; Taylor discovered 16 per cent in Plymouth in 1938; the Merseyside survey reported 16 per cent in 1934; Rowntree in York discovered some 15 per cent in 1936 and Herbert Tout some 10 per cent in prosperous Bristol in 1944. Whatever inquiry was studied and whatever measure of poverty was taken, the message was clear: that in the 1920s and 1930s in both prosperous and depressed towns a significant proportion of the working-class population remained in impoverished conditions.

On the question of the causes of poverty Booth was no more scientific than had been attempts half a century before (see for example Clay (1839), who investigated the various causes of crime in a similar manner). The analysis was of the frequency of the occurrence of the 'immediate' causes that Booth himself felt were operating. There were three broad classes of cause: those that resulted in lack of adequate income, those that resulted in mismanagement of income such as drunkenness and thriftlessness (the latter apparently attributable only to women), and those circumstances which, for the moment at least, were beyond the control of the individual, such as illness and large family. These broad classes he referred to as 'questions of employment', 'questions of habit' and 'questions of circumstance'. The figures that emerged were from a subset of just 4,000 cases of the poor known to selected (how, it is not known, but it seems there were nine) school board visitors, and reflected the attitudes of those gentlemen as to the categories of Booth's 'causes' each family fitted into. Not surprisingly, the major cause of poverty was low or irregular income since having low or irregular income were the major defining characteristics of Booth's 'poor' and 'very poor' classes in the first place. A result that may have occasioned more surprise was that only 13–14 per cent of poverty was caused, in the opinion of the school board visitors, by either 'Drink (husband, or both husband and wife)' or 'Drunken or thriftless wife'. Such a finding ran counter to the current popular wisdom that drunkenness was a major cause of poverty.

Booth, however, was unable to dissociate himself from accepted Victorian ideology. In his only reflection on the findings, he observed: 'To those who look upon drink as the source of all evil, the position it here holds as accounting for only 14 per cent of the poverty in the East End may seem altogether insufficient; but I may remind them that it is only as a principal cause that it is here considered: as a contributory cause it would no doubt be connected with a much larger proportion' (Booth, 1902–3, Poverty Series, Vol. 1:148). Unemployment was explained in terms of personal incapacity for work or personal disability. Low pay was attributed to those 'who could never learn to do anything well' or who were 'slow'; irregularity of employment to 'those who cannot get up in the morning' and who were 'too restless to keep any employment long'. Indeed, the unemployed were a 'selection of the unfit, and, on the whole, those most in want are the most unfit' (Booth, 1902–3, Poverty Series, Vol. 1:149–50).

It is usually claimed by historians that Rowntree improved on the survey as a tool of social investigation. That may be true in some respects, but in terms of his analysis of the causes of poverty, Rowntree's study, although apparently more scientific, was in fact more limited. The analysis was largely restricted to primary poverty, which meant that drink and gambling were excluded, narrowing the possible field of causes to low wages, and absence, sickness or unemployment of a wage earner. This served to compound further the problem of circularity – Rowntree found that over 50 per cent of cases of inadequate incomes were due to low wages! He made no attempt to probe those factors that underlay the immediate causes. He simply declared (Rowntree, 1901:152): 'It is not part of the object of this chapter to discuss the ultimate causes of poverty. To attempt this would be to raise the whole social question.' The immediate causes of secondary poverty, which Rowntree considered only very briefly, were 'drink, betting and gambling. Ignorant or careless housekeeping, and other improvident expenditure, the latter often induced by irregularity of income' (Rowntree, 1901:176).

In his second study of York, Rowntree dropped any pretence of measuring secondary poverty, but his causes of primary poverty remained the same as they had been in 1899. Llewellyn Smith was more concerned than Rowntree had been with comparability with Booth's findings, but even so he did not venture to replicate Booth's analysis of the causes of poverty in the street survey. In the sample survey, conducted by Bowley, the analysis was very similar to that of Rowntree. Tout, in his Bristol inquiry, gave a much more detailed breakdown of the causes of poverty, but otherwise his analysis was essentially the same. Taylor in his study of Plymouth reviewed the causes in terms of just the number of earners in the family. Thus 42 per cent of those in poverty had 'no wage earner', 39 per cent had a 'chief wage earner who was unemployed or casually employed', 11 per cent had 'no adult male earner' and so on (Taylor, 1938:61).

Work, leisure and religion

Those who carried out surveys on the nature and extent of poverty before 1939 were all agreed that it had a lot to do with conditions of employment – low or intermittent wages, casual work, underemployment or unemployment. Booth, however, was aware that his 'immediate' causes needed themselves to be explained in terms of deeper, underlying factors. He set out to connect a social classification of the workers (based on his 'overcrowding' index) to their terms and conditions of employment. He plunged into a detailed analysis of the industrial structure, making studies of individual trades or groups of trades. However, after four published volumes of findings, Booth was still no nearer to discovering the causes of poverty, and concluded that it must be 'to other quite as much as to industrial remedies that we must look for the cure or relief of poverty' (Booth, 1902–3, Industry Series, Vol. V:318).

Booth had long felt that religion would have a strong influence on the morals of the people and in mitigating the effects of personal failings, and he turned to the study of the 'forces for good and evil that are acting on the conditions of the population'. After six further years of patient inquiry Booth, sadly, came to the conclusion that the churches had failed in their attempts to affect the working classes in any way. The ultimate causes of poverty remained as elusive as ever.

Rowntree, in his various studies in York, made no attempt to study its industrial structure, although he did later, with Bruno Lasker, turn his attention to the problem of unemployment in that city (Rowntree and Lasker, 1911). Llewellyn Smith devoted three of his volumes to detailed accounts of each of London's chief industries, trades and services, but confined his attention to showing how the industrial structure itself had changed since Booth's day. The final volume was devoted to 'life and leisure', but Smith did not consider religion at all. The same themes emerged again in Caradog Jones's Merseyside survey, although he did go some way beyond Booth's Industry Series by measuring the extent of occupational mobility. He also went beyond the industrial scene by studying various 'special' groups in the population – infants, schoolchildren, adolescents, pensioners, families without a male head, the deaf, blind, alcoholic and criminal.

None of the social investigators, however, succeeded in linking poverty to anything more tangible than the somewhat obvious 'immediate' causes.

Attempts to show the link between poverty, the industrial structure, religion and other social influences proved to be abortive. The next section will attempt to show that the explanation for this failure probably lies in the shortcomings of the methods and techniques of investigation that they used.

Methods and techniques of investigation

Whatever the motives of the social investigators and whatever social reforms they had in mind as the eventual end-product of their endeavours, the surveyors of poverty all agreed that it was the physical conditions and moral character of the working classes that needed to be studied. Such inquiry was to be scientific, systematic and objective and would discover what proportion of the working classes really were 'in poverty' – and why. But who *were* the 'working classes'?

Booth never actually referred to the 'working classes' as such. He did use the term 'middle class', but inconsistently. Only the 'upper middle' classes were clearly distinguished – on the basis that they kept servants. In his description of the eight classes A to H he said that the 'lower middle' class referred to 'shopkeepers and small employers, clerks etc. and subordinate professional men' (Booth, 1902–3, Poverty Series, Vol. 1:60). However, in his description of class E, who had 'regular standard earnings', he claimed that in the East End, it 'may be noted that classes D and E together form the actual middle class in this district, the numbers above and below them being fairly equally balanced'. So 'middle' appears to mean 'average' for the district rather than any absolute style or standard of living or occupation. Again, in referring to his class F, 'higher class labour' he included some small shopkeepers who were 'in the greatest poverty' (Booth, 1902–3, Poverty Series, Vol. 1:59). This confusion was no doubt a consequence of his collapsing together two systems of classification – one by 'sections' according to character of employment, and another by 'class' according to 'means and position of heads of families'. In short, Booth never really distinguished between the 'working' classes and the 'middle' classes in the contemporary sense. He was more concerned with those people, from whatever class, who were in poverty, in want or in distress.

Rowntree did, however, make such a distinction and he did so entirely on the basis of whether or not the household kept domestic servants. Thus, unlike Booth, he was able to distinguish between the percentage of the 'wage earning' class who were below the poverty line and the percentage of the total population who were in that condition. In Rowntree's later studies he made the distinction in terms of actual incomes. In his second survey of York he defined 'working class' families as those families whose chief wage earners were in receipt of not more than £250 a year.

In Bowley's first five towns study, the household was judged to be 'working class' if the principal occupant was an hourly or weekly wage earner. Thus clerks, travellers, teachers, shop managers, insurance agents and employers were excluded from the inquiry. The rule, however, was not invariable, and marginal cases were apparently treated on their merits. Shop assistants were included only if they were working for butchers and grocers. In his later study Bowley included as 'non working class' all 'professional men or women, clerks, draughtsmen, managers or wholesale agents, and all shop assistants except butchers', fishmongers', grocers', greengrocers' and bakers' ' (Bowley and Hogg, 1925–28). This was an interesting comment on Bowley's view of class and status. Shop assistants clearly straddled the line between working class and middle class and it depended on whether or not they were involved in the sale of foodstuffs.

The repeat of Booth's study by Llewellyn Smith got itself tied up in knots over the distinction between middle and working class. In the street survey the main criterion used was income (earning more or less than £5 per week), while in the sample survey it was the occupation of the head of household. This included as 'middle class' those families of which the head was in commercial or other 'black coated' occupations whatever his income – and there were many such persons who did not earn £5 per week.

The level of sophistication in the application of the poverty line generally rose between 1887 and 1939, with researchers taking into account differences in family composition, rents paid, and various sources of income; the main problem, however, in terms of methods of investigation was that the social investigators did not have any clear notion of what a 'cause' was, and this is probably the major reason why they never successfully got beyond the immediate circumstances that produced inadequate incomes. Furthermore, they did not have at their disposal *any* statistical technique for the measurement of the degree of correlation between variables. It is only too easy to underestimate just how much of a limitation this was. Not only did they not have the statistical techniques, but they had no clear notion of even what a 'correlation' *was*. It is difficult for us to imagine nowadays what this would be like, but some inkling may be obtained from a closer look at Booth's well-known table which measures the 'causes' of poverty (Table 3.1).

Booth has simply listed his causes down the left-hand side and grouped them into 'questions of employment' etc. on the right. If we ask 'What is being correlated with what?' then it becomes clear that it is in fact a one-way table that simply lists each category of independent variable (nature of possible causes) as illustrated in Table 3.2. The dependent variable, poverty, is not varying; in fact there are separate tables for 'great poverty' (classes A and B) and for 'poverty' (classes C and D).

Table 3.1. *Charles Booth's analysis of the causes of 'great poverty' and of 'poverty'*

Analysis of causes of 'great poverty' (classes A and B)

		Per cent		Per cent	
1. Loafers	—	—	60	4	
2. Casual work	697	43			
3. Irregular work, low pay	141	9	878	55	Questions of employment
4. Small profits	40	3			
5. Drink (husband, or both husband and wife)	152	9	231	14	Questions of habit
6. Drunken or thriftless wife	79	5			
7. Illness or infirmity	170	10			
8. Large family	124	8	441	27	Questions of circumstance
9. Illness or large family, combined with irregular work	147	9			
	—	—	1,610	100	

Analysis of causes of 'poverty' (classes C and D).

		Per cent		Per cent	
1. Loafers	—	—	—	—	
2. Low pay (regular earnings)	503	20			
3. Irregular earnings	1,052	43	1,668	68	Questions of employment
4. Small profits	113	5			
5. Drink (husband, or both husband and wife)	167	7	322	13	Questions of habit
6. Drunken or thriftless wife	155	6			
7. Illness or infirmity	123	5			
8. Large family	223	9	476	19	Questions of circumstance
9. Illness or large family, combined with irregular work	130	5			
	—	—	2,466	100	

Source: Booth, 1902–3, Poverty Series, Vol. 1:147

If these two tables are now put together in a modern format, putting the independent variable at the top and the dependent variable down the side, the result will be as in Table 3.3. Two points immediately become clear: first, Booth has percentaged in the 'wrong' direction (i.e. not within the categories of the independent variable); second, there is a missing category

Table 3.2. *Causes of 'great poverty' in simplified format*

Cause	Per cent	Frequency
Employment	55	878
Habit	18	291
Circumstance	27	441
	100	1,610

N.B. 'Loafers' have been included under 'questions of habit'.

Table 3.3. *Degree of poverty by cause, in modern format (percentages)*

Degree of poverty	Cause			
	Employment	Habit	Circumstance	Total
Great poverty	55	18	27	100
Poverty	68	13	19	100

in the dependent variable – those *not* in poverty (classes E to H). Taking the first point, Booth concludes from his table that poverty was due largely to questions of employment since 55 per cent of poverty in classes A and B and 68 per cent of poverty in classes C and D was due to questions of employment. Similarly, that only 13–14 per cent of poverty was due to questions of habit. What Booth omitted to take into account was the considerable differences in the numbers relating to the different causes, that is, a total of 2,546 were questions of employment and only 613 were questions of habit. If the tables are re-percentaged (using the raw numbers), then the result is as in Table 3.4.

Not only do the differences between Booth's causes of poverty almost disappear, but in the case of those in great poverty (classes A and B), it can be said that 34 per cent of those whose poverty is due to questions of employment are in 'great poverty' compared with 47 per cent of those whose poverty was due to questions of habit. In other words, questions of habit are *more* important than questions of employment as far as great poverty is concerned, thereby reversing Booth's original conclusion! From this table Booth might have been able to conclude that 'great poverty' was caused more by questions of habit, and 'poverty' more by questions of

Table 3.4. *Degree of poverty by cause, re-percentaged*

Degree of poverty	Cause		
	Employment	Habit	Circumstance
Great poverty	34	47	48
Poverty	66	53	52
Total	100	100	100

employment. In either case, questions of habit play a much greater role than Booth was able to claim from his original tables, and the same is true of questions of circumstance, whose proportions are similar to those of habit. Even this analysis is largely vitiated because Booth did not measure (or at least did not present the figures concerning) how far each of his causes prevailed amongst those who were *not* in poverty, but who were in comfort.

Booth's successors in effect all made the same mistake when they analysed the 'immediate' causes of poverty. Rowntree did not even distinguish different levels of poverty; still less was he able to make comparisons between those above and those below the poverty line. The later surveys in the inter-war period did no better. Probably the most sophisticated statement on the causes of poverty was that offered by Ford in his Southampton survey where he admitted that poverty was 'a product of many variables, and the real significance of any ascertained volume of it is apparent only if it is understood as an expression of a complex of economic and other social forces'. In consequence, Ford claimed that his study 'went beyond the immediate facts relating to it, and investigates some of the factors which have influenced the growth of population, the earning strength of families, and the elements of costs which attract and repel industries'. In spite of these brave words, the analysis of the causes of poverty followed established lines, focusing on the 'apparent' causes of poverty – unemployment, death or disability of chief wage earner, and insufficiency of wages.

Sociological surveys and academic sociology

Sociological surveys from Booth to Caradog Jones, then, were somewhat standardised affairs, strong on the collection of empirical data of a largely quantitative kind, but decidedly weak on subsequent analysis of the correlations between variables and on their bearing on any form of general theory whose significance went beyond the immediate findings. As Selvin points out in the next chapter correlational statistics had been developed in the 1890s by Galton, Pearson and Yule. Yule, in an article published in 1895, had even gone to the trouble of calculating a correlation coefficient for one of Booth's tables that had appeared in his book *The Aged Poor in England and Wales* (1894). Yet there is no evidence that Booth even acknowledged Yule's article. At no time did Booth, or indeed any of his followers, utilise correlational statistics for investigating the relationship between poverty and other potentially causative factors (see Kent, 1981).

While Rowntree, like Booth, was outside academia, and hence unlikely to receive institutional support for the application of new techniques, the same could not be said for Bowley, Llewellyn Smith, Ford, Caradog Jones and several others who were all attached to the universities. Perhaps the most curious case was that of Bowley, who was teaching statistics at the London School of Economics when the first Department of Sociology was set up there in 1907. Three years later Bowley published *An Elementary Manual of Statistics*, which contained no reference to Yule, Galton or Pearson. Indeed, the word 'correlation' did not appear in the index and the topic was not mentioned, still less covered, anywhere in the book. More curious was that Yule also wrote a book on statistics – *An Introduction to the Theory of Statistics* (1911). Most of the book was, of course, concerned with correlation, and even though he covered the topic of sampling in several chapters, he made no reference to its pioneer – Arthur Bowley. It is likely that each just did not see the significance of what the other was doing for their own fields of interest. Bowley's interest was in handling government statistics and in collecting raw data by way of sample surveys. Galton and Pearson were eugenicists whose aim – the improvement of the human stock by utilising the principles of heredity – would have been anathema to those interested in social reform.

The social survey, then, did not connect at all with the developments in correlational technques; but it did not connect with developments in academic sociology either. The Sociological Society was founded in 1903. At its early meetings eminent men from all walks of life were gathered together – including the eugenicists Galton and Pearson. Charles Booth was himself a prominent member along with others who were conducting sociological surveys at the time. Edward Westermarck and Leonard Hobhouse were also active participants. The scene was thus set for all three elements to come together, but in the end each went their separate ways.

When the Department of Sociology was set up at the L.S.E. it became clear that establishing the academic status of sociology was to be given priority and the two men who were appointed – Hobhouse and Westermarck – were both eminent philosophers. The first sociology syllabus in 1909 in effect offered an introduction to evolutionary philosophy and comparative anthropology. There was no place given to the sociological survey or to methods of research. When social survey methods did enter the universities it was in departments of social administration devoted to the training of social workers. It was from such a department that Caradog Jones operated in Liverpool University.

Academic respectability for the sociological survey might have come from two other sources: the Webbs and the town-planners. Beatrice Webb (or Potter as she then was) had been one of Booth's assistants in his early inquiry into Tower Hamlets, and in 1887 made an inquiry into dock labour for him, followed by a study of the 'sweated' labour in the East End of London tailoring trade. Beatrice, however, became convinced that only collective action would solve the problem of poverty and low wages. She parted company with Booth and made a study of the co-operative movement in Britain. In 1892 she married Sidney Webb and together they turned to historical and institutional inquiry such as their studies of trade unionism and local government (see Kent, 1981). However, the Webbs never engaged in social surveying in the manner of Booth and his successors. Their textbook, *Methods of Social Study* (1932), contained no commentary on the social survey as such. It was more concerned with what would nowadays be called participant observation and the use of historical and other documents. Nor did the book connect well with developments in academic sociology. On the contrary, the Webbs suggested that the correct way to proceed was 'not to focus the enquiry upon discovering the answer to some particular question in which you may be interested', but rather to discover 'every fact' concerning a social institution and its relation to the environment. This was the very antithesis of the deductive mode of reasoning championed by Westermarck and Hobhouse.

The town-planners, led by Patrick Geddes, could have provided another source from which a link between sociological surveying and academic sociology might have been forged. Geddes saw applied sociology (civics as he called it) as combining several disciplines together – geography, economics, anthropology, demography and eugenics. The evolutionism of Comte, the functionalism of Spencer and the idea of family, place and work from Le Play would all be combined into empirical surveys of the city. However, instead of following through this admirable programme he immersed himself in the town-planning movement, mounting exhibitions and stimulating local communities to conduct surveys on a do-it-yourself basis. Most of the ensuing surveys were of rural villages and gathered geological and geographical information, data on land use and institutional facilities, on economic demands and resources, on transportation and occupational patterns. Most of the statistics were not even social; still less were they given any sociological interpretation in the way Geddes had earlier envisaged.

Conclusion

By 1939, then, little progress had been made in terms either of making sociological surveys more analytically sophisticated or in terms of linking them with the development of academic sociology and sociological theory. The late nineteenth- and early twentieth-century studies of poverty *were* sociological rather than just social; investigators did attempt to explain their findings by looking for causes, but the attempt was not very successful. Partly this was a result of their lack of methodological sophistication and in particular of their failure to utilise developments in statistical correlation techniques, but it was also a result of their suspicion of theory and what they derided as *a priori* reasoning. They had felt that delving in greater detail into the facts would provide an explanation. What they failed to realise was that explanation of the facts could never be based on yet more facts. Such an explanation was always a question of interpretation of the facts, and for that they would have needed the kind of theories being proposed by political economists and academic sociologists of the day.

One consequence of this was that when they proposed remedies, it was more often to proposals for the amelioration of the worst symptoms of poverty than to measures for an attack on its causes that they turned. Another was that Booth and his successors were never able to relate their findings on the incidence of social ills – drunkenness, gambling, crime, sexual immorality – to poverty. They had all *defined* poverty in terms of inadequate incomes and had, for the most part, specifically excluded the way in which the incomes were spent as productive of the suffering they were measuring, yet it was precisely working class proclivities towards 'riotous living' that they wanted most of all to curb. They were never quite clear as to whether they were really interested in the causes of respectably-earned, but insufficient incomes, or in the causes of misspent incomes and incomes earned in less reputable fashions.

BIBLIOGRAPHY

Booth, C. (1902–3), *Life and Labour of the People of London*, 17 vols. London, Macmillan.

Bowley, A.L. (1910), *An Elementary Manual of Statistics*, London, Macdonald and Evans.

Bowley, A.L. and Burnett-Hurst, A.R. (1915), *Livelihood and Poverty. A Study in the Economic Conditions of Working Class Households in Nottingham, Warrington, Stanley and Reading*, London, Bell and Sons.

Bowley, A.L. and Hogg, M.H. (1925), *Has Poverty Diminished?*, London, P.S. King.

Briggs, A. (1961), *Social Thought and Social Action. A Study of the Work of Seebohm Rowntree*, London, Longman.

Brown, J. (1968), 'Charles Booth and Labour Colonies, 1889–1905', *Economic Hist. Rev.*, 2nd series, XXI:349–60.

Brown, J. (1971), 'Social Judgements and Social Policy', *Economic Hist. Rev.*, Vol. 24:106–13.

Butterfield, H. (1963), *The Whig Interpretation of History*, London, G. Bell and Sons.

Clay, Rev. J. (1839), 'Criminal Statistics of Preston', *Journal of the Statistical Society of London*, Vol. 2.

Evans, R. (1933), *Unemployment in Hull, 1923–31*, Hull Community Council.

Ford, P. (1934), *Work and Wealth in a Modern Port. An Economic Survey of Southampton*, London, Allen and Unwin.

Jones, D.C. (1934), *The Social Survey of Merseyside*, Liverpool, Liverpool University Press.

Kent, R.A. (1981), *A History of British Empirical Sociology*, Aldershot, Gower Press.

Lumis, T. (1971), 'Charles Booth: Moralist or Social Scientist?', *Economic Hist. Rev.*, Vol. 24:100–6.

Mess, H. (1928), *Industrial Tyneside*, London, Benn.

Owen, A.K.D. (1931–3), *Survey Pamphlets*, Sheffield Social Survey Committee.

Rowntree, B.S. (1901), *Poverty. A Study of Town Life*, London, Macmillan.

Rowntree, B.S. and Lasker, B. (1911), *Unemployment. A Social Study*, London, Macmillan.

Simey, T.S. and Simey, M.B. (1960), *Charles Booth. Social Scientist*, Oxford, Oxford University Press.

Smith, H.L. (1930–5), *The New Survey of London Life and Labour*, London, P.S. King.

Stedman-Jones, G. (1971), *Outcast London: a study in the relationship between classes in Victorian society*, Oxford, Clarendon Press.

Taylor, R.M. (1938), *A Social Survey of Plymouth*, London, P.S. King.

Tout, H. (1944), *The Standard of Living in Bristol*, London, Arrowsmith.

Webb, B and Webb, S. (1932), *Methods of Social Study*, London, Longman.

Williams, K. (1981), *From Pauperism to Poverty*, London, Routledge.

Young, T.C. (1934), *Becontree and Dagenham*, Becontree Social Survey Committee.

Yule, G.U. (1911), *An Introduction to the Theory of Statistics*, London, Griffin.

4 Durkheim, Booth and Yule: the non-diffusion of an intellectual innovation*

HANNAN C. SELVIN, *with the assistance of*
CHRISTOPHER BERNERT

Except perhaps for a few diehards, no sociologist today would think of conducting a large-scale empirical investigation of numerical data without a firm grasp of statistical methods – or at least a graduate assistant who has such a grasp. The old polemics about statistics in social research have died away and are now lost to view under a blizzard of statistical findings in journal articles and books. Asked to date the period when statistical analysis really 'took over' in social research, most sociologists would probably put the date around 1960, when large computers and efficient programs became widely available. But the date of widespread adoption is perhaps not as significant as the date on which the leaders in the field became convinced of the desirability of using powerful statistical methods in the analysis of standardised data.

To some extent the answers that one gives to this question depend on when and where one was trained. Those sociologists educated at Columbia in the last twenty-five years are likely to date the advent of powerful statistical procedures at the arrival of Paul F. Lazarsfeld in the United States, but this, I believe, is a mistake. Indeed, Lazarsfeld himself argued against such tools as multiple regression for some time after they became widely used and easily available on the computer, and he credits Stouffer with the same views (Lazarsfeld in Stouffer 1962: XVI).

The story of the conversion of sociology to high-powered statistical tools of analysis is too long to tell here, but it is one that should be told and one that will carry some surprises (for example, that Robert K. Merton was apparently the first sociologist to use a test of statistical significance in the *American Sociological Review* (Merton 1940)). The story I want to tell here is not 'When did it happen?' but rather 'When should it have happened?'

One answer to this question is: in 1897, in Emile Durkheim's *Suicide*.

*Reprinted with permission from *Archives européennes de sociologie* XVII, 1976, 39–51.

Now one will not find such a statement in any standard history of sociology. Indeed, I discovered it myself, almost by accident. The way in which I came to do this is worth a brief digression, for it illustrates some of what happens when new modes of thought do diffuse.

In the summer of 1957, Peter H. Rossi, having recently become Editor of the *American Journal of Sociology*, was planning a Durkheim-Simmel centennial issue for the next spring; he asked me to write an article for that issue on the methodology of Durkheim's *Suicide*. I began my work on this article by re-reading *Suicide* and making detailed marginal notes. The model I had in mind during this reading was an extraordinary article by Robert K. Merton and Paul F. Lazarsfeld, in which Lazarsfeld provides a methodological commentary on a theoretically oriented empirical analysis by Merton. Lazarsfeld's formalisation of Merton's analysis led him to suggest a more effective way in which to analyse Merton's data than Merton was then planning to do.[1]

Now may I ask you to turn your minds to Durkheim's Book I, where he demolishes various non-sociological theories of differences in suicide rates. Having found that Germany had a high suicide rate, Durkheim goes on to ask whether or not this might be the result of 'race', some 'hereditary state of the German organism'.

> To attribute the German inclination to suicide to this cause, it is not enough to prove that it is general in Germany; for this might be due to the special nature of German civilization. But the inclination would have to be shown to be connected with an hereditary state of the German organism, and that this is a permanent trait of the type, persisting even under change of social environment [. . .] Let us see whether the German retains this sad primacy outside Germany, in the midst of the life of other peoples and acclimatized to different civilizations. Austria [i.e., the fifteen provinces of Austria-Hungary – H.C.S.] offers us a complete laboratory for answering this question. In differing proportions in the various provinces, the Germans are mixed with a population of totally different ethnic origins. Let us see whether their presence effects an increase in the number of suicides (Durkheim 1951 : 86–7).

Durkheim then presents a table showing the proportion of German-speaking people in each province along with its suicide rate; he reports triumphantly that there is in his table 'not the least trace of German influence' on the suicide rate.

Two points about this passage are worth noting. First, like most of Durkheim's tables, the table here is really an 'array', a listing of cases and the values of two variables for each case. It is not a conventional two-variable table, which, even in a crude fourfold form (dichotomising each variable into 'high' and 'low') would have shown the relation more clearly. Second, Durkheim's demonstration that there is no relation consists essentially in showing that there are some provinces that have high proportions of Germans and only middling or low suicide rates and others that have the reverse combination. In short, the presence of a few cases that depart from a perfect relation is enough to convince Durkheim that there is no relation at all. As Boudon has remarked, Durkheim's methodology was still that of John Stuart Mill's *System of Logic* (Boudon 1967:14). In Mill's 'canon of concomitant variation' there is room only for perfect positive and perfect negative relations – nothing in between.

Even without knowing of Durkheim's dependence on Mill, I could see that this table did indeed show some kind of relation. I decided to make a scatter plot of Durkheim's data – per cent German along the X-axis and suicide rate along the Y-axis.

To my astonishment, the dots did not behave as if they had read Durkheim; instead, they marched up the graph paper from lower left to upper right in what was obviously a strong positive relation. Not a perfect relation to be sure, but far from the zero relation that Durkheim had proclaimed.

In order to make this point most meaningful, it is necessary to show *how far* Durkheim was from being correct. It would not do to rely on the unaided inspection of a scatter plot, as Durkheim had relied on the unaided inspection of a table. What is needed here is a numerical measure of the relation between the variables. I therefore computed a Spearman *rho*; it was 0.57 – again a far cry from the zero relation that Durkheim had seen.

Now how did it happen that Durkheim, whom we now venerate as a methodological virtuoso (Selvin 1958, 1965), did not compute a coefficient of correlation? The Spearman measure had not yet been invented, but much of the work on the Pearson *r* as a measure of association had already been done by 1897 when *Suicide* appeared.

My answer to this question is in two parts. First Durkheim did not invent the tabular procedures that he used in *Suicide*; he took them over from the 'moral statisticians' of the nineteenth century, notably from Morselli (1879), much of whose work on suicide reads like Durkheim's but without the theoretical zest and the imaginative indices that grace Durkheim's work. Second, Durkheim's first publication on suicide came not in 1897 but in 1888, when he published an article in an obscure French journal on comparisons of national happiness, using suicide rates as inverse measures of happiness (Durkheim 1888). In short, Durkheim had already come to deal quantitatively with suicide rates before Karl Pearson had begun to study and refine Galton's coefficient of correlation (Kendall 1968a). Now, as far as sociology is concerned, the crucial work on correlation occurred between 1895 and 1899; Durkheim had long since done all the methodological innovating that he was to do in the area of suicide. However the question of

Durkheim's 'failure' to use correlation is more general than its absence in *Suicide*. Rather, it is why neither he nor any of his disciples ever came to be aware of the defects in the methodology of his quantitative analysis.[2]

A cardinal principle of study design holds that it is bad to have only one case for each combination of the values of the independent variables. With only Durkheim as a non-user of correlation, it would be impossible to identify the general factors in his situation that were responsible for his failure to use correlation and to separate them from the accidental or specific factors. Others who have studied the history of empirical research in Germany have shown that it is possible to replicate this analysis in that country too. Thus Lazarsfeld and Oberschall (1965) have shown that Max Weber, far from being the qualitative purist that he has seemed to be to the anti-quantitativists, was in reality a workmanlike survey analyst; but Weber, too, used only relatively crude tabular methods.[3] Thus the question of the non-diffusion of more powerful statistical methods might also be raised for Weber!

There is, however, a more striking and better documented case of non-diffusion. Durkheim and Weber were separated from the development of correlation in London by both distance and language, but there was someone else doing social research in London at the same time, for whom neither distance nor language nor even time can explain his failure to use correlation.

With the upsurge of interest in the scientific study of poverty in the past decade, the name of Charles Booth has come out of the history books, and people have again begun to leaf through his monumental *Life and Labour of the People in London* (1889–91). Booth had been doing research on poverty ever since the mid-1880s (Simey 1960), when his anger was aroused by the statement of a British Socialist that a third of the people in London were living in poverty. Not finding any governmental data on poverty, Booth set about gathering his own. For today's researcher, the obvious procedure would be to interview a sample of the poor, but Booth felt that such interviewing would be an 'invasion of privacy'. Instead, he interviewed the School Board Visitors, or, as they were later to be called, 'truant officers'. With the passage of the Compulsory Education Act in 1877, the British Government felt impelled to keep track of poor children in order to see that they were getting the required education; the children of the rich were assumed to be getting such an education. To this end, the School Board Visitor kept a detailed record of every poor family in his district, noting such details as the occupation of the father, his income, the number, ages, and sexes of the children, the parents' habits of sobriety, the cleanliness of the household and so on and on. Starting in 1886, Booth and his assistants interviewed the School Board Visitors for each district of London, slowly and methodically working their way across the entire city.

Sometime in 1895 Booth's work came to the attention of a young Scottish mathematical physicist named George Udny Yule, who was then working with Karl Pearson, learning and helping to develop the new field of statistics. Before 1890, statisticians were largely curators of museums of numbers, odd people who delighted in reporting odd facts, much as baseball 'statisticians' now do when they tell us who holds the record for the largest number of unassisted triple plays. The transformation of statistics from this magpie-like collecting of facts to the development of tools for analysing complex data had already begun in the work of Edgeworth and Galton, but it is Pearson and his less celebrated student Yule who are the fathers of modern data analysis, especially as it is used in the social sciences.

By 1895, Yule had published six papers on electromagnetic theory. Once he published his paper (1895) on Booth, however, Yule never again did any work in physics but remained a prolific and imaginative statistician for the rest of his long life (for a brief but informative biography, see Kendall 1968b).

Yule's attention was drawn to a statement that Booth made about a set of two-variable tables, that there was 'no relation' between the variables. This impressionistic assessment of a table is couched in almost the same language as Durkheim's statement that drew my curiosity more than sixty years later. Yule did almost the same thing as I did: he computed a coefficient of correlation.

There is, however, one important difference. At the time of Yule's paper the correlation coefficient had not yet acquired its interpretation as the proportion of explained variation. It was, as it had been for Galton, a property of a bivariate normal distribution fitted to the joint distribution of the two variables. Now Yule saw immediately that the bivariate distribution in Booth's table was far from normal, and so he said that it was not legitimate to compute a correlation coefficient. But Yule had no other choice at that time if he was to measure the degree of association quantitatively, and so he went on to compute the coefficiencts of correlation for several tables in which Booth had found no relation. The Pearson r for these tables turned out to be about 0.30 – again, a far cry from zero!

This paper marks the beginning of Yule's career as a statistician. In 1897 he published what one may now consider the cornerstone of statistical data-analysis. Yule did two things in this paper. First he showed that the coefficient of correlation need not be tied to a bivariate normal distribution as everyone had thought. Starting with the idea of fitting a least-squares regression line to a set of points – the approach now used by most teachers of elementary statistics – Yule showed that one gets exactly the same value as if one starts with a normal distribution fitted to the observed bivariate frequency distribution.

The normal distribution now appears almost incidental. In other words, Yule freed the coefficient of correlation from its dependence on the normality of the joint distribution of X and Y, and thus made it into a general-purpose tool for analysing any kind of data.

Yule's second contribution in this paper was to present the formulas for multiple regression and correlation, but without any empirical example. The first published example of the use of multiple regression comes in another paper of Yule's in 1899. He used it to explain changes in the incidence of poverty in the poor-law districts of England between two censuses. In this paper Yule even took note of the relatively heavy computation required in multiple regression and suggested ways to lessen it. It therefore is not a sufficient explanation of the late appearance of multiple regression as a major tool of sociological analysis.

One obvious answer is that both Booth and Durkheim had already settled on their methods by the time that Yule's work appeared, but this merely leads to a sharper question: how was it that neither of these men, nor any of their followers, ever acknowledged the existence of these analytic techniques that would have been so useful to them? Both men continued working for some years after their statistical works were published, and it is only reasonable to expect that they or their followers would at least have made some reference to the development of statistical methods.

It seems fruitful to try to explain why the statistical ideas of Yule did not diffuse to Booth and Durkheim by looking at the conditions under which they *would* have diffused and asking what went wrong. This is essentially what I have done. Adapting a conceptual scheme for the study of diffusion set forth by Katz, Levin, and Hamilton (1963), I have tried to discern the requirements for diffusion that were not met and to assess their relative importance. There are four elements in my conceptual scheme:

1. *Channel*: There must be some path of communication for the item or message to travel between the source (Yule) and the potential adopters (Booth and Durkheim).

2. *Comprehensibility*: The potential adopters must understand the message.

3. *Value consonance*: The potential adopters must perceive the message as legitimate and useful.

4. *Social support*: There must be some social structure that will support and reward potential adopters for changing their ways.

Although it is impossible to answer all of these questions unequivocally, there is enough evidence to make reasonable guesses.

Channel

Is there any evidence that the message of the value of correlation could have reached Booth and Durkheim? For Booth, the answer is certainly yes. For one thing, he was a member of the Royal Statistical Society from the middle 1880s – and thus received its *Journal*.[4] For another, Yule, a courteous, even courtly man, used Booth's data in his 1895 paper, and it is inconceivable that he did not at least inform Booth by letter of what he had written. Finally, there is another blocked pathway from Yule to Booth that is worth a paper in itself – the failure of Beatrice Webb to become what she clearly wanted to be, the first mathematical and statistical sociologist. The story is too long to tell here, but consider only these bare facts. Beatrice Potter, later the wife of Sidney Webb, was a cousin of Booth's wife and worked for him as a research assistant for some months. Early on, she saw her vocation as becoming a 'social investigator' (a social scientist, not a social worker). Recognising the importance of mathematics in this task, she set about learning it on her own. And, even after she left off working for Booth and began the research for her *History of the Cooperative Movement*, she kept in close touch with him about his work. In her collected papers there is a letter from Booth, one of many, in which he says, almost wistfully, that the main difficulty he faced in 'discovering the causes of poverty' was to 'find a statistical framework for organizing the data' (Simey 1960).

Moreover, Beatrice Webb was something that Charles Booth never was: an intellectual in touch with the leading figures of British thought. Thus she was even Spencer's literary executrix before she became engaged to that notorious socialist, Sidney Webb, and thus cut herself off from both Spencer and Booth. And, as a socialist, if not as an intellectual, she was sure to have met Karl Pearson, who, at least in his early years, thought of himself as a socialist too (Semmel 1958). Had she remained friendly with Spencer and Booth, it is inconceivable that she would not have told Booth about the importance of Yule's work. In short, the answer to the question of whether or not there was a path connecting Yule and Booth is certainly yes.

Only one small bit of evidence is available for Durkheim. The citations in *Suicide* show that he or his assistants combed the pages of the *Journal of the Royal Statistical Society*; and one of Yule's 1899 papers was published there. Moreover, the Statistical Society of Paris had been in existence well before 1890, and it seems likely that one or another member of that group might have read Yule's earlier work and told Durkheim about it. At the very least, some such pathway is plausible, and so it seems safe to rate the existence of a channel between Yule and Durkheim as 'probable'.

Comprehensibility

If the message reached Booth and Durkheim, would they have been able to understand it? For Booth, the best guess is 'probably yes'. Although he probably knew no mathematics beyond arithmetic, he needed none to understand Yule's crucial paper of 1895. And, by virtue of his long-time membership in the Royal Statistical Society, he must have known many men who could have explained Yule's later papers to him. (Incidentally, he was elected president of the Society in 1892.)

The evidence is more conjectural for Durkheim. I do not know whether or not the education he received included any advanced mathematics, but, as a professor at Bordeaux and at the Sorbonne, he had many colleagues who could have explained any mysteries in Yule's work. For him, too, the verdict must be 'probably yes'.

Value consonance

Assuming that the message of Yule's work could have reached Booth and Durkheim and that they could have understood it, how would they have reacted to it? Would the idea of calculating coefficients of correlation and other statistic measures have seemed legitimate, useful, and important to them?

Anything labelled 'statistics' and written by a fellow-member of the Royal Statistical Society would surely have seemed legitimate to someone who had recently been president of that organisation. However, one must beware of taking 'statistics' before the turn of the century as comparable to the field of the same name today. In particular, the question of whether or not the practice of statistics required some background in mathematics was not yet settled. As late as 1918 many eminent 'statisticians' still paid no attention to the algebra of correlation. In that year the American Statistical Association published a volume on the history of statistics to commemorate its seventy-fifth anniversary. This volume contains nothing on correlation, on Pearson, or on Yule, and Galton appears only as the author of an 1885 paper on graphical methods (Koren 1918). Similarly, the *Journal of the Royal Statistical Society*, while publishing mathematical derivations in the 1880s, always relegated them to the back pages of the journal; and they were never among the major papers delivered and discussed at the monthly meetings of the Society.

Moreover, we know from Booth's accounts of his own work and from his contemporaries that he was a man of limited intellectual powers. As one British historian remarked to me: 'Charles Booth's greatest contribution to social science was to spend £30,000 of his own money.' All this and what I have said about Beatrice Webb leads me to conjecture that, left to himself, Booth would have been unlikely to see much value in the arcane mathematical symbols of Yule's work. Even Yule's 1895 demonstration that Booth had misread his own tables might well have led Booth only to resolve to be more careful in the future. Thus, despite writing to Beatrice Webb that he needed a 'statistical framework' for organising his data, there is no evidence that he ever consulted anyone who might have been able to help him in this task. Second, had Booth not alienated Beatrice Webb by disapproving of her engagement to Sidney, she might well have provided the intellectual support that he needed (and the obvious importance of elementary algebra in understanding Yule's work might well have motivated her to continue her study of mathematics). The tentative verdict, then, must be that Booth probably would not have thought Yule's work important and useful but that he might have been led to do so had he and Beatrice Webb not parted company.

For Durkheim, the argument is even more conjectural. Again, there is a bit of solid ground in what is known of his desire to make sociology a discipline independent of all others, especially mathematics. Hence, it seems unlikely that he would have even considered seriously any claim that Yule's statistical formulas might have helped him. As with Booth, however, it is conceivable that his friends and colleagues might have persuaded him otherwise, had those around him been part of a free market of ideas. However, as Henri Peyre has pointed out (1960), after 1900 the Durkheim school was closed to any new ideas from outside, concentrating instead on developing the ideas of the master and applying them to new problems.[5]

Social support

One function served for individual scientists by scientific meetings is to provide social support for venturing into new areas. In such meetings and in seminars and colloquia at individual institutions they can launch trial balloons and see whether they are shot down or whether the applause and approval are sufficient to keep them aloft. How different it was for Booth! Working with one or two untrained assistants and apart from any intellectual or scientific organisation, Booth was under-integrated into the scientific community that might have approved his venturing into new modes of research. Part of the difficulty lies in the weak and speculative state of English sociology, at the time still under the influence of Herbert Spencer, but another part undoubtedly lies in Booth's orientation to the world of newspaper editorials and Royal Commissions that vigorously applauded his publication of detailed data on the poor, even without any shred of the causal structure he had originally set out to find.

Durkheim, the great theorist of social integration, certainly did not lack integration into an intellectual milieu, but, as I have said, it was not a milieu that was linked to the wider scientific community. Nor was Durkheim himself interested in tying his work to that of other sociologists. Thus he seems to have remained uninterested in Weber's work, although he almost certainly knew of it (Lukes 1972:397). In the many citations to other investigators in *Suicide*, there is not one that I can recall in which Durkheim gives credit to someone else for an idea. Instead, he acknowledges sources of data and condemns the mistakes of other writers on suicide like Wagner and Morselli. In short, both personally and socially, Durkheim was over-integrated into a closed intellectual world. Had Yule's ideas penetrated it and been considered sympathetically by Durkheim, it is unlikely that the social world he created about him would have supported these strange ventures.

Implications

The moral of this analysis seems almost too obvious to need explicit statement. No matter how convinced an investigator is of the correctness of his procedures, no matter how simple and obvious they appear to him, he should always consider the possibility that better ones may be available. Early airing of new ideas is important, especially before audiences of one's professional peers. The diversity that links one to other 'schools' of thought is valuable in a department or research institute.

Lest these platitudes seem unworthy of repetition, let me close with a striking insight that my colleague at Stony Brook, Jerome Singer, calls 'Herring's Law'. Formulated by Pendleton Herring during his term as president of the American Social Science Research Council, it says simply: 'Every discipline does worst that which is at the putative center of its field.' Historians forget the past, psychologists cannot handle their emotions, economists unbalance their budgets, and sociologists cannot organise social relations. One of our tasks for the future may well be to provide a definitive test of this law. The cases of Booth and Durkheim clearly support it.

NOTES

1 For a further discussion of this paper and of what mathematical and statistical formalisations can contribute to theory, see my paper on Formalising Theory (in Selvin 1975).

2 One might also wonder why neither Durkheim nor his followers seem to have thought of applying the quantitative approach of *Suicide* to other social phenomena. My own guess is that they classified the study of suicide rates as part of moral statistics and considered the method used in *Suicide* as suitable only for the limited domain, in which they lost interest after 1897.

3 Weber's failure to become statistical is all the more striking in view of his apparent familiarity with the mathematical theory of probability. See his reference to the 'law of large numbers' (Weber 1951). I am grateful to Wallace Davis for making available a translation of this passage.

4 The Statistical Society of London was founded in 1835, and began publishing its *Journal* in 1838; in 1885, it became the Royal Statistical Society of London; and its journal was thereafter known as the *Journal of the Royal Statistical Society*. Modern sociologists who browse through its early volumes will see that 'statisticians' were the empirical sociologists of the nineteenth century.

5 In their writings and other activities, Durkheim and his colleagues showed great disdain for most persons not collaborating with the *Année sociologique*; they thereby contributed to crystallising French social scientists into outwardly aggressive and inwardly self-satisfied schools (Clark 1972: 156). See also Clark (1973) and Besnard (1983) for a fuller picture of Durkheim and his social circle.

REFERENCES

Besnard, Philippe (ed.), *The Sociological Domain: the Durkheimians and the founding of French sociology* (Cambridge: Cambridge University Press, 1983).

Booth, Charles *et al.*, *Life and Labour of the People in London* (London, Macmillan, 1902–1903 [1st ed. 1889–1891]), 17 vols.

Boudon, Raymond, *L'analyse mathématique des faits sociaux* (Paris, Plon, 1967).

Clark, Terry N., Emile Durkheim and the French University: the institutionalization of sociology, in Anthony Oberschall, *The Establishment of Empirical Sociology* (New York, Harper and Row, 1972), pp. 152–86.

Clark, Terry N., *Prophets and Patrons: the French university and the emergence of social science* (Cambridge, Mass., Harvard University Press, 1973).

Durkheim, Emile, *Suicide: a study in sociology* (Glencoe, Ill., Free Press, 1951 [1st ed. 1897]).

Durkheim, Emile, Suicide et natalité: étude de statistique morale, *Revue philosophique*, XXVI (1888), 446–63.

Katz, Elihu, Levin, Martin L. and Hamilton, Herbert, Traditions of Research on the Diffusion of Innovation, *American Sociological Review*, XXVIII (1963), 237–52.

Kendall, M.G., The History of Statistical Methods, *International Encyclopaedia of the Social Sciences* XV (New York, Macmillan/Free Press, 1968), pp. 224–32. Quoted as 1968a.

Kendall, M.G., G. Udny Yule, *International Encyclopaedia of the Social Sciences* XVI (New York, Macmillan/Free Press, 1968). Quoted as 1968b.

Koren, John, *The History of Statistics* (New York, Macmillan, 1918).

Lazarsfeld, Paul F., Notes on the History of Quantification in Sociology – Trends, sources and problems, in Harry Woolf (ed.), *Quantification: a history of the meaning of measurement in the natural and social sciences* (Indianapolis, Ind., Bobbs-Merrill, 1961), pp. 147–203.

Lazarsfeld, Paul F., The Analysis of Attribute Data, *International Encyclopaedia of the Social Sciences* XV (New York, Macmillan/Free Press, 1968), 419–29.

Lazarsfeld, Paul F. and Oberschall, Anthony, Max Weber and Empirical Social Research, *American Sociological Review*, XXX (1965), 185–99.

Lécuyer, Bernard and Oberschall, Anthony R., The Early History of Social Research, *International Encyclopaedia of the Social Sciences* XV (New York, Macmillan/Free Press, 1968), pp. 36–53.

Lukes, Steven, *Emile Durkheim: his life and work* (New York, Harper and Row, 1972).

Merton, Robert K., Fact and Factitiousness in Ethnic Opinionnaires, *American Sociological Review*, V (1940), 13–28.

Morselli, Enrico, *Suicide* (New York, Appleton, 1882 [1st ed. 1879]).

Oberschall, Anthony, *Empirical Social Research in Germany*: *1848–1914* (The Hague, Mouton, 1965).

Peyre, Henri, Durkheim: the man, his time, and his intellectual background, in Kurt H. Wolff (ed.), *Emile Durkheim, 1858–1917* (Columbus, Ohio State University Press, 1960), pp. 3–31.

Selvin, Hanan C., Durkheim's *Suicide* and Problems of Empirical Research, *American Journal of Sociology*, LXIII (1958), 607–19.

Selvin, Hanan C., Durkheim's *Suicide*: further thoughts on a methodological classic, in Robert A. Nisbet (ed.), *Emile Durkheim* (Englewood Cliffs, N.J., Prentice-Hall, 1965), pp. 113–36.

Selvin, Hanan C., On Formalizing Theory, in Lewis Coser (ed.), *The Idea of Social Structure*: papers in honor of Robert K. Merton (New York, Harcourt, Brace, Jovanovich, 1975).

Semmel, Bernard, Karl Pearson: sociologist and Darwinist, *British Journal of Sociology*, IX (1958), 111–25.

Simey, T.S. and Simey, M.B., *Charles Booth* (London, Oxford University Press, 1960).

Stouffer, Samuel A., *Social Research to Test Ideas* (New York, Free Press of Glencoe, 1962).

Weber, Max, *Gesammelte Aufsätze zur Wissenschaftslehre* (Tübingen, Siebeck, 1951), I : Roscher und Knies und die logischen Probleme der historischen Nationaloekonomie, p. 68.

Yule, G. Udny, On the Correlation of Total Pauperism with Proportion of Outrelief, *Economic Journal*, V (1895), 477–489.

Yule, G. Udny, On the Significance of Bravais, Formulae for Regression, and e., in the Case of Skew Correlation, *Proceedings of the Royal Society of London*, LX (1897), 477–89.
Yule, G. Udny, An Investigation into the Causes of Changes in Pauperism in England, chiefly during the last two intercensal decades. Part I, *Journal of the Royal Statistical Society*, LXII (1899), 249–86.
Yule, G. Udny, On the Association of Attributes in Statistics: with illustrations from the material of the Childhood Society, etc., *Philosophical Transactions* [*Royal Society of London*] *Series A* CLXXXXIV (1900), 257–319.
Yule, G. Udny and Kendall, M.G., *An Introduction to the Theory of Statistics*, 14th edition revised and enlarged (London, Griffin, 1969 [1st ed. 1911]). – M.G. Kendall has been a joint author since the 11th edition (1937): the 1958 edition was revised by Kendall.

5 The Government Social Survey

FRANK WHITEHEAD

Introduction

The Government Social Survey, now the Social Survey Division of the Office of Population Censuses and Surveys, is one of those anomalous institutions that came into being as a wartime expedient and survived into the post-war world because it had demonstrated that it was too useful to do without. It now carries out the main continuous social surveys required by Government and a wide variety of one-off or *ad hoc* surveys. It also acts as a centre for advice on survey methodology and management, provides a link between Government and private sector research firms and keeps closely in touch with academics concerned with the development and improvement of survey methodology.

The Social Survey is proud of its tradition and the standards it has helped to set for sample survey research in Great Britain. Its present approach is characterised by an adherence to probability sampling, the use of well motivated and well trained interviewers, the careful piloting and development of field procedures, the use of structured questionnaires, careful attention to detail in processing and analysing the data and a firm belief that those who collect data should also analyse and report on it if they are to learn from experience. These standards have tended to make it appear costly on some occasions and misunderstood on others. Yet over the 40 years of its existence it has produced a steady stream of reports on the surveys it has undertaken that demonstrate its ability to complete projects on a wide range of topics.

The purpose of this essay is to trace the development of the Social Survey from its origins in the early 1940s to the present day, to draw attention to the changes in the environment in which it has had to operate, to describe the main features of its work and to indicate its future prospects. Fortunately, a fuller history of the Social Survey is currently being prepared by Louis

Moss, who was its director for some 30 years. This thumbnail sketch owes much to his memory and advice.

Origins

The origins of the Social Survey in the early days of the Second World War are surrounded by some mystery. The Government had planned in the event of war to create a Ministry of Information, and part of its function was to be the collection of civilian intelligence on the state of 'public morale'. For this it was able to use such organisations as Mass-Observation and the British Institute of Public Opinion, who carried out the Gallup Poll in Britain. The Wartime Social Survey came into being as a means of gathering quantitative information to supplement the more qualitative data coming from other sources. At first the organisation operated under Professor Arnold Plant at the London School of Economics with funds granted by the MOI and the tacit support of the National Institute for Economic and Social Research (NIESR). This seems to have been intended to lend academic respectability to the organisation but undoubtedly led to the belief in some quarters that the Government wished to keep its existence secret. Controversy flared in 1941 when Ritchie Calder, a well known journalist (later Lord Ritchie Calder) revealed the existence of a Ministry of Information survey team 'prying around and asking a lot of silly questions about morale and upsetting the public'. These interviewers were inevitably named 'Cooper's Snoopers' after Duff Cooper, the Minister of Information.

In an adjournment debate on 1 August 1941, Sir Archibald Southby alleged that Government Surveys were 'not only an invasion of privacy but unnecessary when Government could call on the press and MPs for information'. In their defence it was argued that without such surveys there would be no statistical check on the generalisations made about public opinion as a whole. Among topics on which the Social Survey had provided useful information were the need for more news about air raid casualties, the need for a consistent siren policy, the treatment of aliens and refugees and the anxieties of parents with children evacuated. However, eventually the critics had their way and there was a complete reorganisation. The link with the NIESR was broken and Louis Moss was brought into the Ministry of Information as a permanent official to run the Social Survey. Its role was restricted to work explicitly commissioned by departments. Most of the existing staff resigned in protest. However, the new organisation survived and by 1944 had carried out over 100 surveys and very nearly 300,000 interviews.

A very full and interesting account of the activities of the Social Survey over this period was given to the Royal Statistical Society in 1944 by Kathleen Box and Geoffrey Thomas.[1] From the beginning it sought advice through a Scientific Advisory Panel, which included Seebohm Rowntree. The earliest enquiries reflected the immediate administrative needs of the wartime Government. For example, there were problems arising out of the control of consumer goods which led to studies such as that into the special clothing needs of workers in occupations where conditions of work caused extra wear and tear.[2] Again, concern about nutrition led to surveys on the diets of young workers, on typical wartime meals, on the use of prepared foods and methods used for cooking vegetables.[3, 4, 5, 6] Another urgent requirement arose out of the need for complete mobilisation of man and woman power. A very early survey was concerned with the objections to service in the ATS of women who were eligible for recruitment.[7]

Health was another important topic for research. In 1942 surveys were undertaken to discover what difficulties parents had experienced in getting their children immunised against diphtheria.[8] Moreover, the Social Survey also played a part in finding out the best way to enlist the voluntary help of the public whether in collecting salvage[9] or digging for victory[10] or preventing the spread of venereal disease[11] or in the use of cod liver oil and orange juice.[12] In the organisation of important publicity campaigns, the Social Survey was used to gauge the extent to which the public understood issues and what obstacles there were to the complete success of programmes.

It became clear at a very early stage of its history that the methods which the Social Survey was developing were capable not only of providing information of immediate relevance but of providing data necessary for long term projects also. After the critical days of the war had passed, the attention of many departments began to turn to the problems which would face the country in peace time. Many surveys were therefore more concerned with the provision of data for the tasks facing administrators in the years ahead than with immediate needs. For example, the Social Survey, working with the scientists and technicians of the Building Research Station of the Department of Scientific and Industrial Research, made several enquiries into such subjects as 'The Lighting of Domestic Buildings',[13] 'Domestic heating',[14] and 'Sound in Dwellings'.[15] The purpose of these enquiries was to provide reliable data about the present installations in houses throughout the country and to estimate the extent to which such present installations were adequate. The co-operation of technicians and physical scientists with social scientists made it possible to devise methods of work which, for the first time, were capable of providing a picture of the housing situation of the country in detail.

During the war it became clear to the Ministry of Health that the regular flow of information concerning the incidence of infectious diseases could usefully be supplemented by information about the state of health of the population as a whole, and experiments were carried out by the Social Survey to test the possibility of regular surveys of illness. These experiments were successful and from the beginning of 1944 the Survey of Sickness[16] studied regularly the amount of illness in the general population. This survey was very successful in achieving its objectives. So much so that the American and Canadian Census authorities began to think seriously of setting up apparatus to produce the same kind of information for their own countries. It was stopped in the early 1950s, but similar data has been obtained more recently by means of the General Household Survey.

By the end of the war Louis Moss was able to claim that social surveys had provided useful information to Government in many fields.[17] The techniques of sampling and personal interview had been demonstrated to be feasible for collecting both factual information and data on opinions. Moreover, it had been shown that the public were interested in these enquiries and prepared to co-operate in them. Finally, and most important, after early upsets the Government had discovered the type of organisation or infrastructure needed to carry out social enquiries. The lesson was an important one to carry over into peace time.

The post-war Social Survey

From as early as 1942 some officials, notably Stephen Taylor, Director of Home Intelligence up to 1944, urged that the Social Survey should be retained after the war. It was foreseen that economic and social restrictions would continue for some time and it would require effective social research to ensure that the Government might reach sound and just decisions. It was felt that such a body would greatly facilitate the working of democracy in that objective research reports, especially if freely published, would off-set both press misrepresentation of public opinion and the necessarily inaccurate impressions of MPs; that legislators and civil servants would come to see that the public was far more sensible and far more reasonable than it had been given credit for in the past; that administrative and legislative action would be in closer accord with the needs and wants of the public; and that explanation of Government decisions, leading to public co-operation, would be made possible. These arguments were persuasive and the Social Survey survived.

Nevertheless a period of post-war expansion came abruptly to a halt in 1951 when the first post-war Conservative Government initiated a wide reaching exercise to reduce the activities of Government. The Social Survey was reduced to half its size. It survived further cuts because its usefulness was being recognised. It had been given responsibility for the National

Food Survey[18] from 1953 and been asked by the Treasury to co-operate with the Oxford Institute of Statistics in three savings surveys.[19] Moreover, it had become involved in the plans to carry out more consumer expenditure surveys.

The development of the Family Expenditure Survey

One of the major statistical developments of the 1950s was the creation of the continuous Family Expenditure Survey (FES). This was important for the Social Survey in demonstrating the importance of an organisation capable of carrying out a succession of experimental studies and providing a substantial continuous fieldwork and processing capability. Responsibility for the FES gave stability to the Social Survey programme which, since the Survey of Sickness had been abandoned, had consisted entirely of ad hoc projects.

We are so used to measures like the Retail Prices Index these days, when inflation is of such national concern, that it is often forgotten that the production of a reliable and non-controversial index number is a fairly recent statistical development. Up to 1947 the index number was based on patterns of working class expenditure obtained in 1904 and modified for 1914 conditions. In 1947 the Ministry of Labour discontinued this Index. It was probably reasonably valid up to 1939, but by 1947 it had become quite discredited. Some items with heavy weights had received subsidies during wartime and the index had failed quite badly to measure the true increases of prices during the war. The old index was replaced by an interim index of retail prices based on patterns of consumption obtained from a family budget enquiry, conducted among some 10,000 working class in 1937–38 by the Ministry of Labour.

The 1937–38 enquiry had been intended to be the basis for revising the Cost of Living Index but by the time results were available Britain had been at war for 18 months. After the war it was not held to be sensible to hold a new household expenditure survey immediately as many goods were unavailable or in short supply and food rationing was still in force. In the meantime there was scope for methodological research into how best to carry out expenditure surveys. The Social Survey played a full part in this programme. This research confirmed that household expenditure could not be collected from the housewife alone; methods involving the co-operation of other household members would be necessary. It was established also that postal methods would produce a very low response and that payments to co-operating record keepers would improve response. It was also found that extending the record keeping period from one week to four weeks hardly affected response. Differences were observed, however, between expenditure patterns in the first week of recording and subsequent weeks. Finally it was found impossible to reconcile expenditure and income.

These experiments prepared the way for the Ministry of Labour Household Expenditure Survey in 1953/54 and for the introduction of the continuous Family Expenditure Survey in 1957. The Cost of Living Advisory Committee, fully recognising the deficiencies of base weighted type index numbers, recommended that in future the index number weights should be kept continuously under review and revised annually to reflect changes in living standards.[20] Thus the continuous Family Expenditure Survey was born.[21, 22]

The Family Expenditure Survey is now one of the most widely used Government surveys, also available (with other continuous surveys) to academic researchers through the SSRC data archive at Essex University.[23] As it contains data on both household income and expenditure it is an important source of data for the assessment of the impact of fiscal measures on the distribution and redistribution of income. It is also an important source of data on low income groups and on the prevalence of poverty.

In the 1950s there was a general belief that full employment and the introduction of social insurance had abolished poverty in Britain – at least as it was experienced in the 1930s. However, social researchers using household surveys began to challenge this by drawing attention to the fact that not everyone entitled to National Assistance was receiving it and that there were even families with the head in full time employment whose income was lower than it would be if they received assistance. Abel-Smith and Townsend used the 1953/54 Consumer Expenditure Survey and the 1960 Family Expenditure Survey to underline these arguments.[24] They were not believed initially and it required the results of the Allen Committee into the Impact of Rates on Households[25] and the official enquiries by the Ministry of Pensions and National Insurance and the National Assistance Board[26, 27] to confirm that a large number of people were apparently entitled to National Assistance and not getting it.

Since the late 1960s the FES has been exploited regularly to obtain data on the prevalence of poverty and the take-up of means-tested benefits, and has played an important part in justifying changes in social security provision since then.[28, 29] The methodology has been further applied to study the income and expenditure of low income families and other underprivileged groups in ad hoc studies. Recently, as part of the effort to improve the value for money in Government statistics, the feasibility of combining the Family Expenditure Survey with the National Food Survey was studied. The results of this study showed that a combined survey would have lower response than the FES and that it would record lower average expenditure. On balance it was decided not to combine the two surveys.

The International Passenger Survey

The 1960s saw the introduction of the International Passenger Survey (IPS).[30] This was a new departure for a household survey organisation and one that consistently raises the eyebrows of the sceptical, who wonder that any Government can really expect to sample and collect reliable data from travellers in a hurry. Yet the IPS has consistently justified itself. The IPS sets out to interview a probability sample of those who arrive in Great Britain, or leave it, temporarily or permanently, by sea and air. This poses considerable sampling and field organisation problems. The purpose of the exercise is to establish the number of, and characteristics of, visitors to Britain and British visitors to overseas and so provide essential information to the tourist industry. It also provides estimates of those arriving to settle permanently in this country (immigrants) and those leaving to settle permanently abroad (emigrants) in order to revise the annual population estimates. Finally it provides information for the Balance of Payments accounts on the expenditure of foreign visitors in Great Britain and the expenditure of British visitors abroad.

To carry out the IPS a special field force of interviewers work continuously at the main airports and seaports interviewing a sample of passengers leaving or arriving on a sample of flights or boats. Airports are busy places and travellers are usually in a hurry. The information requirements have to be strictly curtailed to what can be feasibly collected in a short interview of a few minutes – or 25 yards as some interviewers put it. There can be no doubt that the survey fills important gaps in Government information. The Tourist Industry is an important one and the IPS provides key statistics on those who visit Britain, where they come from, where they go to and what they spend. Moreover without the IPS, estimates of gross and net migration would be largely guesswork. Measurement of flows between the UK and specific areas is becoming increasingly important and more recently larger samples have been selected at Heathrow III to increase the number of observations on those going to and coming from the Indian sub-continent.

Methodology

The 1950s also saw the development of a series of methodological publications setting out in detail the methods used by the SSD and how they had been developed.[31] An inspection of this list shows how prolific the staff in those days were and the variety of topics they studied. Some such as Sampling for the Social Survey by Gray and Corlett,[32] the Interviewer's Handbook[33] and the results of the FES experiments[34] are well known and frequently quoted, but there were others, such as the note on the length of cigarette ends by Gray and Parr,[35] that were more off-beat. There were papers on the use of postal methods, the use of telephones and innumerable papers on interviewing. The wide range reflected the individual interests of a talented group of social survey researchers at the peak of their professional ability. They underlined the importance of the Social Survey at that time as a centre of advice on sampling, questionnaire design and interviewing technique. Apart from a unit at the London School of Economics there was no academic centre of interest in these subjects in the 1950s and the Market Research Society was in its infancy. In the last quarter of a century academic interest in survey methodology has expanded considerably, and moreover private sector firms have developed their own expertise. From the early 1960s the Social Survey methodological programme lost its impetus, and little was published. However, the situation changed in the late 1970s when a *Methodology Bulletin*[36] was started and a methodological report series reintroduced.

Organisational change

There were considerable changes in the fortunes of the Social Survey in the period 1965–70. This was the period in which social science became increasingly respectable. Two official reports had considerable influence. First there was the report of the Heyworth Committee into the use of social scientists in Government which led to the creation of the Social Science Research Council and made recommendations that led to a marked increase in the employment of social scientists in Government.[37] Social research groups were established in the main Government departments and began to play a major part in determining social research requirements, including the need for surveys. The Heyworth Committee paid special attention to the Government Social Survey. It was in no doubt that Government departments needed the services of the Social Survey, but felt that its purpose was not properly understood and it was used inefficiently. Moreover, there was no means by which a coherent programme of surveys could be developed. The committee felt that the Social Survey was not brought in at an early enough stage to contribute to departmental plans and that its contribution to the development of survey methods, training of research workers and creation of an accumulated body of knowledge was being lost because it was regarded purely as a service organisation.

To remedy these criticisms it was recommended that responsibility for the Social Survey be transferred to the Treasury and that an interdepartmental committee under Treasury chairmanship be set up to advise on the programme of work. The Social Survey became a separate department responsible to a Treasury Minister in 1967. However, this lasted only until 1970 when it was merged with the General Register Office to form the Office of Population Censuses and Surveys.[38]

The committee chaired by the Treasury did operate for a few years but with mixed success and it ceased to exist after 1970. The problem of ensuring a coherent programme was then left to the head of the Social Survey to tackle by means of bilateral discussions with departments. An important Treasury circular reminded departments that they should consult the Social Survey before undertaking or commissioning social surveys.

The second major report of the 1960s was that of the Estimates Committee on Government Statistics which recommended greater use of, and higher status for, Statisticians in Government departments.[39] The 1964 Labour Government implemented many of its specific recommendations. Professor Claus Moser was brought in from the London School of Economics as Director of the Central Statistical Office and Head of the Government Statistical Service, following which there were several major initiatives to improve social statistics including the production of *Social Trends* (an annual compendium of social statistics) and the development of a continuous multi-purpose survey which became the General Household Survey. The Social Survey was merged with the General Register Office to create the Office of Population Censuses and Surveys as an office of demographic and social statistics to match the newly created Business Statistics Office.

The 1960s had in fact already seen closer collaboration between the two partners of the merger. The Social Survey had carried out a post-enumeration survey on the 1966 Sample Census[40] and had been closely involved in planning for the 1971 Census. The mid-1960s also saw the first Family Intentions Survey[41] carried out for the General Register Office to help in the prediction of births. These renewed connections that had been broken when the Survey of Sickness had been abandoned in the early 1950s.

Ad hoc surveys

This chapter includes much about the main continuous surveys, but for many who know the Social Survey it is the regular output of ad hoc surveys that has been its main characteristic for the past 40 years. Since 1941 some six to seven hundred such surveys have been tackled by the Social Survey on a wide variety of topics. Many of these have been carried through to the publication of a report. The results of others can be found in the published reports of Royal Commissions and Committees of Enquiry; the results of others were published in journals. In the earliest days of the Social Survey, when there were no continuous enquiries, the programme consisted entirely of ad hoc surveys which encouraged a breed of researchers prepared to use the basic household survey technique to tackle whatever problem was put to them by Government departments. Very often an ad hoc survey requires the construction of an appropriate sample frame, perhaps obtained from administrative records or the identification of a minority like an immigrant group or the disabled. Frequently there are completely new problems of questionnaire design to face.

Ad hoc surveys have been carried out in all the major areas of social and economic policy, such as health and welfare, housing, employment and labour relations, transport, financial circumstances, crime, the police and prison services and many others. Practically every department of state, including even the Foreign Office and the Ministry of Defence, has commissioned a survey at some time.

In the health area, surveys have been carried out to establish the prevalence of conditions such as deafness,[42] physical disability[43] and dental disease,[44] and have examined the particular problems faced by such groups as the blind[45] and the users of surgical footwear.[46] Other surveys have concentrated on the public use of and attitudes to particular services, such as the Home Help Service,[47] the Meals on Wheels Service,[48] the special services provided for the elderly[49] and the Family Planning Services,[50] to name but a few. Another range of surveys have investigated behavioural characteristics that can affect health such as smoking,[51] drinking[52] and weight in relation to height.[53] Problems affecting different groups employed in the health services such as nurses and midwives,[54] and mental handicap nurses[55] have also been studied.

Numerous housing surveys have sought to describe the housing stock at both the national and regional level. In 1945, immediately after the war, an enquiry was mounted which provided figures for each of the 12 civil defence regions on the size and composition of families in relation to the number of rooms occupied.[56] Detailed surveys were carried out in 1960 and 1964 to provide national figures on occupancy, tenure and house conditions.[57] A similar survey was undertaken for the first time in Scotland in 1965.[58] Other housing surveys have looked in greater detail at housing conditions in the major conurbations such as that carried out for the Milner Holland Committee into aspects of rented accommodation in London[59] and the regional surveys in the West Midlands, SE Lancashire and West Yorkshire. There have also been surveys of particular sectors such as the private renters,[60] empty houses,[61] and of special groups of people such as those who have moved house recently[62] or who share accommodation with another household or family unit.[63] The more recent of these were based on samples identified in the course of the 1977–79 National Dwelling and Housing

Survey, a large scale survey carried out by the Department of the Environment.[64]

In the late 1950s, and all through the 1960s, educational issues figured prominently in the Social Survey programme. In 1957 a survey into the use of further education by adolescents was carried out for the Crowther Committee.[65] Then in 1962 surveys among students and teachers in universities and other institutes of higher education were carried out for the Robbins Committee on Higher Education.[66] Another major committee under the chairmanship of Lady Plowden commissioned a survey of the parents of primary schoolchildren, their home circumstances and attitudes to Education.[67] The Department of Education and Science commissioned a similar survey in Wales and also a follow-up survey among the parents selected for the original Plowden Survey.

The Schools Council, concerned with the development of the curriculum and the examination system, was also an important customer and commissioned surveys among parents, teachers and children in connection with the raising of the school leaving age,[68] and among sixth form teachers, pupils and former pupils, and students and teachers in further education in an enquiry into sixth form curricula and examinations.[69]

In addition there have been surveys of the youth service,[70] the employment of leavers from art and design courses,[71] and fifth form girls.[72] Detailed income and expenditure surveys have been carried out among undergraduates[73] and postgraduates[74] to provide information relevant to the determination of the level of student grants.

Employment and industrial relations have also been recurrent themes for ad hoc surveys. Two major surveys have dealt with women's employment patterns and attitudes to work.[75] Another theme has been the employment patterns of older men and women, and attitudes towards retirement and continuing at work on which major enquiries were undertaken in 1953 and 1975.[76] The experience and problems of young people in finding work on leaving school have also been surveyed regularly.[77] Surveys of industrial relations, which pose special problems of sampling and analysis since they cover the views and characteristics of both managers and workers, have also been undertaken.[78]

The Social Survey helped to develop the methods for investigating travel patterns with the use of diaries and these procedures are now incorporated in the periodic National Travel Surveys.[79] It has also studied pedestrian behaviour in order to help interpret the risks of traffic accidents to pedestrians.[80]

Many surveys have been undertaken for the Home Office over the years. These have ranged from surveys of the attitudes of prison officers[81] and people employed in the fire service,[82] to more general studies of public attitudes towards the police[83] and into special topics like drunkenness.[84] The Home Office is responsible for electoral registration; two surveys have examined the accuracy of the electoral register in the light of census results,[85, 86] while surveys have also been carried out into the methods used by electoral registration officers to compile the register[87] and into the feasibility and acceptability of collecting more information by means of the electoral register canvass.[88]

Although most surveys cover Great Britain as a whole, special steps have been taken, when required, to provide separate results for Scotland and surveys have, therefore, been carried out specifically for Scottish departments. Recent examples include a survey into Debt Recovery in Scotland[89] and a survey of attitudes towards the ownership of family property.[90]

In the review of the Social Survey Division that was held in the course of the recent Rayner review of the Government Statistical Services,[91] the view was taken that it was doubtful if the Government needed as many ad hoc surveys as the Social Survey capability provided. It was recommended that the aim should be to contract out such surveys to the private sector where they could be done at cheaper cost than in the public service; and it was also recommended that in future departments should repay OPCS for the full cost of ad hoc surveys. Nevertheless it was recognised that the Social Survey Division should retain an ad hoc capability, and a modified repayment scheme which ensures this will be introduced shortly.

The General Household Survey

A major development of the 1970s was undoubtedly the establishment of the General Household Survey (GHS). The original plans for a continuous multi-purpose household survey were ambitious; they implied a large scale continuous household survey that would provide quarterly data on the main social and demographic characteristics of the population and the facility for rotating ad hoc topics in and out of the survey quickly in response to the changing needs of Government. Analyses would be available quickly after the end of the appropriate fieldwork period. The reality was less spectacular. The size of the survey was restricted by staff shortage to about 15,000 households a year – and it was very quickly learned that regular quarterly analyses were not really practicable or useful. To ensure stability of fieldwork and processing, the questionnaire had to be kept unchanged for at least a year. The GHS aims to interview all those aged 16 or more in the selected households and in addition collects information on the household as a unit. It therefore avoids the problems that arise when one representative adult is required to provide data for all household members –

but it is more expensive as a result. The data collected in a typical year could cover housing conditions, employment characteristics, leisure activities, smoking and/or drinking patterns and health of the respondents. A feature of recent years has been the development of the family information section with questions on the number of children born or expected, and questions designed to identify the existence of one parent families and the extent of cohabitation.

From the beginning the plan was for the Social Survey Division to carry out analysis on behalf of departments and write an annual report, and this has been the pattern for the past 10 years.[92] Ideally the annual report for any calendar year should be available soon after the end of the year's fieldwork, but it has never proved possible to publish the report sooner than 18 months after the end of fieldwork and the delay has sometimes been longer. As a compromise, a press release of the key national results is now issued some five to six months after the end of each year's fieldwork. The main report comes later.

The content of each year's General Household Survey is settled by interdepartmental discussion after proper pilot studies have been held. There can be no doubt that the GHS has avoided the need for certain types of periodic survey and considerably increased knowledge of the structure of society in between censuses. Despite its failure to deliver as many results as quickly as was hoped, it can be counted as one of the statistical successes of the last decade. In the recent review of the Government Statistical Service it was considered to be worth preserving, subject to some economies, and provided it was used by departments fully, to avoid the need for ad hoc surveys.

The GHS cannot tackle topics to the same depth as a specialist survey concentrating on a single topic, so it has not removed the need for ad hoc surveys entirely, but it can complement them by including periodic questions to monitor changes since a base line survey. It also provides a sampling frame for special populations that can then be followed up by an ad hoc survey later. Respondents are now asked automatically if they are prepared to be interviewed again.

Epilogue

Any historical review of the Social Survey would be incomplete without recognition of the contribution of the two former directors, Louis Moss and C.G. Thomas, who each spent over 35 years working in the organisation from its very earliest days. The Social Survey owes a considerable debt to both of them. Thomas in particular developed the International Passenger Survey and did much to establish the Labour Force Survey.

Moss, after 30 years as director, devoted himself to the establishment of the General Household Survey as the comprehensive source of data it is today. Two other names deserve mention, P.G. Gray and W.F.F. Kemsley, who, in their different ways, helped to establish the Social Survey as a centre of technical excellence. Gray was an acknowledged sampling expert but in addition carried out a wide range of ad hoc surveys to a high standard. Kemsley was an authority on household expenditure surveys and his name will always be associated with the Family Expenditure Survey. Their presence on the staff, for over 30 years, sustained the reputation the Social Survey still enjoys as a centre for advice on sampling and survey methods. By the mid-1970s they had reached retiring age and their places had been taken by a new generation of researchers, less experienced undoubtedly, but capable of building on the foundation they found.

In this brief review much of importance has had to be omitted. In particular very little has been said about the development of sampling, interviewing and processing methods – key tools for the Social Survey's work. A full discussion of these and a full description of the important role of the interviewers themselves will have to wait another occasion.

REFERENCES

1 Kathleen Box and Geoffrey Thomas, 'The Wartime Social Survey', *Journal of the Royal Statistical Society A* Vol. 107 (1944) pp. 151–89.
2 Clothing Needs in 15 Occupational Groups (NS 14): The Social Survey, COI, London, 1942.
3 Food – An enquiry into a typical day's meals and attitudes to wartime food in selected groups of the English Working Population (NS 16 and 19): The Social Survey; COI, London, 1942.
4 Feeding of Young Workers 14–18 years of Age in Factories, Offices and Shops: The Social Survey (NS 4), London, 1942.
5 Manufactured Foods Investigation (NS Reports Nos 26 and 28): The Social Survey, London, 1942.
6 Investigation into Household Cooking Habits for Certain Vegetables (NS 27): The Social Survey, London, 1942.
7 ATS – An Investigation of the Attitudes of Women, the General Public and ATS Personnel to the Auxiliary Territorial Service: The Social Survey (NS 5), London, 1941.
8 Diphtheria Immunisation Enquiry (Report No 21 NS): Wartime Social Survey; London, 1942.
9 Salvage (Report No 35 New Series): Wartime Social Survey, London, 1943.
10 'Dig for Victory' (Report No 20 New Series): Wartime Social Survey, London, 1942.

11 The Campaign Against Venereal Diseases, by Pixie Wilson and Virginia Barker (NS 42): The Social Survey, COI, 1944.
12 Food Supplements – An enquiry for the Ministry of Food into the use of Fruit Juices and Cod Liver Oil, by G. Wagner and A.H. Reynolds: The Social Survey (Reg H 25); COI, London, 1944.
13 Lighting of Dwellings, by Dennis Chapman and Geoffrey Thomas (NS 24): The Social Survey, COI, London, 1943.
14 Heating of Dwellings Enquiry, by Dennis Chapman and Geoffrey Thomas (NS 13) (Reprinted from Post War Building Studies No 19 'Heating and Ventilation of Dwellings'): The Social Survey, London, 1942.
15 Sound in Dwellings, by Dennis Chapman (NS Region S6): Wartime Social Survey, 1943.
16 The Survey of Sickness 1943–52, by W.P.D. Logan and Eileen M. Brooke, General Register Office Studies on Medical and Population Subjects No 12, London, HMSO, 1957.
17 The Government Social Survey – a lecture to the Institute of Public Administration, by L. Moss, 1946 – available from OPCS.
18 Reports are published every year, the latest being Household Food Consumption and Expenditure in 1980 with a review of the six years 1975 to 1980, HMSO, London, 1982. ISBN 0 11 241480 X.
19 H.F. Lydall, *British Incomes and Savings* (Basil Blackwell, Oxford, 1955).
20 Cost of Living Advisory Committee Report on the proposals for a new index of retail prices (Cmnd 9710). HMSO, London, 1956.
21 Report of an Enquiry into Household Expenditure in 1953/54 by Ministry of Labour and National Service, HMSO, London, 1957.
22 Family Expenditure Survey reports are prepared annually by the Department of Employment and published by HMSO.
23 W.F.F. Kemsley, R.U. Redpath, and M. Holmes, *Family Expenditure Survey Handbook* (HMSO, London, 1980. ISBN 0 11 690744 X).
24 Brian Abel-Smith and Peter Townsend, *The Poor and the Poorest* (Occasional Papers on Social Administration No 17. G Bell and Sons Ltd, London, 1965).
25 *Committee of Enquiry into the Impact of Rates on Households* (Chairman Professor R.G.D. Allen) Cmnd 2582, London, HMSO, 1964.
26 *Financial and Other Circumstances of Retirement Pensioners* – Report of an enquiry by the Ministry of Pensions and National Insurance with the Cooperation of the National Assistance Board. HMSO, London, 1966.
27 *Circumstances of Families*. Report of an enquiry by the Ministry of Pensions and National Insurance with the Cooperation of the National Assistance Board. HMSO, London, 1967.
28 *Two parent Families*. A study of their resources and needs in 1968, 1969 and 1970. DHSS Statistical Report No 14. HMSO, London, 1971.
29 Take-up of Supplementary Benefits. Supplementary Benefits Commission Administration Paper No 7, London, 1978.
30 Some results are published regularly by OPCS. See, for example, 'International Migration' 1981 (Series MN No 8), London, HMSO, 1982. An early article giving a brief description of the survey can be found in the *Board of Trade Journal*, 23 August 1963.
31 See list of published reports and papers of the Social Survey Division – available free from OPCS.

32 P.G. Gray and T. Corlett, 'Sampling for the Social Survey', *Journal of the Royal Statistical Society, A*, Vol. CXIII, Part II, 1950.
33 *A Handbook for Interviewers* (M.136), by Jean Atkinson (London, HMSO, 1968, SBN 11 700028 0).
34 See for example W.F.K. Kemsley and J.L. Nicholson, 'Some Experiments in methods of conducting Family Expenditure Surveys', *Journal of the Royal Statistical Society, A*, Vol. 123, Part 3, (1960).
35 See list of published reports and papers of the Social Survey Division, available free from OPCS, for a complete list of methodological reports.
36 Survey Methodology Bulletin published by OPCS two or three times a year since December 1977.
37 *Report of the Committee on Social Studies* (Chairman Lord Heyworth). Cmnd 2660, HMSO, London, 1965.
38 Philip Redfern, 'Office of Population Censuses and Surveys', *Population Trends* No 4, Summer 1976.
39 Fourth Report from the Estimates Committee. Session 1966–67, *Government Statistical Services*. HoC paper No 246, London, HMSO, 1966.
40 *A Quality Check on the 1966 Ten Per Cent Sample Census of England and* Wales, by Percy Gray and Frances A. Gee. London, HMSO, 1972. ISBN 0–11–700141–4.
41 Karen Dunnell, *Family Formation 1976* (London, HMSO, 1979. ISBN 0–11–701018–9).
42 Survey of the Prevalence of Deafness in the Population of England and Scotland and Wales, by Leslie T. Wilkins, London, COI, 1948 (rev. 1949).
43 Handicapped and Impaired in Great Britain Pt 1, by Amelia Harris with Elizabeth Cox and Christopher Smith (SS418). London, HMSO, 1971. ISBN 0–11–700045–0.
44 Adult Dental Health in England and Wales in 1968, by P.G. Gray, J.E. Todd, G.L. Slack and J.S. Bulman (SS 411), London, HMSO, 1970. ISBN 0–11–700043–4.
45 Mobility and Reading Habits of the Blind, by P.G. Gray and Jean Todd (SS 386), London, HMSO, 1968. ISBN 0–11–700032–9.
46 National Health Surgical Footwear, by Sheila Bainbridge (SS 1088), London, HMSO, 1979. ISBN 0–11–701020–0.
47 The Home Help Service in England and Wales, by Audrey Hunt and Judith Fox (SS 407), London, HMSO, 1970. ISBN 0–11–700042–6.
48 Meals on Wheels Service (S 288). National Corporation for Care of Old People, 1961.
49 Social Welfare for the Elderly, by Amelia Harris and Rosemary Clausen (SS 366), London, HMSO, 1968. 2 Volumes. ISBN 0–11–700035–3 and ISBN 0–11–700036–1.
50 Family Planning Services in England and Wales, by Margaret Bone (SS 467), London, HMSO, 1973. ISBN 0–11–700680–7. Also The Family Planning Services: changes and effects, by Margaret Bone (SS1055), London, HMSO, 1978. ISBN 0–11–700826–5.
51 Adults' and Adolescents' Smoking Habits and Attitudes, by A.C. McKennell and R.K. Thomas (SS 353/B); London, HMSO, 1967.
52 Drinking in England and Wales, by Paul Wilson (SS 1128); London, HMSO, 1980. ISBN 0–11–690740–1.
53 Adult Heights and Weights Survey. OPCS Monitor SS81/1 issued October 1981.

54 Nurses Working in the Community, by Karen Dunnell and Joy Dobbs (SS1141); London, HMSO, 1982.
55 Report of the Committee of Enquiry into Mental Handicap Nursing and Care: Vol. 11, OPCS Survey, by Paul Wilson (SS 1085). ISBN 0–10–174681–4.
56 Housing Survey 1960. London, COI, 1962.
57 The Housing Survey in England and Wales 1964, by Myra Woolf (SS 372), London, COI, 1967.
58 Scottish Housing in 1965, by J B Cullingworth (SS 375); London, COI, 1967.
59 Privately Rented Accommodation in London: a report on enquiries made in December 1963 and June 1964 for the Committee on Housing in Greater London, by Percy Gray and Jean Todd (SS361); London, COI, 1964. See also Appendix V of Cmnd 2605, HMSO, 1965.
60 The privately rented sector in 1978, by J.E. Todd, M.R. Bone and I. Noble (SS 1118), London, HMSO, 1982. ISBN 0 11 690917 X.
61 Empty Housing in England, by Margaret Bone and Val Mason (SS1109); London, HMSO, 1980. ISBN 0–11–701019–7.
62 A report on a survey of people who had moved house is in preparation and will be published shortly.
63 A report on households sharing accommodation is in preparation and will be published shortly.
64 National Dwelling and Housing Survey. 2 volumes, Phase I and Phases II and III published separately in 1978 and 1980 respectively. London, HMSO. ISBN 0–11–751487–X.
65 15 to 18 Report of the Central Advisory Council for Education – England; Volume II (Surveys), London, HMSO, 1960.
66 Report of the Committee on Higher Education (Chairman Lord Robbins) 7 volumes (Cmnd 2154), London, HMSO, 1963–4. Includes results of four surveys carried out by the Government Social Survey (SS 340).
67 Children and their Primary Schools; a report of the Central Advisory Council for Education (England) – Chairman Lady Plowden. Vol 2, Appendix 3; Survey Among Parents of Primary School Children by Roma Morton-Williams (SS 365); London, HMSO, 1967.
68 Young School Leavers; an enquiry carried out for the Schools Council, by Roma Morton-Williams and Stewart Finch et al (SS 389), London, HMSO, 1968.
69 Sixth form pupils and teachers, by Roma Morton-Williams, John Raven and Jane Ritchie (SS403). Sixth form leavers, by Jane Ritchie and Roma Morton-Williams (SS423).
70 The Youth Service and similar provision for young people, by Margaret Bone assisted by Elizabeth Ross (SS 437); London, HMSO, 1972. ISBN 0–11–700128–7.
71 The Employment of Art College Leavers, by Jane Ritchie; assisted by Chris Frost and Sue Dight (SS 448); London, HMSO, 1972. ISBN 0–11–700130–9.
72 Fifth form girls: their hopes for the future, by Irene Rauta and Audrey Hunt (SS 495); London, HMSO, 1975. ISBN 0–11–700693–9.
73 Undergraduate Income and Expenditure, by Peter Bush and Susan Dight (SS 1039); London, HMSO, 1979. ISBN 0–11–700833–8.
74 Postgraduate Income and Expenditure, by Susan Dight and Peter Bush (SS 1068); London, HMSO, 1979. ISBN 0–11–700289–X.

75 A Survey of Women's Employment in 1965, by Audrey Hunt, London, HMSO, 1968. 2 Volumes ISBN 0–11–700029–9. (Another major survey on this subject was carried out in 1980 but the report has still to be published.)
76 Older workers and retirement, by Stanley Parker (SS 1086); London, HMSO, 1980. ISBN 0–11–701020–0.
77 Looking forward to work, by Roger Thomas and Diana Wetherell (SS 427); London, HMSO, 1974. ISBN 0–11–700684–X.
78 Workplace Industrial Relations – an enquiry undertaken by the Royal Commission on Trade Unions and Employers Associations in 1966 (SS 402); London, COI, 1968.
79 See, for example, National Travel Survey 1975/76 Report. London, HMSO, 1979. ISBN 0–11–550504–0.
80 People as pedestrians, by J.E. Todd and A. Walker (SS 1066); London, HMSO, 1980. ISBN 0–11–701023–5.
81 A major survey of attitudes of prison officers was carried out in 1982 but the report has not yet been published.
82 The Fire Service and its personnel, by Margaret Thomas (SS 417B); London, HMSO, 1969.
83 Relations between the police and the public – an enquiry carried out for the Royal Commission on the Police (SS 321). London, COI, 1962.
84 The Drunken Offender in Britain, by H.D. Wilcock (SS 356); London, HMSO, 1972.
85 Electoral Registration for Parliamentary Elections, by P.G. Gray and Frances A. Gee (SS 391): London, COI, 1967.
86 Electoral Registration in 1981, by Jean Todd and Bob Butcher (SS 1168); London, OPCS, 1982. ISBN 0–903933–31–4.
87 The Electoral Registration Process in the United Kingdom, by J.E. Todd and P.A. Dodd (SS 1171); London, OPCS, 1982. ISBN 0–903933–28–4.
88 Extending the Electoral Register–2: two surveys of public acceptability, by A.J. Manners and I. Rauta (SS 1096, 1105 and 1114); OPCS Occasional Paper No 21; London, OPCS, 1981. ISBN 0–906197–21–X.
89 Survey of defenders in debt actions in Scotland: research report for the Scottish Law Commission No 6, by Janet Gregory and Janet Monk (SS 1024); London, HMSO, 1981. ISBN 0–11–690774–6.
90 Family property in Scotland, by A.J. Manners and I. Rauta (SS 1139); London HMSO, 1981. ISBN 0–11–690779–7.
91 Review of Government Statistical Services, Report to the Prime Minister by Sir Derek Rayner, London, 1980.
92 See, for example, *General Household Survey 1980* (London, HMSO, 1982. ISBN 0–11–690926–9).

6 Methodological research on sample surveys: A review of developments in Britain

GERALD HOINVILLE

Survey research methods are now widely used in Britain; survey agencies have a well established survey methodology; the standards of survey research interviewing, sampling, coding, and other procedures are high. Yet much of the methodology is based on conventional wisdom and ease of operational performance. Have we done enough to test the methodology and to review alternatives? This chapter examines the evolution of survey methods in Britain and identifies contributions to methodological research of survey practitioners, academics and survey users. It discusses the conditions required for effective methodological research and shows how organisational and financial factors have inhibited those conditions in Britain.

The expansion of survey research

Since the 1950s there has been a considerable increase in the use of survey research to assist social policy, to describe and explain social conditions, to aid production, marketing and advertising decisions, to improve civic planning and to help develop and test economic, social and psychological theories. The Market Research Society, for example, has grown rapidly: from 114 members in 1953 to 1,300 by 1963, 2,500 by 1973 and 4,000 by 1983. The growth in membership reflects the growth in the market and opinion research industry as a whole, much of which is based on survey research. Commissioned survey work has been estimated as growing from about £3m annually in the mid 1950s to well over £100m today. Even allowing for changes in the value of money, that represents a considerable expansion.

Developments in the social policy and public sector domains in the last 20 years have both stimulated and reflected growth in survey activity. The Skeffington report on Public Participation published in 1967 encouraged the notion of public involvement in planning; survey research was seen as one of the means of enabling people to participate. Transport and town planning requirements imposed on local authorities by central government created additional demands for large-scale surveys. In an era of capital investment in roads, new towns and other civic projects, policy makers were eager for data to allow them to monitor urban patterns and to predict growth trends.

Social policy research created additional needs for information, particularly about the disadvantaged groups in society – the poor, the handicapped, the unemployed, ethnic minorities, and about the impact of health, education and other public sector provisions. The Government Statistical Service was much expanded during this period as were the social services and research departments in local authorities.

The expansion of the social sciences in universities and polytechnics in the 1960s created a corresponding increase in social research. Independent research institutes and university research centres emerged or expanded. The Social Science Research Council, which funded most academic social research, was created in 1965. By 1969, the number of institutes and centres was large enough to warrant the encouragement of informal links through the Association of Social Research Organisations (ASRO).

A flourishing survey research industry has thus evolved during the past 20 years or so, built on foundations laid down chiefly during and immediately after the Second World War.

The pathfinders

The origins of survey research are to be found at a much earlier period. The introduction of population censuses in Europe and the United States around the close of the eighteenth century, and the attempt to quantify and describe the living conditions of the poor as early nineteenth-century industrialisation spread, provide the backcloth. The early social enquiries were a mixture of investigative journalism as described by Marsh (1982) and statistical enquiry. The 1840 *Journal of the Statistical Society of London*, for example, contains a report from one of the society's committees on the state of the working classes in the parishes of St Margaret and St John, Westminster. Two agents visited dwellings in the area occupied by the working classes to look at their living conditions and to ask questions of the families.

The conduct of the enquiry showed a concern for statistical accuracy.

> Both the agents visited dwellings of the working classes together and they thus became mutually a check on the accuracy of the statistical information obtained. (Statistical Society of London 1840:14)

The method of enquiry was a combination of observation and interview:

> Many of the houses in the districts were subdivided into single rooms and each room contained frequently a separate family; the street door leading to the interior apartments was usually closed, and the agents were often obliged to knock or ring in order to obtain admission into the house; they afterwards visited the various families within the house in their separate apartments. (Statistical Society of London 1840:14)

The agents collected information from each family on the occupancy and density of dwellings, housing conditions and amenities, household furnishings, reading material and pictures in the home, children's education, religious denomination, rents, occupation of workers, country of birth and length of residence.

These nineteenth-century social enquiries pre-dated sampling. In a subject matter index, published by the Statistical Society, of works contained in the society's catalogue up to December 1883 the word sampling did not appear. And Booth's famous study, begun in 1887 to describe the life and labour of the people of London, was not a sample survey. Booth's aim was to describe the conditions of *all* families (with children) in an area, street by street. Most people agree, however, that the systematic, large scale documentation of social conditions carried out at the end of the nineteenth century by Booth and Rowntree, which was built upon the earlier less rigorous enquiries, laid the foundation for survey research in Britain as we recognise it today.

In Booth's study data were collected indirectly, chiefly from the reports of school board visitors on the families they had visited. The Rowntree study in York, which began in 1898 and was published in 1902, about the same time as Booth's study, introduced the notion of direct interviewing but not sampling.

The theoretical and practical development of survey sampling in Britain was pioneered by Professor A.L. Bowley following initiatives by the International Statistical Institute (ISI) to investigate and recommend (in 1903) a sampling approach. He linked survey sampling and inference, provided a theoretical justification for random sampling, and introduced sampling into his own social conditions enquiry (1915) which followed on from the work of Booth and Rowntree. This leap forward was underlined by his approach to questioning, which was more rigorous than anything that had gone before.

Subsequent use of sample survey methods in Britain was limited and slow to develop. The Director of Statistics at The Ministry of Labour, Mr J. Hilton, carried out several studies of the unemployed during the early 1920s and, with advice from Professor Bowley, introduced sampling into government research. In a paper to the Royal Statistical Society (1924),

Hilton described the results of a survey of 10,000 people registered for unemployment benefit at employment exchanges. Although probability sampling methods were used, the sampling method adopted was a biased one in order to overcome the practical difficulty of coping with the uneven distribution of claimants between towns. Hilton acknowledged the shortcomings of the process but accepted them as a fact of life.

Comments made after Hilton presented his paper to the RSS underline the rudimentary state of the art. Yule, proposing the vote of thanks, said:

> How much more difficult it would be to carry out such a sample investigation where there was not already available what might be called a directory of the persons to be sampled . . . If, for example, a wages census were to be taken by way of a sample, I can foresee considerable difficulties in pitching on a series of individuals who could be regarded with confidence as an unbiased sample. (Hilton 1924: 562–3)

and Bowley, seconding, said:

> I hope that the result of this example will be that the method will be adopted in other branches of statistics in this country and other countries. (Hilton 1924: 563)

He went on to say:

> It is a very good thing that this subject has come up for public discussion by the Society, for the method of enquiry by sample . . . is of special importance in these times of economy . . . A little quiet thinking in terms of algebra, a little quiet organisation in an office, and you can examine ten thousand individuals instead of a million. (Hilton 1924: 563)

In his reply, Hilton referred to colleagues' reservations about the survey method in Britain:

> Many members of the Society must find it difficult to realise the degree of scepticism that had to be overcome in even extremely intelligent and able people, who did not happen to have had occasion to use and test the sampling method, that a small sample, properly taken, could yield results which were sufficiently trustworthy for many practical purposes. (Hilton 1924: 569)

In an article on the development of sampling in Britain, Moser (1949) pointed out that Hilton's experiment with sampling made little immediate impact in government circles and that no real progress was made until the mid 1930s. By that time the theory of sampling had been developed extensively following a report (Jensen, 1926) of a Commission appointed by the ISI. Bowley was a main contributor to that work. The Commission's report was followed by a number of separate and progressive developments including contributions by Neyman, Mahalanobis at the Indian Statistical

Institute, Cochran and Hansen and Hurwitz in the United States, and agricultural and biological researchers in Britain including R.A. Fisher and F. Yates. The first edition of Yates's book on sampling methods for censuses and surveys (1949) commissioned by the UN Statistical Commission, was another major landmark in the development of sampling theory and practice in Britain. (Several authors have reviewed these developments including Yates (1946), Moser (1949), Smith (1976) and O-Muicheartaigh and Wong (1981).)

The theoretical basis for sampling was thus developed gradually during the period between the First and Second World War. Its application was also developed during this period, but the main thrust came immediately after the Second World War. The time lag between the emerging theory and its practical application is well illustrated by a contribution to the discussion of Yates's paper to the Royal Statistical Society in 1946. Mr A.P. Zentler said:

> It would not be an exaggeration to say that by and large market research firms were blissfully unaware of the fact that the very foundation of sample investigation was probability theory . . . they were very many years behind the times in their methods. Even the resolutions adopted by the National Institute of Statistics in 1924 – which Dr Yates naturally considered outdated – would seem new, strange and much too theoretical to the practical market research man. (Yates 1946: 35)

In fact, this account was an exaggeration; probability sampling was in use, particularly for government surveys carried out by market research agencies. Even so, it illustrates the gap between theory and widespread application of probability sampling methods.

The limited application of sample surveys up to the mid 1930s is apparent from a report of the 1934 committee set up by the Sir Halley Stewart Trustees, and chaired by Professor Carr Saunders, to appraise work based on social surveys. The report mentioned only 32 social surveys, most of which had been undertaken by groups of individuals with a special interest in a locality (Wells, 1935). One recommendation of the 1934 committee, to improve the quality of survey methods, was that a permanent professional centralised social survey organisation should be set up and given continuing financial support, but no such organisation appeared until the Wartime Social Survey was formed in 1941, discussed in chapter 5.

Other parts of the survey industry had taken tentative steps forward immediately before the Second World War. Market research activity increased – predominantly within three advertising agencies (London Press Exchange, J. Walter Thompson and Lintas) and with the Nielsen Retail Audit Service. Media research was launched by the Institute of Incorporated Practitioners in Advertising; several major surveys of readership of newspapers and periodicals were carried out between 1930 and 1939. The BBC Listener Research Department started at the end of the 1930s. Public opinion research began with the creation in 1936 of the British Institute of Public Opinion, one of the international Gallup Institutes. Only one newspaper, however, the *News Chronicle*, published poll results. In 1937, the formation of Mass-Observation, a new type of research organisation, focused attention on the argument about the respective merits of qualitative anthropological research and statistical sampling and interviewing. Mass-Observation, discussed in chapter 7, used a variety of opinion research methods but emphasised the anthropological study of social conditions and behaviour by getting ordinary people to keep diaries of their everyday lives.

Although the foundations were being laid for a survey research industry and the pace of development had begun to increase, the general picture of pre-Second World War survey research in Britain is one of limited application, limited methodological development and a limited organisational structure for the conduct of surveys. The information needs of wartime increased the amount of survey research carried out in Britain, and provided the sort of impetus to applications that the ISI Commission had given the development of sampling theory.

In the years before the Second World War, there had been much more survey activity on the other side of the Atlantic. The US equivalent of the pathfinding British poverty studies was the Pittsburgh survey, carried out between 1909 and 1914 and supported by the Russell Sage Foundation. The use and application of surveys mushroomed after 1914. A bibliography of surveys carried out in the USA up to the beginning of 1928 listed more than 2,500 titles. Topics covered included:

adolescence	city planning	gangs	race
age	clinics	garbage	recreation
blindness	dance halls	insurance	welfare
burial	deportation	kindergartens	unemployment

The introduction to the bibliography stated:

> The growing conviction that control and improvement can be more intelligent if based on knowledge have combined to make the social study or survey almost one of the indispensable activities of the modern community. (Eaton and Harrison 1930: xiv)

A key difference in approach between the two countries was the way in which survey research was funded and sponsored. In Britain before the Second World War, social surveys were generally seen as a charitable activity. The Booth, Rowntree and Bowley studies reflected the philanthropic and charitable attitudes of the late Victorian period. Booth and Rowntree financed their own work; Bowley's money came from charitable funds. In each case the survey team consisted of the initiator working with an assistant or with a small secretariat and supported by volunteers from social/welfare organisations. When Booth's survey was repeated in 1928 it was financed by charitable foundations and City trusts. In the United States in the 1930s and 1940s the increased growth in government expenditure created an environment in which the survey was increasingly used as an instrument of social policy, and government and other public bodies funded several long-term programmes of research. A similar increase in the use of surveys resulting from growth in government expenditure did not occur in Britain until the 1960s.

Election and public opinion polls grew in parallel with social surveys in the United States. They began to emerge at about the same time as Booth's, Rowntree's and Bowley's reports appeared in Britain. By 1916 the *Literary Digest* had begun a regular poll that continued for 20 years. The poll examined public opinion on current affairs, an aspect that became a feature of other polls in the United States. By 1928 there were six national polling organisations and countless regional ones; the American Institute of Public Opinion was established by George Gallup in 1935; other independent polling organisations soon followed. *Public Opinion Quarterly* was launched in 1937 at Princeton University. One of the results of all these polls was to make sampling and surveys more noticeable and more acceptable to the American public.

This contrast between the pace of development and acceptability of surveys in Britain and the USA was to have important implications for the next phase in the development of survey methods, the pioneering phase of the 1940s and 1950s.

The pioneers

If the period leading up to the Second World War can be seen as the pathfinding era of survey research, the period that followed was the pioneering one. During the 1940s and 1950s the basic methodologies for the conduct of sample surveys in Britain were refined and developed; the staffing and divisions within survey agencies were tailored to fit the survey tasks, and knowledge was acquired about the way survey techniques could be used to collect descriptive, behavioural and attitudinal information from different segments of the population about different subjects.

Two strands of methodological development are distinguishable. One strand is work on the *measuring instrument* (and sometimes the special sample) to be used for a particular class of surveys, the other is more general *methodology related to the survey process*. There is no hard division between the two, and findings on one side support work on the other. Nevertheless, the distinction is helpful in examining the development of survey methods research in Britain.

One of the best examples of extensive project-specific methodological work on the measuring instrument is that concerned with household budget surveys. This started in the first decade of this century, with Board of Trade enquiries into household budgets to provide weights for the cost of living index. An enquiry by the Ministry of Labour in 1936/7 to update the weights was overtaken by the war. Development on the government's Family Expenditure Survey (FES) began in earnest during the mid 1950s after Kemsley joined Government Social Survey. He reviewed the budget enquiries and developed the survey measuring instrument (diaries and questionnaires) through pilot and experimental studies. At about the same time the Department of Applied Economics at Cambridge and the Institute of Statistics at Oxford carried out studies on personal incomes, savings and expenditure in consultation with Government Social Survey. Papers by Cole (1956) and Lydall (1956) show the overlap between work on a specific measuring instrument and more general methodological work. At Government Social Survey Kemsley built into the FES a programme of methodological work to refine and improve the survey, publishing the results at frequent intervals during the 1960s.

There are numerous other examples from government, university and commercial research of work on the measuring instrument, for example to measure travel behaviour, poverty, quality of life, racial discrimination, child development and educational attainment; social mobility and social class; cigarette, alcohol and food consumption; voting intentions; consumer buying intentions; readership; environmental trade-off preferences. This work extends to the method of data collection (e.g. by diary, panel study, self-completion methods) and on the ways in which the data can be analysed and interpreted.

In contrast, methodological work on the survey processes – interviewing, sampling, coding – of a more general kind has been sporadic. In the United States the academic interest in survey research in the 1940s resulted in the setting up of several university-based survey research centres which carried out their own large scale survey work. They stimulated an academic interest in research into the survey processes which was closely linked to survey practice and application. There were no British counterparts. In Britain most surveys have been conducted in agencies outside the universities, with a few notable exceptions. Only the market research companies, Government Social Survey and – since 1969 – Social and Community Planning

Research (SCPR), have built survey agencies engaged full-time in designing and carrying out surveys of the population.

Agricultural survey work particularly at Rothamsted Experimental Station has, however, contributed greatly to the theory and the practice of sample surveys. The contribution to sampling of Yates, head of the Rothamsted Department of Statistics, has already been mentioned. An article by Kempthorne (1946) showed that the unit also made practical contributions to data processing during the development period, this was followed by significant work on data analysis and computer software.

Academic centres provide more opportunity and incentive for research publication than survey agencies. Block grants give the former academic freedom whereas the need to keep to individual project budgets imposes time restrictions on the other. As a rule, researchers in academic centres are able to spend more time reviewing their subject and developing theoretical and conceptual frameworks; their teaching requirements encourage this.

Whereas research on the measuring instruments can be carried out in isolation from a survey agency, to do methodological work on the survey *process* researchers need to be closer to that process. In Britain, during the pioneering phase, very few institutions had this proximity and those that did – notably Government Social Survey and one or two of the leading market research agencies – were faced with the project pressures of a survey agency. Their funding was on a project basis, encouragement to publish methodological work was not part of the career reward system on a par with academics, and depended more on professional interest of researchers, and these agencies were removed from a teaching environment. Thus the individual methodological contributions which emerged from these agencies – and there were many – were not encouraged by the financial and organisational system.

In Britain societies such as the Royal Statistical Society and the Market Research Society provided an important stimulus for methodological work. These were particularly important as a forum for discussion and outlets for publications. The dominance of academic survey research centres in the USA and the much larger survey activity in the United States, meant that most of the published work on survey research during the pioneering phase came from that side of the Atlantic.

For instance, one of the first sets of guidelines on questionnaire design appeared in an American textbook entitled *Scientific Social Surveys and Research* (Young, 1939). This was followed by Cantril (1944) who provided a list of weaknesses of questionnaire construction and remedies for their resolution. Payne's *The Art of Asking Questions* (1951) was the first textbook devoted to question construction.

Other American publications in the 1940s covered various aspects of the survey process – sampling, interviewing, coding, non-response. Articles by Sheatsley (1947–8; 1949), Durant (1946) and others on interviewing, interviewer bias and cheating appeared in *Public Opinion Quarterly*, *The International Journal of Opinion and Attitude Research*, and in the *Proceedings of the American Philosophical Society*. Hansen and Hurwitz (1946) and Politz and Simmons (1949) published papers on non-response and call-back procedures in the *Journal of the American Statistical Association*. Kish (1949) published a paper on respondent selection methods, and Lazarsfeld (1948) one on the use of panel methods. Hansen and Hauser (1945) published a paper on sampling and Deming a book on the theory of sampling (1950). A comprehensive publication on survey methods was Deming's paper (1944) 'On Errors in Surveys'. Deming reviewed the 'factors affecting the usefulness of a survey' and outlined, for the 13 factors he listed as contributing to errors, the methods to be used to avoid them in designing a survey. His factors (updated only in terminology in the list below) provided a framework for investigating the survey process.

1 variability in responses between people and over time
2 the effects of the survey mode (interview, postal, length of questionnaire, depth or structured interviews etc)
3 interviewer bias and variability
4 bias due to the sponsorship
5 questionnaire design
6 changes in behaviour/attitudes etc. after the survey, that make the results obsolete
7 bias from non-response
8 bias arising because interviewers fail to question as many respondents as they are supposed to because of time pressures
9 bias because the period covered by the survey is unrepresentative
10 bias in the sampling frame
11 sampling errors and biases
12 data processing errors
13 errors in interpretation

The US Census Bureau, at which Deming worked, was an important contributor to sampling and to other aspects of survey methodology. However, much of the groundwork done in the United States before 1950 originated from four key American university centres of survey research – Michigan, Chicago, Princeton and Columbia, where close links were established between academics and survey practitioners. These centres provided three essential ingredients for methodological work on surveys: an academic approach, practical expertise in survey work and research opportunity. The Survey Research Center at the University of Michigan, part of the Institute for Social Research (ISR), was created by Rensis Likert and his colleagues. They had worked together on surveys in a wartime agency, the Division of Program Surveys in the Bureau of Agricultural Economics, where they had gained professional expertise. The new Survey Research Center carried out its own surveys. The National Opinion Research Center (NORC) was an established opinion and market survey agency before it moved from Denver to Chicago University in 1947 to link with a strong sociology department. At Princeton there was no direct merger with a professional agency, but there were close links with Gallup's American Institute of Public Opinion. The Columbia University Bureau of Applied Social Research was headed by Paul Lazarsfeld, who joined the university just before the Second World War. As one of the pioneers of social research he had a keen interest in survey methods and data analysis. He was actively engaged in media research and used a panel survey to measure the impact of the mass media on people's attitudes and behaviour at the 1940 presidential election. He also made a major contribution to *The American Soldier* (Stouffer, 1949), a landmark in measurement and analysis methodology in survey research.

Lazarsfeld, Likert, Kish, Cannell, Deming and their colleagues are good examples of Americans who combined their academic approach with their practical experience of surveys to use the research opportunity offered by their survey work to enhance the survey process. It is that contribution of 'scholarship', 'professionalism' and 'research opportunity' which has brought the major developments in methodological research on the survey process.

In Britain Government Social Survey took the lead in methodological research on the survey process immediately after the Second World War (see chapter 5). In 1943 the Government Social Survey carried out 36 surveys, many of them concerned with clothing and clothes rationing, food and food rationing and health education campaigns (Box and Thomas, 1944). By the end of that year it had an interviewing panel of 55 and a technical administrative and clerical staff of around 40. In spite of its small scale it took a professional approach to surveys, and research staff managed to use the research opportunity created by those surveys to do and publish methodology work in a practical and scholarly way.

The growth in the Government Social Survey in the next few years was considerable. The interviewing panel had increased to about 250–300 when Gray and Corlett wrote their paper on 'Sampling for the Social Survey' (1950). An agency department structure had emerged with specialist sampling, interviewing, coding and data processing branches that became increasingly expert in these specialist tasks. The large collection of early methodological working papers in the Government Social Survey's library cover many aspects of the survey process – sampling, interviewing, coding, and so on. A major difference it would seem between the American and British scenes at this time was that Social Survey researchers failed to publish in a more widely available form.

The early methodological working papers include:

M.5 (1945): *The design of Social Surveys with supplementary notes on interviewing and the recording schedule*
This paper discussed the elements involved in designing surveys, described the interviewers' tasks (making contact, securing the information and recording) and provided guidance on how each aspect of the task should be tackled. The paper also provided a classification of information needs – facts, behaviour, reported behaviour and attitude, and discussed ways of collecting each type of information.

M.9 (1947): *A report on the field observation of interviewers and an experiment in mock interviewing*
This paper reported on an experiment that used observers alongside interviewers to monitor the level of error. Its conclusions led to improvement in the training of interviewers in the use of probing without prompting.

M.17 (1948): *The open interview as a method of investigation*
This paper reviewed the use of depth interviewing as a precursor to the design of a structured survey and to provide amplification of qualitative results.

M.28 (1949): *Some objective tests of interviewer efficiency*
This paper describes a thorough investigation of interviewer biases and efficiency, including validity checks using fuel consumption data.

M.29 (1949): *Probing in opinion enquiries*
An experiment is described in which field supervisors repeated questions used by interviewers on an economic opinion survey to look at the effect of probing. The paper contains a good discussion of question types and probing guidelines for each type.

M.36 (1950): *Research on interviews*
This paper was in the format of a proposal setting out the needs for a continuous programme of research on interviewing. It pointed out that many research data on methodology were a by-product of work on normal commissioned surveys, and advocated the need for a more systematic, long term programme with specific aims.

M.58 (1950): *Sampling for the Social Survey*
This paper by Gray and Corlett, published in the *Journal of the Royal Statistical Society*, reviewed sampling practices.

M.59 (1950): *The register of electors as a sampling frame*
This paper by Gray, Corlett and Frankland later appeared in Edwards (1956).

M.69 (1952): *A use for the Jury qualifications in sample design*
This paper was published in *Applied Statistics*.

M.67 (1953): *The work of a coding section*
This paper was read at a weekend sampling school held by the Association of Incorporated Statisticians.

Some of Social Survey's methodological working papers were published in journals. Other published papers included Scott's on mail surveys (1961), and Kemsley's report on his experimental work on record keeping on budget surveys (1961). Dissemination was also achieved through seminars and conferences. Nevertheless, much went on behind the scenes in those early days that did not receive wide circulation.

The merging of the academic and the practical was present too in the pioneering market research agencies, encouraged in those early days by links with a powerful group of statisticians at the London School of Economics which included Maurice Kendall, Alan Stuart, James Durbin and Claus Moser. Later examples of that combination of 'scholarship', 'professionalism' and 'research opportunity' are found in the work of William Belson's Survey Unit of the LSE, at the World Fertility Survey and through its links with Colm O'Muircheartaigh from the LSE, and at SCPR, through its links with Graham Kalton from Southampton University.

Significant contributions to the methodology of the survey process have rarely occurred within a university setting totally removed from the practice of survey work. Conversely, in most of the busy survey agencies the research staff seldom have the opportunity to do more than isolated and fragmented methodological work on the survey process; often there is not the time to transform a report on a practical experiment of procedure into the type of more learned articles demanded by journal referees and editors.

As Moser pointed out (1949), the demands of project work in an agency often conflict with the need for general methodological research on the survey process, although survey projects offer the opportunity for such research.

> As it is difficult to experiment with methods in a survey the results of which have been requested and are to be used by a department, there is not as much methodological research as appears desirable. It is hoped that the Social Survey will be able to spend more and more of its time on research into sampling techniques, interviewing methods, questionnaire biases and all the other problems associated with surveys.

The difficulty of incorporating methodological work into projects requested by clients holds for most project work. In busy survey agencies project work restricts the time available for general methodological research; the project team's interests are necessarily concentrated on the project for which they are being funded. The methodological work that does emerge often falls under the *measuring instrument* category rather than the *survey process* category, but that is not always the case. Scott's work on mail surveys, for example, was a by-product of five projects that used that data collection technique. His experiments with that aspect of the survey process had implications beyond the specific projects he was working on.

In the early days of market research, survey researchers in agencies such as the British Market Research Bureau, Research Services and Gallup Poll made time for methodological research on the survey process and published results in the form of working papers or journal articles. These organisations were fairly active in the immediate post-war government research programmes, working directly for the Ministry of Food and the Board of Trade. In 1956 the British Market Research Bureau published a collection of *Readings in Market Research* (Edwards, 1956) that included contributions from British authors on sampling, interviewing, coding and other aspects of the survey process.

The introduction to the collection described the collaboration between academics at the London School of Economics and survey practitioners in Government Social Survey, market research agencies and the BBC audience research department. In 1949, a Division of Research Techniques – later to become the Survey Research Centre (SRC) – was formed under the direction of Professor Maurice Kendall. The division was founded to study the methodology of research into economics and other social sciences. Professor Kendall's strong team of statisticians made the LSE the main university centre for research on survey methods in Britain. The principal difference between the LSE and the key American university centres was that the LSE did not develop its own survey capacity. To overcome that weakness the Survey Research Unit was formed as a committee to link the academic researchers at the LSE with survey practitioners. The link produced one of the few continuous programmes of research by British academics on the survey process, and it led to publications on aspects of survey methods by Moser, Stuart and Durbin.

The LSE division was later transformed into the LSE Survey Research Centre under the direction of Dr William Belson, a psychologist. The Centre, which operated through the 1960s, provided a unique opportunity in Britain for people working in an academic centre to directly involve themselves in survey work. Its aims were stated as:

i) to conduct studies of the techniques of survey research, with a view to assessing their overall efficiency and to develop modifications and new procedures as necessary;
ii) to provide courses of training in the techniques of survey research;
iii) to conduct social investigations, particularly where these call for special methodological preparations;

iv) to provide an information and advisory service with regard to research techniques and procedures.

Dr Belson carried out a number of surveys and collaborated with survey agencies, on readership surveys in particular. He did important pioneering work on recall error, interviewer behaviour, prompted recall and on the respective merits of open and closed questions. He developed the double interview technique, pioneered the use of tape recorders for evaluation and contributed to the analysis of multivariate data. Institutional difficulties eventually prompted Belson to move the centre away from the LSE, at which point he concentrated more on training than on methodological work.

More recent developments

Since the pioneering days the methodological contribution of academics in Britain to the survey process has been sketchy and largely the work of individuals rather than of academic centres. An example is the link between Colm O'Muircheartaigh, based at LSE, and the World Fertility Survey (WFS). His collaboration with the WFS has made important contributions to sample design, the calculation of complex sampling errors, and the measurement of response errors, particularly interviewer variability. Another example is the link between Graham Kalton, then based at Southampton University, and Social and Community Planning Research (SCPR). This collaboration yielded important contributions to response errors and to sample design and led to the creation of the Survey Methods Centre at SCPR.

Recognition of the limited contribution of the academic sector to survey methodology was made by the SSRC when it set out the case for its own survey unit in 1970. A background paper drew the following conclusions:

> The steady increase in the use of the sample survey method by academic researchers and the likelihood of work of this kind expanding very substantially within the next few years have led the Council to give special thought to how present and future needs in this respect can best be met. At the moment relatively few students of social science in this country receive any formal training in survey methods . . . The contributions to survey methodology from the academic world in Britain have also been disappointingly sparse . . . An SSRC Unit could provide training in survey methods and build up a substantial contribution to survey methodology.

On the basis of advice from American colleagues and because of the cost and funding difficulties involved, the SSRC decided against making the survey unit a survey agency:

> Careful thought has been given to whether or not the Unit should have its own field force of interviewers . . . The cost of this, however, would appear to be prohibitive; at least at the outset.

In setting up the survey unit, the SSRC thus created the opportunity for an academic approach but removed it from a survey agency environment where it could also have benefited from professional survey expertise and research opportunity. The unit's main contributions to survey methodology were focused on the measuring instrument category (particularly for quality of life measurements) and not on methodology of the survey process.

The SSRC Survey Unit (which closed in 1976) could have become a survey agency only by accepting contract work. Grant funding alone was inadequate to generate the necessary scale and continuity of operations. But contract work would have brought the Unit into direct competition with the market research industry, and enlarged it in ways that would have exposed it to entrepreneurial risks and commercial pressures.

The way in which survey research is financed has undoubtedly played an important part in limiting methodological work; competitive tendering and the small scale of funding in the public and private sectors have led to intense competition with pressures to reduce quality and ignore methodology. Harry Henry, a market research pioneer in Britain, underlined one of the reasons for poor methodological research in a paper he gave to an ESOMAR conference in 1964.

> Because of rapid expansion of the business of market opinion research, many of the rather more senior people who would be primarily and essentially concerned with developing and refining their own technical repertoires and with training new generations to assist and succeed them became so heavily involved in matters of administration and selling that the quality of work becomes an almost secondary consideration.

This tendency has increased as the market research industry has become more fragmented and as it has expanded to meet the overall growth. To some degree the growth in the volume of surveys in the commercial sector has acted against rather than in favour of methodological work. It is to the credit of many individuals in market research that they have continued to do methodological work and to publish despite these constraints.

An encouraging recent development is the creation by the Market Research Society of a Research and Development Committee with its own small research budget. The Committee has commissioned reviews of sampling practices and of telephone interviewing procedures among market research agencies, useful first steps in a programme of methodological evaluation. Some market research companies have also subscribed to a methodological research fund to enable Dr Belson to continue with his research on survey methods.

Government Social Survey continues to undertake research work on survey methods. In 1970 it became the Social Survey Division of the new Office of Population Censuses and Surveys. After a period in the later 1960s and early 1970s when methodological research and development had no formalised structure, Social Survey Division formed a methodological unit in 1976 to carry out a programme of methodological work aimed at improving the cost effectiveness and quality of survey research. The programme covers a range of survey issues including sampling error methodology, investigation of non-response, evaluation of proxy interviews and other aspects of the quality of the data. The results of this work are published in Social Survey Division's *Methodology Bulletin*. Some of Social Survey's methodological work – particularly that on measuring instruments – is funded by government departments. But Social Survey is also able to devote some of its central funds to this purpose. It remains to be seen how far financial restrictions and the government review of its statistical service will impinge on these recent methodological developments.

Another organisational development occurred at SCPR. This independent institute was formed as a charitable trust in 1969. Its founders and first members of staff came from survey agencies and were willing to carry out contract work and engage in competitive tendering. SCPR was able to expand and develop as a survey agency operating within the non-profit sector. In 1975 SCPR received from SSRC a 3-year programme grant (extended to five years) to do work on survey methodology. That programme led to the setting up of SCPR's Survey Methods Centre, in association with The City University, as one of the SSRC's newly constituted Designated Research Centres. For the first time in Britain a survey organisation outside government was given funds that were not project-specific, to pay for a small team of people working exclusively on survey methodology.

Since the Survey Methods Centre was created in 1980 the activities of SCPR have widened to include teaching and training. SCPR now runs a postgraduate M.Sc./Diploma course in survey methods at The City University and organises workshops and seminars on different aspects of survey methods. It also publishes a *Survey Methods Newsletter* three times a year.

The main activity of the Survey Methods Centre is a co-ordinated programme of research into survey practice, particularly interviewing, sampling, coding, questionnaire design and telephone surveys. The programmes involve observing the process; looking at data from a range of surveys to see the results of current practices; experimenting with different methods in a variety of surveys, evaluating efficiency, cost and reliability of existing and alternative methods and feeding the results into training and practice.

The Survey Methods Centre at SCPR is only one of the recent initiatives of the Social Science Research Council to develop survey methods research and to foster links between academics and survey research users and practitioners. Its Research Resources and Methods Committee has also funded a series of survey methods seminars (administered by SCPR in collaboration with the London School of Economics and the City University) since 1979, which regularly brings together about 75 research workers from a wide variety of backgrounds; a group of statisticians based at Edinburgh University has received funds to run a northern series of seminars in survey methods; Professors Holt and Smith, at Southampton University, have received programme funding to develop survey data analysis models; and links have been forged with the Market Research Society to investigate joint methodology workshops.

The financial climate in Britain for survey research in the public, commercial and academic sectors as we enter the 1980s is distinctly gloomy. Yet the initiatives of the SSRC and developments at OPCS Social Survey Division, the Market Research Society and SCPR indicate that some of the organisational barriers to methodological research are beginning to break down.

ACKNOWLEDGEMENTS

The paper has been prepared as part of the Survey Methods Centre's work at SCPR, funded by the Social Science Research Council. I would like to thank the many people who were kind enough to comment on an earlier draft of this paper, in particular Louis Moss, Tom Corlett, Alan Stuart, Aubrey McKennell, Chris Scott and Bill Kemsley. They provided information based on their own knowledge of and involvement in the pioneering phase and helped me clarify my thinking about methodological development. I would also like to thank Isobel Campbell for her invaluable editing. I must assume full responsibility, however, for this account and for any errors or omissions.

REFERENCES

Abrams, M.A. (1951) *Social Surveys and Social Action*. Heinemann, London.

Booth C, ed. (1889–1902). *Life and Labour of the People of London*. 17 volumes. Macmillan, London.

Bowley, A.L. and Burnett-Hurst, A.R. (1915). *Livelihood and Poverty: a study in the economic conditions of working-class households in Northampton, Warrington, Stanley and Reading*, Bell, London.

Box, K. and Thomas, G. (1944). 'The Wartime Social Survey', *Journal of the Royal Statistical Society*, 33: 151–89.

Cantril, H. ed. (1944). *Gauging Public Opinion*. Princeton University Press, Princeton.

Cole, D.E. (1956). 'Field work in sample surveys of household income and expenditure', *Applied Statistics*, 5: 49–61.

Deming, W.E. (1944). 'On errors in surveys'. *American Sociological Review*, 9: 359–69.

Deming, W.E. (1950). *Some Theory of Sampling*, Wiley, New York.

Durant, H. (1946). 'The theater problem', *Public Opinion Quarterly*, 10: 288–91.

Eaton, A.H. and Harrison, S.M. (1930). *A Bibliographv of Social Surveys: reports of fact-finding studies made as a basis for social action*, Russell Sage, New York.

Edwards, F. ed. (1956). *Readings in Market Research: a selection of papers by British authors*. The British Market Research Bureau, London.

Gray, P.G. and Corlett, T. (1950). 'Sampling for the Social Survey', *Journal of the Royal Statistical Society A*, 113: 150–206.

Hansen, M.H. and Hauser, P.M. (1945). 'Area sampling – some principles of sampling design', *Public Opinion Quarterly*, 9: 183–93.

Hansen, M.H. and Hurwitz, W.N. (1946). 'The problem of non-response in sample surveys', *Journal of the American Statistical Association*, 41: 517–29.

Hilton, J. (1924). 'Enquiry by sample: an experiment and its results', *Journal of the Royal Statistical Society*, 87: 544–70.

Jensen, A. (1926). 'Report on the representative method in Statistics', *Bulletin of the International Statistical Institute*, 22: 359–77.

Kempthorne, B.P. (1946). 'The use of a punched card system for the analysis of survey data; special references to the analysis of the National Farm Survey', *Journal of the Royal Statistical Society, A* 109(3): 284–95.

Kemsley, W.F.F. (1961). 'The household expenditure enquiry of the Ministry of Labour: Variability in the 1953–54 enquiry', *Applied Statistics*, 10: 117–35.

Kish, L. (1949). 'A procedure for objective respondent selection within the household', *Journal of the American Statistical Association*, 44: 380–87.

Lazarsfeld, P.F. (1948). 'The use of panels in social research', *Proceedings of the American Philosophical Society*, 92: 405–10.

Lydall, H.F. (1956). 'The methods of the savings survey'. In *Readings in Market Research* (ed. F. Edwards). The British Market Research Bureau, London.

Marsh, C. (1982). *The Survey Method: the contribution of surveys to sociological explanation*. Contemporary Social Research Series No. 6, George Allen and Unwin, London.

Moser, C.A. (1949). 'The use of sampling in Great Britain', *Journal of the American Statistical Association*, 44: 231–59.

O'Muircheartaigh, C. and Wong, S.T. (1981). 'The impact of sampling theory on survey sampling practice: a review', *Bulletin of the International Statistical Institute* 40(1), pp. 465–93.

Payne, S.L.B. (1951). *The Art of Asking Questions* (Studies in public opinion No. 3) Princeton University Press, Princeton.

Politz, A. and Simmons, W. (1949). 'I. An attempt to get the "not at homes" into the sample without callbacks. II. Further theoretical considerations regarding the plan for eliminating callbacks', *Journal of the American Statistical Association*, 44: 9–31.

Rowntree, B.S. (1902, new ed. 1922). *Poverty: a study of town life*, Longmans, London.

Scott, C. (1961). 'Research on mail surveys', *Journal of the Royal Statistical Society A*, 124: 143–205.
Sheatsley, P.B. (1947–8). 'Some uses of interviewer-report forms', *Public Opinion Quarterly*, 11: 601–11.
Sheatsley, P.B. (1949). 'The influence of sub-questions on interviewer performance', *Public Opinion Quarterly*, 13: 310–13.
Smith, T.M.F. (1976). 'The foundations of survey sampling: a review', *Journal of the Royal Statistical Society A*, 139: 183–204
Statistical Society of London (1840). 'Report on the state of the Working Classes in the parishes of St Margaret and St John, Westminster', *Journal of the Statistical Society of London*. 3: 14–24.
Stouffer, S.A. *et al* (1949). *The American Soldier*, 4 volumes. Princeton University Press, Princeton.
Wells, A.F. (1935). *The Local Social Survey in Great Britain*. Allen and Unwin, London.
Yates, F. (1946). 'A review of recent statistical developments in sampling and sampling surveys', *Journal of the Royal Statistical Society A*, 109: 12–43.
Yates, F. (1949, 3rd edition 1960). *Sampling Methods for Censuses and Surveys*. Griffin, London.
Young, P.V. (1939, 4th edition 1966). *Scientific Social Surveys and Research*. Prentice-Hall, Englewood Cliffs, N.J.

7 Mass-Observation 1937–1949

ANGUS CALDER

Mass-Observation was formed early in 1937 by three young men: Charles Madge, well-known as a poet but earning his bread and butter as a Fleet Street journalist; Humphrey Jennings, a lesser poet, who was learning under John Grierson, in the GPO Film Unit, the skills which would make him Britain's most distinguished documentary film director; and Tom Harrisson, self-taught ornithologist and anthropologist, a publicist – and self-publicist – of genius.

Mass-Observation was planned as an independent, scientific organisation. Its early activities had two main centres. In Bolton, Harrisson led a shifting team of full-time and part-time 'Observers' in a detailed study of every aspect of life in a Northern working class environment. Madge, then living at Blackheath, presided over the 'national panel' – hundreds of volunteers who reported on their own views, dreams, taste in clothing, daily activities and so on, in response to regular 'directives'. Jennings' involvement was brief, but he did organise Mass-Observation's first book, *May 12*, a collage of reports on the Coronation of George VI in May 1937.

By 1939, the organisation was in some ways well-established, and had become a household word. Its Penguin Special, *Britain*, had sold well. The press took an interest in Mass-Observation's homely findings – about smoking habits, for instance, or that current dance-craze the Lambeth Walk. For some volunteer observers, 'Mass-Observation' had become habit forming. However, crisis was at hand. Madge and Harrisson, not dissimilar in background, were polar opposites in personality. Getting money to keep the organisation going was difficult and already it was carrying out market research, in violation of its high scientific aims. The four planned books on Bolton commissioned by Victor Gollancz had proved very hard to pull into shape. Then war broke out. Only one Bolton book appeared, in 1943, *The Pub and the People*. But Mass-Observation found a role. Volunteers were asked to keep 'war diaries' and send them in monthly. Madge and Harrisson collaborated on a lively survey of the early, 'phoney' months, published early in 1940 as *War Begins at Home*. The Ministry of Information soon employed Mass-Observation to help it compile reports for the government on public opinion and 'morale', and with Government support, Mass-Observation survived through the hectic months of the Battle of Britain and the Blitz. (For an anthology, see Calder and Sheridan 1984.)

Madge drifted away in this period. The surrealist poet had become absorbed in hard, 'positive' social science – research on working class saving and spending habits, which he pursued, under the influence of J.M. Keynes, in a research project for the Institute of Economic and Social Research. The Ministry of Information ceased to use Mass-Observation systematically during 1941. But other government departments employed it from time to time, and it received crucial support from the Advertising Service Guild, a combination of seven independent advertising agencies who aimed to promote the advertising industry by publicising its alleged social value. Under Advertising Service Guild auspices, Mass-Observation published, during the war, several books and booklets of wide ranging significance – on *Clothes Rationing* and *Home Propaganda* in 1941, on *People in Production* in 1942, on *People's Homes* in 1943, on demobilisation, *The Journey Home* in 1944 and on *Britain and Her Birthrate* in 1945. Meanwhile, Gollancz brought out, in 1943, an account from the inside of women's work in a *War Factory*. As reporters in depth on public opinion in wartime, Mass-Observation had served an obviously useful purpose, and it may be that its greatest significance in the history of social science in Britain is that its reputation accustomed people to the idea that such surveys should be taken seriously. The Government's own Wartime Social Survey, founded in 1940, had worked far more obscurely, after the early furore in the House of Commons raised by MPs who objected to 'snoopers' (see chapter 5).

Harrisson had entered the army in 1942, and while he nevertheless remained remarkably close to the centre of things until he was sent to the South Seas in 1944, day to day running devolved upon others, notably on H.D. ('Bob') Willcock. The Mass-Observation 'style', which was punchy and provocative, undoubtedly owed much originally to the journalistic skills of Madge and Harrisson, but it became the common possession of those who worked for the organisation. If before the conflict 'Mass-Observation' had seemed a two man show with Harrisson more and more threatening to make it a one man show, during the war team spirit kept it alive. The National Panel of volunteers was of course disrupted by call up and bombing; conscription also led to a rapid turnover of full-time personnel. But a conviction that, in a most concrete way, Mass-Observation was helping to make history, by preserving so much detail of war-time life from oblivion, was one of the altruistic motives which sustained the organisation's still-precarious existence.

In peace time, the impetus had to be routinised. Mass-Observation could only survive, it transpired, in competition with commercial market research organisations. Willcock and its other full-timers fought hard to preserve its distinctive character – which meant trying to sell its 'qualitative' methods of investigation. Harrisson came back from Borneo in 1946, couldn't settle down, and soon returned there to act as curator of the Sarawak Museum and turn his versatile hand to self-taught zoology and archaeology. (The fullest account of his extraordinary career can be found in Green, 1970.) In 1949, 'Mass-Observation' became Mass-Observation *Limited*, with Harrisson retaining ownership of all the material previously gathered. In the mid 1960s, Paul Addison, the historian, tracked this material down to a basement in West London under the offices of Mass-Observation (UK) Limited, where only a couple of previous researchers had, lightly, disturbed it as they compiled books of popular social history. The material was in a muddle, and its preservation seemed at risk. I pointed this out to Professor Asa Briggs, now Lord Briggs, who was then my supervisor. Leonard England, then head of Mass-Observation Limited, who had joined Mass-Observation as a schoolboy before the war, was glad to agree to the transportation of much of it to the keeping of the University of Sussex. When Harrisson returned from Sarawak in 1970, the rest of the surviving material was gathered in, and he himself, eventually from a personal chair, presided over the setting up of a special archive.

There it still thrives, despite the sudden death of Harrisson in 1976, in a road accident in Thailand. The material, under the immediate care of Dorothy Wainwright, has still not been fully ordered and catalogued, but has already proved of great value to researchers in many fields. In 1981, Professor David Pocock, the director of the Archive, revived the National Panel, and there is now a new body of hundreds of volunteers, responding to invitations to send in notes on their daily lives and opinions.

This is not the first revival. In 1960, Harrisson himself, during a brief return visit to Britain, took a team of former Mass-Observers to Bolton to look at changes there since the 1930s, and in 1977 Philip Ziegler recruited diarists to provide material for his book, *The Crown and the People*, on popular attitudes to royalty.

The core of material in the archive can be divided as follows. Firstly, there are 45 boxes full of material collected in Bolton and Blackpool during the 'Worktown' survey of 1937 to 1940. Secondly, there are over 3000 File Reports, in a series stretching from 1939 to 1951 – mostly typewritten papers, mostly summarising Mass-Observation investigations and almost all written by full-time observers. Some are very short, some are book length. Thirdly, there is a body of 'day surveys' collected when Charles Madge was running the Panel, members of which were asked, from February 1937 to February 1938, to send in detailed reports on their activities on the twelfth day of each month. From January 1939, Mass-Observation sent volunteers a monthly questionnaire, called a 'Directive', covering a particular topic, or maybe several. This was the basic use made of the Panel throughout the forties, and 'Directive Replies' form a fourth major type of material. From August 1939, numerous volunteers – some 500 at one time or another, though never so many at any one time – sent in war diaries, commenting freely on their personal lives. These, a few of them carried on after the war, fill 160 storage boxes. To sample them is fascinating and tantalising; Mass-Observation repeatedly failed in attempts to find systematic use for them. Sixth and last, there are numerous boxes of 'topic collections', in which are gathered material used by full-time personnel in their investigations of particular subjects – for instance, 'Housing', 'Pacifism', 'Wall Chalkings', 'Dreams'.

Altogether, this huge assemblage – more than 1000 boxes of raw material – forms an impressive monument to the vision of Mass-Observation's founders. It has the same fascination for the historical imagination as the great *Statistical Account* of Scotland compiled by Sir John Sinclair in the 1790s, and Madge and Harrisson 'thought even bigger' than Sinclair. Their aim was nothing less than to achieve a complete understanding of modern society, neglecting nothing as unimportant. They were hampered as they set off on their quixotic quest by very little knowledge of what social scientists before them had done. A note in the bibliography of *The Pub and the People* reveals Mass-Observation's conscious indebtedness to American sociology:

> Actually responsible for the greatest section of field work to date are Chicago's Park and Burgess . . . Perhaps the most penetrating work on method is that of Thomas, Loomis and Arrington (Yale, 1933). Dollard's *Class and Caste in a Southern Town*, Thomas and Znaniecki's volumes on the Polish peasant, the Lynds' *Middletown* and *Middletown Revisited*, Gosnell and Merriam on the non-voter in American politics, the University of North Carolina's Society Study Series, and the volumes of the Payne Fund's Cinema Research are significant also. (Mass-Observation, 1970, p. 350).

Madge and Harrisson believed that they were, in Britain, pioneers, and with the Gallup Poll in its infancy, and market research hardly much in the public eye, they were able to convince others that they were right.

Both men were what we would now call 'dropouts' from Cambridge University, both had been born abroad – Madge in South Africa, Harrisson in Argentina – both had soldiers for fathers. They were children of empire;

they were also more metaphorically 'children of the sun', to adopt the term used by Martin Green in his suggestive book of that name about British intellectuals of the inter-war years. That is, they shared in the widespread revolt of young men of the dominant classes against the values of their fathers and of the public schools to which they had been sent. Madge, joining the Communist Party as an inactive member, already a famous poet in his mid twenties, conformed to the type defined by Green as 'naif' – sensitive in manner, generous in sympathy, quiet and vulnerable, like Stephen Spender and Philip Toynbee. Harrisson was, in Green's terms, a classic 'rogue', determined to be outrageous, and succeeding, dominant even in the company of the formidable Richard Crossman (Green, 1977, pp. 26–36). Evelyn Waugh, that mordant observer of the follies of the 1930s, valued *May 12*, Mass-Observation's first substantial book, much more highly than most other reviewers. What stodgier men saw as formlessness, Waugh praised as 'a new way of writing a book'. He revelled in its 'funny footnotes' (*Spectator*, 15 April 1938).

After dropping out of Cambridge, Harrisson had migrated to live in Oxford, where, in 1933, he had published a jokey, provocative *Letter* to the university's denizens, teasing them for their tameness, their propensity to talk, not *do*:

> I am intelligent, reasonable, and independent. Since I was 15, I have been doing things, living in slums and in Charlotte Street, on trawlers, desert islands, South America, Lapland, and the East, bicycling in Europe, rock-climbing, hop picking, playing a barrel-organ, feeling hungry, staying at Shepheards Hotel (Cairo), studying vice in London, sleeping in lavatories and the baths of hotels, writing articles (and a book) on natural history and scientific subjects. I am a scientist. I have no politics and no axe to grind. I believe vaguely in life. I can live on practically nothing, but am fond of spending a great deal. I believe in action – in doing a thing as well as saying it, in seeing something wrong and trying to put it right. That is, indeed, the purpose of this present enterprise. My contemporaries are sayers, not doers. (Harrisson, 1933, p. 13)

Walking round Oxford in sandals with painted toenails, Harrisson had identified himself as a rogue. Yet he was also a real 'doer'. While at Harrow School he had published a book on the birds of Harrow and its district. He went on to organise important ornithological surveys – one study involved a team of 1000 nationwide observers. He was 25 when Mass-Observation was founded, and had already gone on scientific expeditions to the Arctic and to Borneo. He had spent a period on the island of Malekula in the New Hebrides, living with 'cannibals', from which experience he produced a best-selling work of popular anthropology, *Savage Civilisation*. Returning from the Pacific, he decided to study British people anthropologically, and 'went bush' to this end in Bolton. His later activities there, punctuated by orgiastic trips to Paris, could credibly, though not fairly, be seen as those of a rogue 'child of the sun', expressing his personal style through the manipulation of others.

Madge, by contrast was quiet, and seemed shy. However, he had expressed revolt in his own way. He wrote poetry from the age of 8. At Winchester, he had been refused permission to study science; nevertheless, he had insisted on studying science after he got a classics scholarship to Cambridge. He was attracted to Magdalene College by the presence of I.A. Richards there and, while denying any direct connection, he would agree that Richards' experiments in *Practical Criticism* – involving the use of volunteer guinea-pigs to establish truths about the way people read poetry – may have had some influence on the trains of thought which led him to Mass-Observation. He met J.D. Bernal at Cambridge and published him in his own magazine *Cambridge Left*. This is an indirect but suggestive link with the movement, in the 1930s, to bring science and the masses together, of which Bernal was a leader (interviewed by A. Calder, March 1979). He left Cambridge without a degree, already married to the beautiful poet Kathleen Raine, and they lived in Blackheath close to the GPO Film Unit for which their friend Jennings worked.

With their shared interest in the new, outrageous surrealist movement, Madge and Jennings might also seem to have conformed to type as 'children of the sun', and the Oxford Collective Poem, produced by Madge as one of Mass-Observation's early fringe activities might seem almost 'roguish' in its conception; twelve undergraduates spent weeks over it, collecting images day by day and eventually bringing their collections together and noting overlaps. They took six common images, and each wrote one pentameter line on each of them. They voted on the best six lines, then each proceeded to write a poem of not more than eighteen lines using them. They amended each other's poems before finally voting for the best final version. The result was a surrealistic poem not unlike some which Madge himself had published, concluding:

> And on our heads the crimes of our buried fathers
> Burst in a hurricane and the rebels shout.
>
> (Symons, 1960, pp. 114–16)

Madge and Harrisson were brought together by precisely such a coincidence as fascinated the surrealist temperament. The Abdication Crisis of 1936 seemed to reveal the continuing role of myth and superstition in 'civilised' mass society. A Cambridge schoolmaster called Geoffrey Pike published a letter in the *New Statesman* which spoke of the 'desperate need' this exposed for an 'anthropological study' of Britain itself. Madge, working on the *Daily Mirror*, had first-hand insight into how badly the press was serving its readers in this important crisis. He shortly took up Pike's idea in another letter to the *New Statesman*, announcing that a group of poets, painters and documentary film makers had formed 'Mass-Observation' to create a new 'science of ourselves'. By sheer chance, Harrisson had in the same issue the only poem he ever published – about 'cannibals'. So of course he saw Madge's letter and wrote to the Blackheath group. On 30 January 1937 a further letter, signed by Harrisson, Madge and Jennings, called in the *New Statesman* for volunteer mass-observers. So this social survey was born.

It looked like a topical cultural fad. It linked up not only with surrealism but also with a documentary impulse in literature, most famously exemplified by Orwell's *Road to Wigan Pier*. The undergraduates, painters and poets who followed Harrisson to Bolton and put in longer or shorter stints of mass-observing in 'Worktown' (as he dubbed it) were motivated by curiosity about the proletarian North, as well as by guilt over mass unemployment. It was a not *very* political way of expressing social concern, and its context was general unease about where modern society was heading, as Hitler, Franco and Mussolini strode on. Mass-Observation's appeal was largely to much the same groups as congregated in the Left Book Club, supported Cripps' plans for a Popular Front, bought the new red and white Penguin Specials, and took an interest in the formation, in 1938, of the British Association's new Division for the Social and International Relations of Science. Unemployment and widespread belief in astrology could both be claimed as factors in the rise of Hitler. Tom Jeffery has argued, in the best account published of Mass-Observation:

> Mass-Observation sprang . . . from a realisation that ordinary people were being misled by a complacent press and indifferent government, both deeply ignorant of the needs of working people and the desires of 'people of good will.' To counteract this situation the people needed to know the facts, about international affairs, government policies, and about themselves; only if the people were given the facts could democracy work. In this sense, M-O was a political challenge of the man in the street, of us against them; it was a populist demand, that democracy should mean what it says, rule by the people, appraised of the facts. M-O originated with the Abdication Crisis of 1936 but it stepped into the centre of populist politics following the Munich crisis of September 1938. M-O was part of the articulation of a popular consciousness which would make its greatest impact in the early years of the war but it also links that 'war radicalism' to the later 1930's. (Jeffery, 1978, pp. 3–4)

Madge and Harrisson were not merely 'children of the sun', playing at roles. Interaction with Bolton people, with earnest young field workers, with 'ordinary people' who sent in reports, deepened a real initial commitment in both men to the scientific study of society. Harrisson was a variously gifted man with a restless passion for travel and change – yet he spent five zestful years working at all hours for Mass-Observation. Madge converted himself within three years from surrealist poet to dogged social scientist, and by 1950 would be Professor of Sociology at the University of Birmingham.

Both men meant business – as Waugh was sorry to see. He perceptively feared when he read Mass-Observation's second book, *First Year's Work*, that 'the movement might degenerate into a "trade inquiry" of the kind organised by sales managers and advertising agents'. But he also deplored the serious ambitions clearly shown in this small volume, the desire to set the world to rights. He was properly witty at the expense of a rather flatulent postscript by the anthropologist Malinowski, who had taken Mass-Observation under his wing (*Spectator*, 15 April 1938). But had he read Mass-Observation's first pamphlet, published a year before, he would have known that Messianism had been there from the outset. Though neither Madge nor Harrisson commonly acknowledged H.G. Wells as master, it was a vision like his, of a world saved by science, to which their early publicity appealed.

Referring to the Abdication Crisis, Madge and Harrisson had spoken of 'the sway of superstition in the midst of science. How little we know of our next-door neighbour and his habits; how little we know of ourselves. Of conditions of life and thought in another class or another district, our ignorance is complete . . . It is left to the intuitions of men of genius to cope with the unknown mess. Such intuitions are to a human science of the future what cookery is to chemistry. The building up of such a science is an urgent problem for mankind.' Current sociology was dismissed as academic. Mass-Observation would do better by making use of 'the untrained observer, the man in the street. Ideally, it is the observation by everyone of everyone, including themselves.'

Urgency was given to the task by 'the atavism of the new Germany and the revival of racial superstition', threatening the extinction of humanity. But the political commitment implied so far was cut across by a further remark that 'It is the task of science not to pass a moral judgement on superstition, but simply to examine and describe it, leaving to others to decide whether they want it or not.' The immediate task was 'patiently [to] amass material, without unduly pre-selecting from the total number of available facts'. The hope was somehow to 'add to the social consciousness of the time' by presenting facts without bias, and making them generally available (Madge and Harrisson, 1937, pp. 9–11, 29, 47).

There was a conflict in Mass-Observation from the outset between a populist wish to show 'us' to 'us' and 'us' to 'them' and a determination to be scientific; and there was a further dilemma arising from the notion that an unbiased social science must be unselective. Both Madge and Harrisson at the outset were preoccupied with myth and superstition – but Mass-Observation never organised itself so as to produce a major study of the subject; that would have required a more selective approach. Harrisson, a bird-watcher originally, believed that people could be understood, like owls, by pure observation, and set his Bolton colleagues on to strange and unprofitable courses such as 'trailing' lone pedestrians and noting their every movement. After a year of Day Reports, Madge, according to a newspaper article 'found himself buried under 1730 reports containing approximately 2,300,000 words and cried out for a year to get them sorted'. As William Walwyn, the journalist in question, went on to remark astutely, this represented 'infinite regress . . . If we could read all the papers and all the books, we could know what we are all thinking. But there never will be time' (*Reynolds News*, 1 May 1938).

Academic social scientists, scoffed at incessantly by Harrisson, were not slow to point out the weaknesses of his methods. Their objection was not that they were wholly novel. As Raymond Firth pointed out, there were surveys already in existence using ordinary people as observers and collectors of statistics (reported in *Newcastle Journal*, 31 January 1939); as T.H. Marshall protested, 'It would be a big task even to make a list of the social enquiries at present in this country: it would be next to impossible to do it for the United States.' The case, as elaborated by Marshall ('Is Mass Observation Moonshine?' *Highway*, December 1937, pp. 48–50) and by Marie Jahoda (*Sociological Review* Vol. XXX, 1938, pp. 208–9) was that Mass-Observation's approach was unscientific. Neither was wholly unsympathetic – both recognised the sincerity of the Observers and approved of the conception of the Bolton survey. Marshall complained, 'Mass-Observation has made things very difficult for its would-be friends.' Like Jahoda he pointed out that one couldn't be both 'scientific' and unselective. Hypotheses, generalisations, were essential. While Marshall denounced the assumption 'that there are things called social "facts" which exist independent of selection and interpretation', Jahoda described as 'nonsense' the Mass-Observers' apparent belief that 'exhaustive observation and description are possible'.

Both based their criticisms on *May 12*, a book which the founders themselves came to see as misguided. However, their Penguin Special, *Britain*, published in 1939, while it still makes lively reading, was hardly a weighty contribution to social science. Both Madge and Harrisson were skilled journalists and the book's handling of public opinion in the Munich crisis, all-in wrestling, and a random assortment of other topics, has the general character of thoughtful 'in depth' reporting.

The war saved Mass-Observation's methodological bacon. It was pushed towards urgent investigations of limited topics. There was no time to survey Portsmouth, say, in the 'Worktown' manner when the full-time team descended on that city to report on morale during the Blitz; nevertheless, like other Blitz reports by Mass-Observation, those on Portsmouth do give a convincing account of the subject under investigation, and the pre-war experience of observing trivia for their own sake showed its value in this and other 'war work' where the need to defeat Germany gave all observations a natural focus: what did trivia point to about morale? However, the Ministry of Information eventually dropped Mass-Observation, whose apparently slapdash methods seemed questionable. To criticism before, during and after the war, Harrisson, Bob Willcock and others retorted with reiterated insistence that while Mass-Observation *used* statistics – its own, Gallup's and so forth – its 'qualitative' approach gave it special status. Mere public opinion polls and market research organisations aimed at rapid results and sought information only on particular issues; Mass-Observation studied people from all angles all the time. Hence it could spot, so the argument ran, long-term trends. A draft of 1947 for a handout designed to attract customers put the point this way:

> A few hundred *ardent* fascists in this country may have more long term effect than a few million passive socialists. An idea may be accepted by millions today, but if their acceptance is shallow, uninformed, weakly held, it may change to rejection tomorrow. This applies to a favoured brand of tinned soup just as much as it applies to a favoured political party or religious group. (Draft together with Ms drafts of 'Polls Apart' in Mass-Observation Archive)

'Observer-unobserved' techniques of watching and overhearing people could often discover their real views, about which they would lie in response to direct questions, and the National Panel of volunteers gave Mass-Observation, so the argument ran, access to private opinions on sensitive topics where social prestige was involved.

In fact, use of Mass-Observation reports alongside other evidence of movements of opinion in Britain during the Second World War suggests that they were not untrustworthy. Quirky though Harrisson may have been, impatient and undisguisedly prejudiced, he showed in an article 'Who'll Win?' published in *The Political Quarterly* in January 1944 that he had achieved much grasp of popular opinion. At a time when most people in politics and in the press found the idea unbelievable, he correctly predicted that the Tories under Churchill would not win a post-war election. This, in retrospect, was Mass-Observation's finest hour.

At about the same time, Harrisson wrote his introduction to *War Factory*. This short book, published by Gollancz in 1943, is essentially the work of a single observer, Celia Fremlin, who worked for a time, *incognito* except by two managers, on the shop floor of a West Country factory. She was an expert writer (subsequently well known for her detective stories) and her text still reads very well. Harrisson explained that this one-woman survey arose from a request by the firm to investigate factors which might be slowing down production. He could report that the firm had found Celia Fremlin's study helpful.

Emboldened, he launched a characteristic attack on academic sociologists, dismissing their craving for statistics as evidence of an inferiority complex, due to their not being true scientists. 'The qualitative approach is used daily by biologists, surgeons, geologists. No-one doubts that in such hands the results are "scientific" . . . Uncontrolled accumulation of figures may actually obscure the HUMAN problem . . . *solely* quantitative methods tend to endless pursuit of the WHAT, while neglecting the vital WHY.' He went on to jeer at Marie Jahoda for her recent paper on 'Some Socio-Psychological Problems of Factory Life' published in the *British Journal of Psychology*. Her findings were invalid, he suggested, because the factory girls whom she had studied had known that she was analysing them.

But, as he acknowledged, Celia Fremlin's work was untypical of Mass-Observation's usual methods. 'Generally, Mass-Observation employs a team of trained objective investigators working simultaneously, checking this with information of a subjective nature from some of the persons actually being observed' (Mass-Observation, 1943, pp. 5–11). *People in Production*, an 'enquiry into British war production' sponsored by the Advertising Service Guild and published in 1942, is thus more representative of Mass-Observation's wartime work.

Twenty investigators were engaged in this enquiry from October 1941 to March 1942, at a time when grave concern was widely voiced over real or supposed inefficiency in Britain's industrial war effort. Information was collected from the managements of some eighty firms, large and small. Supervision staffs, including foremen, were interviewed; so were trade union officials. 'Just over 1,200 workers' were also spoken to (Mass-Observation, 1942, pp. 6–13). The resulting report is wide-ranging and extremely lively. Urgently topical in its original impulse, speedily despatched through the presses, it has a blatant polemical thrust. Its Introduction claims that Mass-Observation 'have tried to adopt an absolutely honest and disinterested attitude' (p. vii), and there is no reason to disbelieve it. But its conclusions are deliberately controversial. Greater self sacrifice, by industrialist and worker alike, are required. The normal economic yardstick of efficiency must be discarded under wartime conditions. Better information, and better propaganda, are needed. Above all, with women so important in the workforce, more attention must be paid to industrial welfare. It is true that these recommendations obeyed the logic of 'People's War' and had support in the highest political circles – in the Ministry of Information and the Ministry of Labour, for instance. It is also true that the ideological tide which they represent swept Churchill out of office in 1945. Tom Jeffery's point, quoted earlier, may be rephrased thus: Mass-Observation itself, as survey and 'movement', was inextricably party to the changes of mood and opinion which it described. People in Production drew some of its details from directive replies and diaries sent in by volunteer members of the National Panel. It is worth looking more closely at the Panel. Though it was small, its existence, besides being crucial to Mass-Observation's claim to supremacy in 'qualitative' methods, gave its surveys an intrinsic 'populist' basis.

The National Panel of volunteer observers, a distinctive, though not unique, device, represented Mass-Observation's insistence (still voiced after the war) that social science should not only be *about* the masses but should be conducted *by* the masses. Dr Nicholas Stanley has done as much as could be done to reduce, or alternatively elevate, this fluctuating, even amorphous, body of men and women into statistical tables (1981, chapter 3).

It was never as large as was claimed on the red and white cover of *Britain by Mass-Observation*, that Penguin Special of 1939 – there were never at any one point 'some two thousand voluntary observers', though by then about that number may have written in at least once. Nick Stanley has identified a 'total population' of all respondents ever replying of 1894 men and 953 women between 1937 and 1945. But if 'once off' replies are excluded, the male Panel descends to merely 680, the female to 415. And many others wrote only a few times, or otherwise erratically.

The original group recruited through the *New Statesman* in 1937 numbered 420. Of these, 97% were middle class, and 72% were male. And in 1937 this group made up 74% of the total Panel. Comparing the Mass-Observation Panel to the British population as a whole, Stanley detects marked discrepancies. 80% of the male Panel was under 35, as compared with 53% of the general population. The female Panel was older. Over the 1937–45 period, the old remained a consistently low proportion among both males and females, and the male Panel younger than the female. But over the war years the Panel moved consistently closer to the national pattern, as young men were swept away by conscription, and as earlier recruits aged.

Regionally, the South East of England was over-represented, but as Dr Stanley suggests, when critics complained that the Panel was unrepresentative, they were not speaking up for Tyneside and Orkney, or protesting on behalf of old-age pensioners. They suspected class bias, political bias, and a bias towards the bored and lonely. The Panel, after all, was self-selected.

Boredom and isolation can be discounted. Work in the Archive suggests that even very copious respondents, who wrote exceptionally full diaries and long replies to directives, were commonly active, sociable people, and that cranks were if anything under-represented. But class cannot be so dismissed. One of the richest crops of material in the archive is the body of replies to a directive Questionnaire on Class in mid 1939. The questions asked were such as to encourage many respondents to provide copious biographical material.

There were just over 400 replies – that was 'the Panel' so far as this questionnaire was concerned. There were eleven men to five women, and other imbalances likewise correspond to those discovered by Dr Stanley. In this particular case, over a third of the whole 400 were in the largest single grouping by age plus sex plus marital status – they were male, unmarried and under 25. Less than one in six defined themselves as 'working class' – about twice as many men, proportionately, as women. A surprising number – about a fifth of respondents – assigned themselves confidently to the 'upper', 'upper middle', and 'professional' classes. About 7 in 16 placed themselves as 'middle' or 'lower middle' class. Altogether then, about five-eighths put themselves into one or other middle class category. This was apart from the one in six who refused to commit themselves or nominated unusual categories; and most of these would clearly, from the evidence they gave, have been judged 'middle class' by others. Dr Stanley's figures show that objectively, as well as subjectively, the Panel were heavily middle class.

Were they politically motivated above the average and towards the left, as might have been assumed of a panel largely recruited through the *New Statesman*? Certainly, as Mass-Observation itself acknowledged on occasion, the Panel was a rather left-leaning group. However, it gives an overall impression, in this and other material, of tentativeness and even puzzlement. Coherent ideologues are rare, committed activists rarer still. There are grounds for supposing, as Dr Stanley does, that the clerks and students and scientific workers who agglomerated in the male section were commonly using Mass-Observation as a substitute for political action rather than as a chance to express strong views of whatever complexion, and this applies equally to the clerks, teachers and housewives who dominated among the women.

Having described the panel as young-ish, left-leaning, and preponderantly middle class one might seem to have confirmed its uselessness as a representative sample. But its real value is suggested by the directive replies on Race which immediately preceded those on Class in 1939. The class questionnaire was not badly designed. The race questionnaire was.

The questions are:-

(1) How do you feel about negroes? (Write down the first thing that comes into your head.)

(2) Vote, in order of preference, numbering from 1 to 10, which of the following races you would prefer the British nation to collaborate with and associate with. Put 1 for the one you most favour and so on down to 10.

French
Italian
Scandinavian
Jewish
American
Irish
Asiatic
Polish
Negro
Russian

(3) Vote, in order of preference, numbering from 1 to 10, the leaders for whom you have the greatest respect, as far as possible forgetting their racial or other associations:-

Daladier
Mussolini
Chamberlain
Stalin
Roosevelt
Beck
Chiang-kai-shek
Hitler
De Valera
Goering

(4) Write down yes or no in answer to the following:-

(a) Would you use a clean handkerchief which you knew belonged to a Jew?
(b) If you knew a negro, would you care if you were seen with him in public?
(c) Would you shake hands with a Nazi in uniform?
(d) Do you ever use the verb "to jew"?
(e) Do you think that Hitler is sane?
(f) Have the recent activities of the I.R.A. influenced you in your attitude to the Irish as a race?

(5) Write down, in a few words, your opinion of:-

Frenchmen, Germans, negroes, cannibals

(6) Give, in a few words, what you consider to be the racial implications of the crucifixion of Christ.

Some Panellists quarrelled quite fiercely with the questions. Were Negroes a 'nation', Americans a 'race'? What sort of 'association' with Britain did the questioners have in mind? What *sort* of Asiatics? Confusion over this latter point was reflected in contradiction, often in the same reply, between low rating of Asiatics and high esteem for Chiang Kai Shek. How could one forget the 'racial associations' of Hitler?

This was, then, an amateurish questionnaire, addressed to an unrepresentative sample. Yet, *if one knows how the Panel was composed*, then the results in part seem highly significant. Responses preceded the Nazi-Soviet pact. Amongst a left-leaning group it is not surprising to see Russians ranked fourth as a race to co-operate with and Stalin third as a leader to be respected. (Chiang Kai Shek came second, I suspect, because the Panel knew so little about him.) What really stands out, however, is the vast popularity of Americans as a race, Roosevelt as a leader. The Mass-Observer at this stage represented particularly well the young middle class elements whose leftward shift helped so much to upset Churchill in 1945. The results of the 'Race' questionnaire might nudge political historians to consider afresh a subject which has been neglected – the appeal in the 1930s and 1940s of America, land of the New Deal, of Steinbeck and Frank Capra and Ed Murrow, where there seemed to be no old school tie, and a vibrant concern at the top of the political structure for the plight of the Common Man.

The very ways in which the panel was unrepresentative may have made it a better instrument for detecting long-term tendencies then, and suggesting them to historians now, than a more perfect sample of the population could have been. The South East set the cultural pace; the young clerks and students of 1939 were the married ex-servicemen of 1945. If Harrisson was able to spot the trends which would overthrow the Tories, this may have been because his own organisation originated from, and appealed to, moving opinion in the late 1930s, and moved with it to 1945. It was more 'involved' than its leaders, who kowtowed to a notion of science as neutral, altogether wanted it to be, and however paradoxical it may seem, this enhanced its value as a survey.

REFERENCES

Calder, A. and Sheridan, D. (eds.) (1984) *Speak for Yourself: a Mass-Observation anthology*. London: Cape.

Green, M. (1977) *Children of the Sun: A narrative of "decadence" in England after 1918*. London: Constable.

Green, T. (1970) *The Adventurers: Four Profiles of Contemporary Travellers*. London: Michael Joseph.

Harrisson, T. (1933) *Letter to Oxford*, privately printed.

Jeffery, T. (1978) *Mass-Observation: A Short History*, Centre for Contemporary Cultural Studies, University of Birmingham.

Madge, C. and Harrisson, T. (1937) *Mass-Observation*. London: Muller.

Mass-Observation (1942) *People in Production*. London: John Murray.

Mass-Observation (1943) *War Factory*. London: Gollancz.

Mass-Observation (1970) *The Pub and the People*. London: Seven Dials, reprinting Gollancz 1943.

Stanley, N.S. (1981) *'The Extra Dimension': a study and assessment of the methods employed by Mass-Observation in its first period 1937–40*. CNAA D. Phil. Thesis, Birmingham Polytechnic.

Symons, J. (1960) *The Thirties*. London: Cresset Press.

8 The Institute of Community Studies

PETER WILLMOTT

The Institute of Community Studies was formally established in 1953, with the creation of a charitable trust bearing that name. It started operations at the beginning of 1954, when Peter Townsend and I joined Michael Young in one room in Oxford House, a settlement in Bethnal Green. We moved within six months to occupy part of the Queen Anne house in Victoria Park Square which we were eventually to buy as a permanent base. This chapter concentrates on the first ten or so years.

Young had raised the initial money, covering his salary, mine and office costs, from the Elmgrant Trust, the Dartington Hall charity. A further grant was obtained from the Nuffield Foundation, for a study by Townsend of old people. Peter Marris completed the quartet of founder members when he joined after about a year.

Why Bethnal Green? It had been selected by Young for the research he had begun in 1951, before the Institute was launched, into the effects of rehousing on working-class family and community life. The district had to be one, in London, which had a predominantly working-class population and from which people had been rehoused. East London was right on both counts, and Bethnal Green (then a separate borough) was chosen partly because Ruth Glass (Glass and Frenkel, 1946) and James Robb (1954) had done research in the area and partly because it was relatively compact (57,000 people in 1953). We were subsequently never explicit about how far it was an extreme case in terms of local kinship and community and how far it was 'typical'. We were certainly able to cite corroborative research in other places, from Wolverhampton to Liverpool and from Oxford to Bristol. Nevertheless, Bethnal Green at that time clearly represented a particularly strong example of 'traditional' social networks, though these probably flourished to a greater or, more often, lesser extent in virtually every district where some working-class people had lived for a generation or more.

Our initial motive was to influence 'policy'. Both Young and I had worked previously at Transport House, in the Research Department of the Labour Party. Our main concern there had been with Party policy for the 1950 and 1951 General Elections. We had both become somewhat disillusioned about the extent of progress towards socialism that could be made even by a determined government, and we thought, innocently no doubt, that the performance would be better if the policy-makers (like the ones we had been and like the politicians we had worked with) were better informed about the needs of their constituents. We considered (arrogantly, I am sure) that many Labour politicians, even those who had sprung from the working class themselves, had a sort of structural blindness which prevented them from taking the part of their own working-class supporters when they got to Whitehall or to the Town Hall. The subject of kinship in particular had been picked out by Young for special mention as one to which any future Labour Government should pay attention when he made his farewell report, entitled *For Richer, For Poorer*, to Labour's National Executive Committee in 1951.

As the Institute's studies developed, so did our views about the relationship between social research and policy, a point taken up later in this chapter. But certainly the initial aim was to find out – and communicate to others – more about the lives, needs and aspirations of working-class people. And that seemed to us to require methods of research and styles of presentation different from those commonly used by sociologists, academic ones in particular.

Methods of research

The work of empirical social scientists usually falls into one of two distinct types: the statistical survey versus the case study, the extensive versus the intensive, the quantitative versus the qualitative. We thought we saw the strengths and weaknesses of each, and we wanted to achieve some combination which would, more successfully than either alone, get a sense of what daily life was like and what mattered to people while, at the same time, leading to conclusions that carried authority and were, at least to some extent, generalisable. At the time, we described what we sought as a marriage between anthropology and sociology. Some years later Young and I (1961) expressed it like this in an article:

> We wanted, on the one hand, to study a smallish community in depth, drawing from people in informal talks the accounts which would make our 'reports' as vivid as we could. We wanted, on the other hand, to collect some basic information from random samples of the population and to analyse it with proper statistical care . . . The particular, as we see it, can only be satisfactorily generalised by means of statistics, the general only become meaningful if based on an understanding of the individual.

This approach meant, first, that our research enquiries were bound to be local ones, the 'community studies' of the Institute's title. Though each piece of research would concentrate on a particular aspect of life or set of issues – housing and planning policy, old age, widowhood, mental illness – we would always try to learn enough about the totality of people's lives and concerns, about the other residents, about the district and its local institutions, to be able to set the main themes in their wider social context. We succeeded only to a limited extent, of course, but this is what we were trying to do, and what we saw as the case for local studies.

The method works best when the researcher is able to emulate the anthropologist to the full extent of living in the community being studied, as I did in Bethnal Green with my family during the research for *Family and Kinship in East London* (Young and Willmott, 1957). Our growing familiarity with the district helped with the other two early studies (Townsend, 1957; Marris, 1958) and with later ones (Mills, 1962; Willmott, 1966). Peter Marris (1961), repeating *Family and Kinship in East London* in another continent, studied an inner district of Lagos, Nigeria, and the new housing estate to which residents had moved; his experience of living in the city showed in the writing. Local studies elsewhere, for example in Woodford (Willmott and Young, 1960) and in Dagenham (Willmott, 1963), lacked something of the same immediacy because we were no more than visitors to the places.

Even without the researcher living locally, the community study approach still seems to me to have many advantages, particularly for research concerned with how social policies affect people. A knowledge of the locality enables the researcher to make better sense of the detailed information gathered about the daily and weekly round, and a knowledge of local institutions makes more intelligible the interaction between the State and its citizens. An obvious limitation is that the research tells only about one place; it is difficult to know how generalisable the findings are. It is also true, of course, that most people belong to social networks – through work, kinship, friendship or common interests – which extend geographically far beyond the locality in which they live, and that a residence-based study might be in danger of ignoring this complexity. But as long as these issues are taken into account in the research, the benefits of local studies – as part of the spectrum of methods available – surely outweigh the disadvantages.

The Institute later moved away from this distinctive approach. The first eight books in its series, published in the first decade, were all local studies, if one includes Jackson and Marsden's (1962) examination of Huddersfield-based scholarship boys and girls. Of the remaining twenty, only three were. Even though some of the later books were certainly distinguished (e.g. Young, 1965; Runciman, 1966; Marris, 1974), the shift now seems to me a matter of regret. It coincided with a growing neglect of the method on the part of other researchers; since about the mid-1960s there have been hardly any British studies giving a sense of people's daily lives and aspirations.

I think the reasons for this neglect are clear enough. For our part, we moved away to aspects of policy which we thought could not be appropriately studied in a local community alone: for instance, university students (Marris, 1964), education (Young, 1965), changes in family life, work and leisure (Young and Willmott, 1973) and poverty in a cross-national context (Young, 1975; Willmott, 1976; Madge and Willmott, 1981; Mitton, Willmott and Willmott, 1983). We were, in our small way, in tune with the wider reaction, though that was based upon assumptions we did not share. By the late 1960s the generally confident spirit of the post-war years had begun to crumble, particularly among intellectuals and idealistic students. The new mood was more radical, often marxist, and community studies were criticised for treating problems in a fragmented way, while distracting attention from more fundamental structural issues. This scepticism has, I believe, continued to influence the great majority of empirical social scientists.

Back in the Institute's early days, our concern to get at the detail of people's lives was reflected not only in the local approach but also in the kinds of samples drawn and interviews carried out. We adopted two main procedures. Where the people we were focusing on could easily be identified in the population – parents with dependent children, for instance – we employed a team of assistants to interview a general sample of a thousand or so, collecting mainly factual information with brief and largely precoded schedules; the statistical data thus collected were supplemented by about 50 semi-structured intensive interviews with willing respondents drawn from the first stage who were called on again to yield detailed personal accounts. Where the required sample was too specialised to recruit in that way – widows, for instance, or mental patients – we selected a single sample of around one or two hundred. Inevitably, some of these interviews had to be more cursory than others. Some people could not spare the time. Other respondents, who were willing to talk at greater length, were encouraged to do so. In addition, with both procedures we often used observation and other methods such as diary-writing (by members of the team or by respondents).

As indicated earlier, the purpose was to create two different sets of material to be drawn upon in the final report, one capable of statistical analysis, the other providing examples of human experience and comment, and adding to the depth of understanding by amplifying statistical results or suggesting possible explanations for them. The senior researcher would normally take responsibility for a study from the initial design to the final report – usually a book – incorporating the material from the various sources. To ensure his familiarity with the subject matter 'on the ground', he was expected to do a large part of the interviewing himself.

It can of course be argued – as indeed it was, by Jennifer Platt (1971) in her book-length evaluation of the Institute's work – that it was illegitimate for us to combine the two kinds of evidence in the way we did. We were, she said, guilty of mixing two methods – each acceptable by itself – into a dangerous concoction. In particular, she accused us of drawing inferences from the intensive interviews that were not supported statistically. Part of the answer, though we cannot have made this clear in our books, is that we used the survey statistics to provide the constraints within which the case studies were interpreted. We drew no conclusion from the qualitative material which was in conflict with the quantitative evidence as formulated in a range of tables, only a few of which were ever published. But, though we never went against such evidence, it remains true that we sometimes went beyond it, usually in an openly speculative fashion. Given the lack of certainty endemic to social research, I still believe we were right to use the mixed method, though I acknowledge that academic readers were sometimes understandably suspicious of what they took to be sleight of hand in the writing, weaving together as it did description, case material, statistical evidence and the author's own interpretations.

The writing style was itself the result of deliberate policy. At that time, there were few social science works which described people's lives and were readable, Zweig's books (e.g. 1948) being exceptions. In an unpublished note in 1953 called 'Draft Proposal for Establishing a London Institute of Community Studies' Young had written: 'A primary object is to make social science intelligible to the interested layman. Every effort will be made to keep reports free from the deplorable jargon which afflicts so much of sociology.' Young had added, in what at the time seemed an over-confident prediction but was later borne out by events, that if money could be found for the new Institute for an initial three years 'the publications would by then be good enough to make it fairly easy to raise money'. (I return to the question of funding later in this chapter.)

We needed to put in a good deal of work to achieve anything like the standard of writing we wanted. Young and I in particular, whether working jointly or separately, went over and over our drafts, sometimes starting again almost from scratch, and we also committed much of our time to editorial work on the manuscripts of our younger colleagues. Most researchers, particularly ones who are inexperienced or cushioned by an academic appointment, think of report-writing as a relatively small final phase in a research project, requiring perhaps the last sixth or quarter of the time, say six months out of a two or three year project. Our own view was and remains that, because of the importance of reaching as large an audience as possible while maintaining proper standards, the balance should be quite the other way – say one third data collection and two thirds writing.

Our first rule was to avoid jargon, to insist that when technical words were used they had first to be defined in lay language. But as well as clarity we sought vitality. One value of the case material and the quotations from informants, in addition to the extra enlightenment they provided, was their ability to humanise and enliven the text. The aim was, while making the exposition readable, also to convey a sense of the lives and concerns of real people.

Research for policy

The search for readability was connected to the interest in policy. We hoped that we might through our publications influence policy and administration in two main ways: directly, by addressing policy-makers and administrators themselves; and indirectly, by reaching a wider public, who if their views were changed might then exert pressure on those responsible for decision. This wider constituency would include editors, journalists and opinion-formers but also the much larger readership whose opinions they – and, through them, we again – might shape. This range of potential audiences created no conflicts of style, since all were composed of laymen rather than of academic social scientists.

We knew, however, that, though it would be gratifying if our books 'sold well', we could never expect them to be read by more than a tiny proportion of the reading population. We recognised therefore that a report's impact largely depended upon the extent to which it was noticed, discussed, criticised and endorsed in the newspapers and weekly journals, rather than upon it being actually read by large numbers of people.

As suggested earlier, at the outset we envisaged the Institute's research providing evidence leading to new policies. As we then saw it, we would carry out our studies, report the results and draw conclusions about how policy and practice should be changed, and if all went well the recommendations would be adopted. We came to recognise that this was somewhat naive. For one thing, the 'policy recommendations' could seldom be in a neatly-packaged form, requiring a Ministerial decision, a new circular to local authorities or a change in statute. A few proposals were of that kind, the most notable success being the abolition of the earnings rule for widows following a parliamentary debate in which Marris's findings about their poverty were quoted by MPs. But the message we drew from our research was usually a broader one. To implement the suggestions of *Family and Kinship in East London*, for instance, would have required action by a host of bodies ranging from central government and local authorities to private developers and public bodies like British Railways.

Although we continued to make detailed recommendations where we could, we began to recognise early on that the research could be more useful to policy for the greater understanding it could sometimes offer of fundamental issues, for example the strength of family and community ties, the extent to which the care of old people was undertaken by relatives and the consequences for all generations when married children were forced to move to another district. Such findings had long-term implications for the thrust of policy rather than suggesting detailed remedies that could readily have been implemented. (As experience showed, however, they were also findings which, despite the attention given to the books, policy-makers found it easy to ignore. For more than a decade after *Family and Kinship* was published, for example, government subsidies continued to encourage high-rise flats, and it was not until the Ronan Point collapse in 1968 that the tide of enlightened opinion unequivocally turned.)

We further realised that in an even more general sense there could be value in a study, like that in Woodford, which showed the reader how other people lived and what mattered to them, even if, as in this case, no direct policy recommendations could be made. In their subsequent research careers, the Institute's first researchers often moved between practical projects and more basic research – examples are Young's involvement in educational experiment and action, and mine in housing studies with architects, before we worked together again on *The Symmetrical Family* (1973). While we continued to be closely concerned with policy issues and policy debate, intervening when we felt we usefully could, we developed a less mechanistic view of the potential influence of research on policy than that with which we had started. As I have suggested, we saw that studies which were not directed to the detail of policies, but were descriptive and analytical, could be of long-term and fundamental value to policy, partly because they might help to change public and official perceptions of the issues – and thus the context of policy-formulation – and also because they could improve understanding of the problems and better inform short-term policy responses when required.

Relationship to academic sociology

The Institute clearly started outside the mainstream of academic sociology in Britain, and remained so. One reason was that none of us belonged to that world. In our previous work – Young and I on policy research for the Labour Party, Townsend at PEP (Political and Economic Planning, now incorporated in the Policy Studies Institute) on empirical studies of working-class people and their incomes, Marris for the Colonial Service as a District Officer in Kenya – we had been more concerned with political action than with the academy. Furthermore, none of us was conventionally trained in sociology. Young had an LSE degree in economics as well as a barrister's qualification; under Richard Titmuss he had also, just before the Institute begun, completed his Ph.D. in social administration (the 'rehousing and family' study, a first draft of *Family and Kinship*). Townsend had a Cambridge degree in anthropology, Marris in psychology. I had no degree at that time.

It was obvious why the unit was not established inside a university. Academics would have judged us poor recruits, untrained and unproven as we were. In 1952, when Young considered a university career as an alternative to starting a new unit, he failed to get appointed as assistant lecturer at Birmingham University or research fellow at Nuffield College, Oxford. The four founder members were however later offered, and accepted, University appointments. Townsend went to a full-time appointment in Richard Titmuss's department at LSE at a relatively early point, in 1957. Young was lecturer in sociology at Cambridge University from 1960 to 1963 and continued as a Fellow of Churchill College until 1966. Marris did some college teaching in Cambridge in the early 1960s, went to Berkeley (University of California) as a regular visitor from 1969 to 1973 and since 1976 has been on the teaching staff at the University of California, Los Angeles. I also did some Cambridge college teaching in the 1960s, had spells in Paris and UCLA as an academic visitor, and have been a visiting professor since 1972, first at University College London and now at the London School of Economics.

Even if we had been academically respectable, it is doubtful whether the work could have been developed in an academic setting in the 1950s. No university departments of sociology then existing showed interest themselves in doing what we wanted to do or in encouraging us to set up the operation inside their walls. (A formal condition of Young's appointment at Cambridge was that the Institute should not move there with him.) As Young and I put it (1971), in a review of Platt's book: 'The only way we could make the inquiries that were not being made by others, and that we were so keen to make, was to get on with them as best we could, with very slender resources, in the unit that we had to establish for ourselves outside the academic world.' Once the Institute was established, and had proved itself capable of attracting both attention and research funding, we might have appealed more to the new university departments then growing up. Some tentative discussions were opened with universities in the late 1950s, in the 1960s and again in the 1970s. But, though we often weighed the advantages and disadvantages of some form of association, we always came in the end to the decision that we valued our independence too much to want a merger.

It is in any case clear that we would not have fitted in. Our aims, and the audience we were addressing, were too different from those of academic social science. We were committed to understanding social problems rather than advancing social theory, to informing politicians and public servants rather than educating a new generation of sociologists. But we were not quite as atheoretical as our critics have suggested. At the beginning we were certainly ill-informed and the little we did know about what Mills (1959) called 'grand theory' inspired little confidence or enthusiasm on our part, then or later. We were also afraid of it, fearing that it might cloud our ability to see and hear.

On the other hand, for our first book Young and I, for example, read widely about sociologists' views on the place of the family, kinship and neighbourhood ties in modern cities, and we also learned from social anthropology about theories of kinship. Marris, likewise, reviewed the theoretical work on grief and bereavement for his study of widows, and Townsend developed a theory of reciprocity in his book on old people. We were not much interested in comprehensive theoretical structures, but to some extent developed 'middle range' theories. We did so pragmatically and eclectically, drawing upon whatever ideas seemed helpful. We wanted to use theory – or, rather, particular theories – to help provide explanations for the behaviour we were studying. We did not turn to the recognised mainstream traditions of social theory as sources of hypotheses or starting points for research. We were, as I have said, not primarily interested in developing either sociology as a subject or the theoretical schemes needed for that; and in the writing we certainly played down such theory as there was, in the sense that we presented it in everyday language. All this did not endear us to most academic sociologists.

This was perhaps particularly so because of the insecurity of academic sociology in Britain in the 1950s and 1960s. As a new academic subject, just being established and struggling for recognition, it was preoccupied with the desire to show that, like economics, it had a body of theory with which all sociologists worked; that it used strictly scientific objective methods which would develop proven laws of social behaviour; that it was a distinct discipline, different from psychology, politics or anthropology; and that its contribution to knowledge would be fundamental, not merely useful. These were the characteristics of the natural sciences which sociology sought to emulate, so as to establish its academic credibility. Sociologists saw their subject, like science, as something esoteric: a specialised body of knowledge which only initiates who had studied it long and hard could expect to understand. From this point of view, the Institute was a threat. We were eclectic, borrowing freely from psychology or anthropology; we were indifferent to the development of theoretical structures; we were pragmatic and interested in reform; we wanted to be widely read and understood, and so avoided jargon; our methods seemed to lack rigour. From an academic point of view, we undermined the credentials sociology was trying to establish, and so it was important that what we did should not be accepted as sociology.

For our part, we played down theoretical issues and were non-conformist because what we were trying to achieve was so different. To quote again from our review of Platt, the criticism that we had neglected theory could, we said, in one particular be turned back on her:

> She says, sharply, that we could have profitably used reference group theory; so could she. She says, quite rightly, that we acknowledge Booth and Rowntree as our intellectual ancestors (more, as she might have said, than Weber or Durkheim). But she does not explore the causes or tie up the consequences of this ancestry . . . She says it was 'inexcusable' that when we first started we did not know about multivariate analysis or, generally, much about the vast amount of work done in America on this or that. It may have been inexcusable, but it was easily understandable, since we had hardly put foot in a sociology department. She complains that we became so attached to Bethnal Green; but we needed a reference group just as Platt needs one, and has one, of a very different sort, in her university. She is irritated by our using only 13 tables in 105 pages; but we were not writing mainly for her, partly perhaps because her sociological predecessors of that time were so few (the boom had not begun) and those there were showed little interest; partly because the audience we were aiming at were the architects and planners, the social workers and the housing managers, the civil servants and the politicians.

This statement gives perhaps an exaggerated impression of separation. We certainly saw ourselves as sociologists, if rather unusual ones. We wanted to contribute to sociological understanding about society, and we hoped that, to this end, the readership for our books would include the growing numbers of students of sociology and related subjects.

What is more, we would have found it difficult to start the Institute at all without the encouragement and backing of friendly academics. We wanted to draw upon all the expertise and support we could and, outside the ranks of conventional sociology, these were generally forthcoming. Some people were particularly helpful. Edward Shils encouraged us from the start, even to the extent of providing money out of his own pocket during an early period of financial stringency, and he supported us in a crucial bid to the Ford Foundation. An eminent theorist himself, his catholic approach found room for new work in the British 'empirical tradition' of Booth and Rowntree. We had, as newcomers to his subject, been excited by an article by Shils in *Pilot Papers* (1947) on American sociology, and Young had attended his famous seminars at the London School of Economics in 1948 and 1949. We benefited from his wisdom and erudition in a series of tutorial sessions that he generously gave us at Bethnal Green during the Institute's first year.

Richard Titmuss was another source of inspiration and support, as the first chairman of the Institute's trustees. The second chairman was Charles Madge, the former editor of *Pilot Papers* and by this time Professor of Sociology at Birmingham. Ann Cartwright (later to join us at Bethnal Green) and Margot Jefferys taught us some of the rudiments of survey technique.

Another link was with Raymond Firth, whose *Two Studies of Kinship in London* (1957) was *the* pioneering work on kinship in modern urban society. Knowing of our common interest, Firth invited us to his LSE seminars on the subject, attended by John Barnes and Ernest Gellner among others. As regular participants during the Institute's first two years, we acquired some slight knowledge of such anthropological concepts as matrilocality, bilateral descent and joking relationships, upon which we drew in the first reports in the Institute's series.

Other advisers included Geoffrey Gorer and John Bowlby. These, and the others mentioned, were prepared to give their open support from the very beginning, before the new venture had any reputation at all.

Funding for community studies

I began by mentioning the crucial grants, from Elmgrant and Nuffield, that made it possible to launch the Institute. There have been difficult periods since then, the most critical of which was immediately after the first funds had run out before the first books had appeared and attracted some interest. It was at this intermediate stage that we received a large grant from the American Ford Foundation, thanks largely to the intervention of Shils. Over the next two decades we received money from many sources. Apart from a further grant from Ford, we were supported by the main British foundations, including Leverhulme, Gulbenkian and, particularly substantially, Nuffield again and the Joseph Rowntree Memorial Trust. From about the mid-1960s we got an increasing proportion of our funds from government departments and, later, from Europe, including the European Commission, the French Government and the Anglo-German Foundation. We had nothing from the then Social Science Research Council until 1973, partly because of a self-denying ordinance during Young's chairmanship of the SSRC from 1965 to 1968, but probably also partly because of the disapproval of most academic sociologists.

Money became more and more difficult to raise, because of increasing competition for the available funds as sociology expanded in the universities and because, in recent years particularly, there has been less to go round. The general squeeze on public spending has in turn put more pressure on the foundations. There has also been something of a reaction against social research, mainly, I suppose, because it is believed to have failed to fulfil its early promise. It has not done as much to 'solve problems', in clear-cut ways, as we and others had hoped it would. On top of all this, the independent institutes were always at a disadvantage once social research started in universities because, lacking basic support from the University Grants Committee (under the so-called 'dual system'), they had to ask for more money for what looked like comparable work. Institutes like ours had, in any case, to keep 'going the rounds' of funding bodies because foundations and the like were always keener to support exciting innovations than to sustain existing operations, however worthy. We found we could stay alive only by regularly discovering a new subject (education, poverty) or a fresh approach (experimental research, applied work with planners). This is perhaps another reason, along with our own restlessness, why we did not remain loyal to community studies.

Yet the case for community studies seems to me stronger, if anything, than it was thirty years ago. Great changes have taken place in patterns of life in Britain. Household structures are more diverse than they were, with more one-parent families, more young single people living away from their parents, more openly homosexual and lesbian menages, and more, though still not many, 'communes' and the like. Ethnic minority 'communities' are more numerous, and probably more diverse, than in the past. In the mid-1950s we thought, correctly, that policy-makers, opinion-formers and the public generally were ignorant about the lives of their fellow-citizens. How much more true that is in the 1980s.

There has also been a development of 'community' in quite a different sense from the one we were using, expressed in heightened neighbourhood and ethnic self-consciousness and in a proliferation of community groups and campaigns for local causes. What is not clear is the relationship between all this activity in the name of community and what happens in the daily lives of the majority of local residents, inside their homes and in their informal networks with relatives and friends. It seems to me that these issues – the greater diversity of life-styles and the upsurge of 'community action' – are among those which could usefully be studied through the kind of locally-based research pioneered by the Institute of Community Studies in the different social and political climate of the 1950s and 1960s.

ACKNOWLEDGEMENTS

The author is grateful to Michael Young, Peter Marris and Phyllis Willmott for their advice and help.

REFERENCES

Firth, R. (editor) (1957) *Two Studies of Kinship in London*. London School of Economics, Monographs on Social Anthropology, No. 15. University of London, The Athlone Press.

Glass, R. and Frenkel, M. (1946) 'How they live at Bethnal Green', *Contact: Britain Between West and East.*

Jackson, B. and Marsden, D. (1962) *Education and the Working Class*. London, Routledge & Kegan Paul.

Madge, C. and Willmott, P. (1981) *Inner City Poverty in Paris and London*. London, Routledge & Kegan Paul.

Marris, P. (1958) *Widows and Their Families*. London, Routledge & Kegan Paul.

Marris, P. (1961) *Family and Social Change in an African City*. London, Routledge & Kegan Paul.

Marris, P. (1964) *The Experience of Higher Education*. London, Routledge & Kegan Paul.

Marris, P. (1974) *Loss and Change*. London, Routledge & Kegan Paul.

Mills, C.W. (1959) *The Sociological Imagination*. New York, Oxford University Press.

Mills, E. (1962) *Living with Mental Illness*. London, Routledge & Kegan Paul.

Mitton, R., Willmott, P. and Willmott, P. (1983) *Unemployment, Poverty and Social Policy in Europe: a comparative study in Britain, Germany and France*. Occasional Papers in Social Administration No. 71. London, Bedford Square Press.

Platt, J. (1971) *Social Research in Bethnal Green*. London, Macmillan.

Robb, J.H. (1954) *Working-Class Anti-Semite*. London, Tavistock.

Runciman, W.G. (1966) *Relative Deprivation and Social Justice*. London, Routledge & Kegan Paul.

Shils, E. (1947) 'The present situation in American sociology'. *Pilot Papers*, Vol II, No. 2. London, Pilot Press.

Townsend, P. (1957) *The Family Life of Old People*. London, Routledge & Kegan Paul.

Willmott, P. (1963) *The Evolution of a Community*. London, Routledge & Kegan Paul.

Willmott, P. (1966) *Adolescent Boys of East London*. London, Routledge & Kegan Paul.

Willmott, P. (1976) (editor) *Poverty Report 1976*. London, Temple Smith.

Willmott, P. and Young, M. (1960) *Family and Class in a London Suburb*. London, Routledge & Kegan Paul.

Young, M. (1965) *Innovation and Research in Education*. London, Routledge & Kegan Paul.
Young, M. (1975) *Poverty Report 1975*. London, Temple Smith.
Young, M. and Willmott, P. (1957) *Family and Kinship in East London*. London, Routledge & Kegan Paul.
Young, M. and Willmott, P. (1961). 'Institute of Community Studies, Bethnal Green'. *Sociological Review*, Vol. I, IX, No. 2.
Young, M. and Willmott, P. (1971) 'On the green'. *New Society*, 28 October.
Young, M. and Willmott, P. (1973) *The Symmetrical Family*. London, Routledge & Kegan Paul.
Zweig, F. (1948) *Life, Labour and Poverty*. London, Gollancz.

9 Provincials and professionals: the British post-war sociologists*

A.H. HALSEY

A continental visitor to the social sciences in Britain after the Second World War would have noticed the secure establishment of economics in Cambridge and politics in Oxford. These subjects also enjoyed a sturdy, if modest, existence in such other universities as Manchester and Glasgow. But at the distinctive London School of Economics and Political Science the visitor's eye might have been caught by about a dozen students of sociology, similar in age but of a style and outlook markedly contrasted with those of their Oxford contemporaries. They took their degrees, and busied themselves around Houghton Street with a novel aspiration. They wanted to become professional sociologists. I was one of them. Fifteen years later Raymond Aron was visiting Oxford and some of us were gossiping about the state of the British sociological art. Aron suddenly cut in to exclaim: 'The trouble is that British sociology is essentially an attempt to make intellectual sense of the political problems of the Labour Party.' Fifteen more years later Ernest Gellner suggested that I write an essay on what turned out to be the first group of career sociologists in Britain. What had been their political and intellectual concerns? What formed their unprecedented and unlikely occupational ambition? And what happend to them and their intentions?

To be more precise by enumeration, the group consisted of thirteen people, twelve of whom graduated from the School between 1950 and 1952, one of whom came from elsewhere to join them as a graduate student. They were J.A. Banks (now Professor of Sociology, University of Leicester), Olive Banks (Professor of Sociology, University of Leicester), Michael Banton (Professor of Sociology, University of Bristol), Basil Bernstein (Professor of the Sociology of Education, University of London), Percy Cohen (Professor of Sociology, London School of Economics), Norman Dennis (Reader in Sociology, University of Newcastle), Ralf Dahrendorf (Director,

* The complete text of the following article has been previously published in *Archives européennes de sociologie*, XXIII (1982), 150–75. Reprinted with permission.

London School of Economics, 1974–84), A.H. Halsey (Professor of Social and Administrative Studies, University of Oxford), David Lockwood (Professor of Sociology, University of Essex), Cyril Smith (Secretary, Social Science Research Council), J.H. Smith (Professor of Sociology, University of Southampton), Asher Tropp (Professor of Sociology, University of Surrey) and John Westergaard (Professor of Sociology, University of Sheffield).

This L.S.E. group became a significant part of the sociological establishment by the mid-1960s. They did not monopolise sociological development between 1950 and 1965; their immediate predecessors remained active – Jean Floud, Michael Young, Donald Macrae, Tom Bottomore, Tom Burns, and Ilya Neustadt. Contemporaries from elsewhere followed similar careers towards the professoriat – Peter Worsley and John Barnes from Cambridge anthropology, Joan Woodward from Oxford, John Rex from South Africa, Stanislav Andreski from Poland. And the School continued to send graduate students to join them – Bryan Wilson, John Goldthorpe, Frank Parkin. But those enumerated began as a more or less self-conscious group, and ended as more or less prominent individuals in the British sociological professoriat, scattered about the country as the heads of newly-created university departments.

The story is therefore restricted to a period, as well as to persons. It is restricted, too, to a short essay which is a personal appraisal of past events; not a complete account but an answer to particular questions about those who graduated from L.S.E. in the early 1950s to be dispersed by professional success during the 1960s.

Who were they? A short answer is that most were provincials: provincial in social origin, provincial in political preoccupation, and provincial in their early jobs. A longer and more adequate answer would recognise the provincial as only one kind of outsider and so would take account of the three others who were foreigners. Native or migrant, they were all initially sleepwalkers, but their education and profession led them towards metropolitan and cosmopolitan recognition which was scarcely attained before their subject and their academic calling had again been transformed. In the 1960s, twenty-eight new university departments of sociology were created. A feverish expansion of staffing went on throughout the decade from each year's output of graduates against a background of new student radicalisms in America and Europe. By the 1970s they had become a middle-aged minority so small as to be barely noticeable among the diverse armies of their younger colleagues.

Yet before their time sociology as an academic profession hardly existed. Its British origins as a mode of thought can, admittedly, be traced into the nineteenth century and beyond. Nor did nineteenth-century Britain lack distinguished political arithmeticians, social philosophers, and social anthropologists. As Philip Abrams has described it,[1] the failure of sociology to develop in Victorian Britain was not a consequence of inadequate intellectual resources. The difficulty was to find recognised sociological posts for able people in a society which

> provided numerous outlets for social concern of a legitimate, satisfying, and indeed, seductive nature; all these were disincentives to role-innovation. Above all it provided, for a large and apparently open class of 'public persons', access to government. Use what indicators you will, it is clear that, whatever happened to the British economy, British government, both amateur and professional, grew continuously and faster than any other throughout the nineteenth century. The political system was growing and malleable. Performing administrative and intelligence functions for government soaked up energies which might have gone towards sociology had such opportunities not been there.[2]

Even when in the Edwardian period (with social anthropology already securely established) sociology began at last to be institutionalised, the men who took the decisive part – Victor Branford and J. Martin White, Patrick Geddes and L.T. Hobhouse, Francis Galton and Frederic Harrison – 'were one of three things: wealthy amateurs with careers elsewhere, academic deviants, or very old men'.[3] Nor did the first half of the twentieth century bring much change. Between the wars the British universities continued to ignore the academic claims of sociology, and it was virtually confined to London.[4] The L.S.E. 1950 group was the first to find adequate institutional support. It was the first set of individuals to be absorbed into the university senior common rooms by the normal processes of undergraduate and graduate education in their own subject.

But what subject, some may still ask, is that? Sociology in the now received view is continental in origin. It has been the European reply to Marxism. Is that the subject which was taught to undergraduates at L.S.E. in the late 1940s? Certainly not directly. On the contrary the L.S.E. syllabus still rehearsed the nineteenth-century battles between the statistical empiricism of the London Statistical Society and the synthetic orthogenic evolutionism espoused by L.T. Hobhouse. 'Classical sociology' as developed on the continent by Weber, Durkheim and Pareto was imported into L.S.E. for the most part by Edward Shils in the form of Parsons' *The Structure of Social Action* An assessment of what the 1950 graduates made of the confused sociological inheritance offered to them is therefore an essential part of the description of their intellectual preoccupations. First, however, we must look at their social and cultural origins.

The ten natives were born in the slump years between the wars on the periphery of English society, not in its central circle of the well-born and well-connected. By no means all of their parents were working class, but none of them, gentile or Jew, sprang from the metropolitan professional or administrative families or from the business class. Some were of wholly uncomplicated provincial proletarian origin – the son of a railway porter in Kentish Town, or a tram driver in Sunderland. Others had their childhood in families on the margin of the working class, their fathers in petty trade or clerical work. Almost all look back on a home dominated by political radicalism and awareness of 'the Labour movement'. All, as Wyndham Lewis would have put it in those days, were 'branded on the tongue'. Short of strenuously sustained efforts of elocution their class and province would henceforth claim ownership of them.

Most, if not all, of them had 'won the scholarship'.[5] There were no 'public' school[6] boys among them. They went to their grammar schools and absorbed the curious provincial patriotism which that experience afforded in the 1930s – a national and nationalistic history and literature which, with science and mathematics, was taught, often with high skill and devotion, in a refined version of the local dialect. 'My country right or left' was as much a principal component of the hidden agenda of the provincial grammar school as it was of Orwell's Eton. And, combined with education in the kitchen from fathers who had served in the First World War, it was effective. J.A. Banks was, exceptionally, a conscientious objector, but the rest completed their pre-university schooling in the armed services. More than one came across the word 'sociology' reading H.G. Wells in a Nissen hut. Most argued themselves into a democratic socialism and enthusiastic support for Attlee's government on His Majesty's ships, airfields, and army camps. Few, if any, of them had any notion while at school of going on to a university. That aspiration was a product of war service and the F.E.T. grant.[7]

They chose to come to L.S.E. They carried a picture of their country as a status hierarchy still strongly entrenched but now outmoded by the social democratic revolution which the war and a Labour Government promised, and for which Laski's L.S.E. was an intellectual instrument. They came to study at a place which, though physically in London, they knew to be outside what Edward Shils later depicted as the 'Oxford–London–Cambridge axis',[8] knowing that sociology had no place in, and was indeed rejected by, the cognoscenti of that golden triangle of politics, power, and letters.

Social attitudes, antecedents, and responses are necessary background, but insufficient explanation of the emergence of their aspirations towards academic careers in sociology. Obviously the experience of the School came closer to *sine qua non* despite some important limitations and discouragements. In the first place, though provincial to the Oxford–London–Cambridge axis, the L.S.E. was an intellectual-cum-political Mecca to them. Its buildings sprawled in grimy liveliness on the East and West sides of Houghton Street off the Aldwych. Demob suits and battle jackets, incongruously adorned by the college scarf, thronged the street between the two main lecture theatres. The library was heavily used, assailing the nostrils with the mustiness of books and the sickliness of human sweat. The students' refectory was a clutter of cheap and unappetising snacks, and the Students' Union pub, The Three Tuns, normally permitted no more than standing in discomfort. But they were indifferent to the chaotic ugliness of the architecture. The inconveniences of a human ant heap were of no significance by comparison with the conversation and the visibility and audibility of great scholars. The tradition of first-year undergraduate lectures by the most eminent professors was fully and conscientiously practised. So they listened to Robbins, Popper, Tawney, Laski and Ginsberg, and absorbed the excitement of the social sciences.

Of course, the intellectual encounters were inextricably interwoven with the social experience of getting to know each other and their tutors. They developed their awareness of establishment attitudes towards the modern universities in general, and sociology in particular, and of the contrast between their own biographies and those of the typical pre-war English don. This sociological generation at the L.S.E. sought and offered an alternative platform of sociological analysis and criticism. It was less brilliant and more conventional in its conscious continuity from the traditions of 'social investigation' into poverty and inequality. But it was less conventional in its avoidance of the use of the academy as a point of entry into a political career. None of the group was active in student union or L.S.E. Labour Club politics. They all read Max Weber's two essays on Science and Politics as vocations and chose the former for themselves while in no way abandoning their political enthusiasms.

But was professional ambition socially possible? The dilemma was one of personal style as well as institutional place. From this point of view the biography of the man among their English mentors who eventually gained their greatest respect for his intellectual stature stood in illuminating contrast to any of theirs. T.H. Marshall was, at least by the external marks of origin and personality, typical of the social stratum and culture to which they were outsiders. As he describes himself,[9] Marshall was born in 1893, the son of a successful London architect. 'Our home was, I suppose, typical of the higher professional classes of the period – intellectually and artistically cultured, and financially well endowed [. . .]. Add to this my conventional schooling, first in a very select preparatory boarding school, and then at Rugby, a solidly bourgeois but not particularly snobbish "Public School", and it is easy to understand how limited, and how naively unsociological was my youthful view of society. I knew nothing of working-class life, and the great industrial north was a nightmare land of smoke and grime through which one had to travel to get from London to the Lake District.'

Neither Marshall nor my citing of him should be misread. His sympathy for working-class people, if not for 'the working class', was absolutely genuine. His eyes had been opened to the realities of class prejudice when he took temporary leave from his fellowship at Trinity College, Cambridge, to campaign in the general election of 1922 as a Labour candidate in a Tory constituency in Surrey. And his *Citizenship and Social Class*[10] disguises in moderated prose a passionate advocacy of the rights of ordinary people on the basis of elegantly interpreted knowledge of the history of social inequality in Britain. The point for them in the early 1950s was that Marshall's world – the Cambridge voice, the shy self-assurance, the faint air of ennui – was no longer to be joined but to be transformed.

It had been different before the war when the handful of English recruits to sociology were isolated individuals, and the possibility of academic expansion and cultural openness was virtually inconceivable. If, like David Glass or Jean Floud, they came from the working or lower-middle classes, they were under strong pressure to assimilate in dress and speech to the culture of the higher metropolitan professionals, and so to be heard by the post-war students as people who used 'telephone' and 'motor' as verbs. Again the continuity of social outlook in the sense of opposition to ancient social hierarchy and inequality was no less important and taken for granted as the ethos of 'the School', at least on the East side of Houghton Street. Moreover, the newcomers were more impressed by Glass's suave erudition and Jean Floud's vivacious intelligence than by their socially elevated appearance. And they were after all of 'humble origin'. But they were assimilators, perforce or by choice, in ways which seemed less available and less compelling to the post-war group.

In any case the social character of their predecessors and teachers, though important to the 'definition of the situation' (a much contemplated jargon phrase of the time), was not crucial to the outcome. The intended journey was an intellectual and professional one: the vehicle and travelling clothes were secondary. No doubt those of the new group who were gentile and low-born were sensitive or over sensitive to the surface *son et lumière* of English gentlemanliness. But some were Jews, some foreign, and some both. The same was true of the tutors and authors who fashioned their intellectual outlook. And these exotic influences were essential signposts to the journey out of provincialism. Among the students, Cohen came from South Africa, Westergaard from Denmark, and Dahrendorf from Germany. Among the tutors Donald Macrae was a Scot (of the same age but with a longer academic biography reaching back to schoolboy precociousness), Ernest Gellner was a Prague Jew, and Edward Shils an American. The head of the department was Morris Ginsberg. Socially and culturally he was an ambiguous figure. To his post-war students he appeared as a remote, anciently established member of the austere English middle class, and his obscure origins as a child of Lithuanian Jewry, entirely Yiddish-speaking until adolescence, had little personal significance for them.[11] If he noticed their ambition at all, it was with a gentle negative sadness. He gave no encouragement.

For some, perhaps the majority of, undergraduates the assured expositions of the professors gave no more than an impression of majestic social-scientific scenery. For the minority which our group persisted to join, two men stood out as guides to further ambition – David Glass and Edward Shils. Both oddly enough were indifferent lecturers, but endowed with a compelling charisma (a convenient word avidly acquired especially by those with no religious education). Glass offered a method, Shils a theory. Glass was the active leader of empirical research on the social structure of Britain. Radical in politics, as privately angry as he was publicly knowledgeable about social inequality, precise in research technique, learned in the L.S.E. tradition of demographic and statistical investigation, he was doing what they aspired to do.[12] Ambition seemed therefore both consistent with their political outlook and practicable to their personal capacities.

An alternative spur to academic aspiration came from Edward Shils who not only presented classical European sociology to them but did so in an American voice which simply assumed that undergraduates would become graduate students and subsequently professionals. His blend of tutorial ferocity and Olympian erudition challenged their still half-formed ambition to fearful effort. His *Current State of American Sociology* (1948) conveyed the idea that a subject of great difficulty and worth was at once both dignified in its European antiquity and accessible in its American modernity. Sociological research was a living practice as well as a hallowed tradition.

It was not so with Ginsberg, whose lucid discourse, so heavily concentrated on L.T. Hobhouse, portrayed a subject both complete and closed to lesser minds. It was an opportunity sadly lost, for the philosophical sophistication and the knowledge of social history which he commanded were, in principle, a theoretical basis for the political enthusiasms of his post-war audience. He was aware that attention was shifting mainly to American work towards which he was gently but firmly dismissive, regarding most of its leading exponents as verbose and pretentious. It was not that his own learning was in any way limited. On the contrary, he was familiar with the major and minor European authors, appreciated the importance of Max Weber in Germany and Emile Durkheim in France, and he had been quick to provide a critical introduction of Pareto to the English speaking world. He was aware of, and lectured on, German phenomenology a generation before it became fashionable in America and Britain.

Yet the weight of his teaching continued to rest on the interests he inherited from Hobhouse and conceded little or nothing to the eagerness of his post-war students to come to grips with the growing volume of American empirical sociology, the development of quantitative methods and, later, of Marxist and phenomenological approaches to sociological theory.

But the idea of progress to which Ginsberg adhered had been maimed in Flanders in the First World War and finally destroyed in Belsen in the Second. His post-war audience heard him as the advocate of a nostalgic rationalist humanitarianism. It seemed as arid as Durkheimianism seemed to Aron between the wars. Vigorous young men wanted a future as well as a past. Their politics assumed the practice of progress, and they were ready to believe in some English, Fabian, Labour-movement version of the idea of progress. Ginsberg's version would not do. They looked elsewhere in sociology for a theoretical answer.

It is questionable and questioned whether they ever found it. Classical sociology may perhaps be best thought of as the liberal reply to Marxism. If so it was a central feature of their provincialism that they were unschooled in, and conditioned to be resistant to, either the Marxist thesis or the liberal sociological antithesis. John Westergaard was the exception. He was an avowed Marxist whose early work was with Ruth Glass in urban sociology. Nevertheless, the aspects of his Marxism which were most apparent were also characteristic of the group as a whole, viz. hostility to social inequality and commitment to empirical research.[13] Some at least of the others have spent their subsequent sociological lives in at least partially successful search for a viable synthesis. A Marxist such as Perry Anderson would dismiss such a claim as preposterous. Insisting on the view that Britain never produced a classical sociology, his judgement in 1968 on the group of sociologists I am discussing was unequivocal:

> To this day, despite the recent belated growth of sociology as a formal discipline in England, the record of listless mediocrity and wizened provincialism is unrelieved. The subject is still largely a poor cousin of 'social work' and 'social administration', the dispirited descendants of Victorian charity.[14]

The point about such a sneering dismissal is not so much perhaps the view of social theory which lies behind it as its rage against any sociology which is not subordinate to revolutionary politics as defined by Marxists. In that sense it is a judgement narrowed by the blinkers of 1968 by which time, after a quinquennium in which the number of social scientists in the British universities had tripled, the character of sociology had shifted decisively towards a chaos of conflicting ideologies. Anderson's prejudice prevents him from appreciating the radicalism of these post-war British sociologists. Theirs was indeed a provincial radicalism but none the less passionate for that, and none the less powerful in its impact on the consciousness of the ruling academic and political elite. The ex-service students had had a childhood in committed Labour families to which was added the experience of war with its siege socialism, the sense of a just cause against Fascism, and the promise of a planned and open society without the unfreedom of a communist state. With these social experiences they felt no need of Marx to support a radical fervour.

They did not hate or reject their country. For all its persistent inequality, the snobbery which branded the tongue of every British child, the stupidity and incompetence of the slump Tories, and the stuffy closedness of the culture, nevertheless they knew Britain as a decent society. They were confident that the democratic institutions invented by the Victorian and Edwardian working class, the Unions, the Co-operative Societies and the Labour Party were the foundations of a New Jerusalem, a free and socialist Britain. If their Party and their Attlee government lagged behind, their idealistic impatience called for renewed radical persuasion. It did not require a total therapy of revolution and the massacre of people by their own countrymen. Resolve, pressure, argument, and firm insistence of democratic action would be repeatedly necessary over a long haul. But democracy and decency need never be abandoned.

It was an elaboration of Popper's view in *The Open Society* and *The Poverty of Historicism* which gave most of them the first theoretical, as distinct from political, engagement with Marxism. Then came Parsons. *The Structure of Social Action* gave them their first synopsis of the sociological tradition. But it is worth recording that they were uneasy with *The Social System*, not because of its weirdly unwieldy and polysyllabic prose (that was attributed to nationality), nor because Glass dismissed it without argument (that was opaque political prejudice), nor because it revolved around norms and values (for their essential politics was ethical socialism), but precisely for the reason that Anderson admired it:

> Sociology, in this sense, came into existence as a science which aspired to a global reconstruction of social formations. This was its *differentia specifica*. It is no accident that it later developed into the monumental architectonic of Parsonian action theory, embracing every dimension of social existence in a single schedule of classificatory concepts. Whatever the concrete outcome of this enterprise, the ambition to provide such a master synthesis was inscribed in its vocation from the start.[15]

But not for them. Both Parsons and Marx offered theories of society as a totality in terms of categories which were surely too arbitrary to carry the empirical weight of social analysis of a particular country in a particular historical period.

Functionalism, it should be added, now ritually slaughtered before first-year undergraduates every Michaelmas, was not the undisputed sociological piety of the 1950s which the fashion of the 1970s made it out to be.[16] True, it was rescued 'politically' for the L.S.E. group by R.K. Merton's ingenious defence of its analytical neutrality in *Social Theory and Social Structure* (among the two or three most exciting publications of their student years). But they were never wholly reconciled to the functionalism Parsons embraced any more than to the Hobhousian harmony offered to them by Ginsberg. Nevertheless, suspicion of a theory which turned on consensus did not imply reactive acceptance of Marxist contradiction. Their general inclination was to reject the totality of both systems, and then to seek a combination of Parsons' abstractions of value with Marx's abstractions of material circumstances.

The most remarkable early expression of this idea, and one which deeply impressed the group as a whole, was David Lockwood's review of Parsons' *The Social System*. Lockwood, effectively for them, placed both Parsons and Marx in the corpus of social theory on the problem of social order descending from Hobbes. For Lockwood, as for Parsons, Marx's fundamental insight into the theory of social change was that the transition from the state of nature (with its endemic and fractionalised conflict) to the state of civil society was one in which conflict became systematic, between the interests of groups through the social relations of production. Conflict was non-normative as well as non-random. The two systems thus appeared in almost polar opposition. A Parsonian social structure is based on dominant value patterns, a Marxist one on forms of ownership and control of the means of production. Socialisation in the one is set against exploitation in the other.

The theoretical question was whether a sociologist had to take the two sets of abstractions as exclusive choices. Lockwood refused, seeing both as particular sociologies.

> On the one hand, it is suggested that society is unthinkable without some degree of integration through common norms and that sociological theory should deal with the processes whereby this new order is maintained. On the other, society is held to be unthinkable without some degree of conflict arising out of the allocation of scarce resources in the division of labour, and sociological analysis is given the task of studying the processes whereby divisions of interest are structured and expressed. The latter view, which seems to be the general import of the Marxian sociology, does not necessarily imply that resources refer only to productive means, or

that conflict is necessary and not contingent. In the expansion of these points it may also be shown that there is no real rivalry between the two sociological systems, but that they are on the contrary complementary in their emphases.[17]

Lockwood's general theoretical development of this position has occupied him ever since. His doctoral thesis on *The Black Coated Worker*,[18] and his later books on *The Affluent Worker*[19] with Goldthorpe and their Cambridge colleagues, are important empirical studies of British class structure within the theoretical framework of non-Marxist radicalism. Dahrendorf's graduate studies yielded *Class and Class Conflict in an Industrial Society*[20] and bore the stamp of a similar theoretical origin. It included a brilliantly argued and empirically based demonstration of the failure of the polarisation thesis. T.H. Marshall's subtle account of citizenship as a principle of social change cutting across class and status conflict had also been assimilated. And his first book already pointed the way towards the liberal (rather than the egalitarian) political position which Dahrendorf eventually took.[21]

My own doctorate was an empirical study of the implications of the 1944 Education Act for social mobility. Jean Floud and I collaborated in the 1950s to give the sociology of education a place in the general development of sociological theory and research. The emphasis was again on egalitarian analysis of social inequality, but in our case consciously carrying on the tradition of political arithmetic – marrying a value-laden choice of issue with objective method of data collection and analysis.[22] The influence of Glass was plain and his programme of research into the modern history of the British occupational hierarchy also covered Tropp's thesis on *The School Teachers*[23] and Olive Banks' *Parity and Prestige in English Secondary Education*.[24] J.A. Banks was also supervised by Glass in preparing a much applauded study of the decline in fertility among the Victorian upper-middle classes,[25] launching a series of enquiries by the Bankses on that remarkable shift in the behaviour of a key status group.[26] Meanwhile, Bernstein began the explorations of class, language, and school performance which were to be so celebrated in the 1960s. And Dennis began his empirical studies of modern urban democracy with a period of fieldwork in a mining community near Leeds.[27]

Taken together, the work of the L.S.E. group in the 1950s can reasonably be thought of as a significant addition to knowledge of the changing social structure of Britain. In one important sense it was a sociological expression of autobiographical experience – a projection of the country they had learned in their families, schools, and local communities. In another sense it was, as Aron suggested, a sociology of the programme of Labour Party reform. But in its most fundamental sense it was the assimilation of international sociology and its application to the understanding of British society. In their labours the group made obeisance to a powerful Pantheon. It was neither a pantisocracy nor a shrine to any particular theoretical orthodoxy. Marx, like Parsons, held an honoured, but by no means dominant, place.

The L.S.E. locus of the group began to disintegrate almost as soon as it was formed. By 1954 it had become a set of research workers and junior lecturers, mainly in the provincial universities – the Bankses were at Liverpool, Banton at Edinburgh, Dennis at Leeds, and I was at Birmingham. Westergaard was at University College, London; Lockwood, J.H. Smith, and Tropp were at L.S.E., Cohen was in Israel and Dahrendorf had returned to Germany. They were in touch with each other through the British Sociological Association (formed in 1951).[28] The L.S.E. itself was passing through one of its phases of institutional self-doubt, and the sociology department was somewhat fragmented. Shils had gone back to Chicago, and was in Manchester in 1952–53. Ginsberg retired, Jean Floud moved to the London Institute of Education, and the unifying and civilising influence of T.H. Marshall was absent from 1956 to 1960. The atmosphere of the department was clouded with obscure hostilities between individuals and small groups generating negative and uncharitable attitudes to each other's work. It is doubtful whether any clear principles of theory or method were involved, though passions could flare occasionally over the value of empirical enquiry.[29] Productivity suffered.

The contrast with provincial university life was marked. Leicester, under the leadership of Neustadt and Elias, became a highly successful teaching department, attracting creative young lecturers like Goldthorpe, R.K. Brown, Percy Cohen, and Anthony Giddens, and producing a flow of graduates to challenge the previous monopoly of the School. Research in the new departments in Birmingham, Liverpool, Leeds and Manchester was developing with energetic enjoyment – the enjoyment perhaps of people with opportunities beyond their expectations, and the energy perhaps of people with nervous resentment of the continuing resistance to sociology of the high establishment. Sociology was finding a bracing but invigorating climate in provincial England in the later 1950s.

NOTES

1 Philip Abrams, *The Origins of British Sociology 1834–1914* (Chicago, University of Chicago Press, 1967).

2 *ibid.*, p. 4.
3 *ibid.*, p. 103. Hobhouse, Westermarck, and Geddes all owed their chairs to Martin White's benefaction. Hobhouse was an academic deviant who left an Oxford career as a college tutor in philosophy to work as a journalist for the *Manchester Guardian* before going to London where he took the L.S.E. chair in 1907.
4 There was a small recruitment to sociology in this period from Bloomsbury – T.H. Marshall, Charles Madge, and W.J.H. Sprott. The resulting connection of sociology to upper-class aestheticism and the Communist Party is a minor, unexplored, element of the history of the subject.
5 A competitive examination for state school children before 1944, giving a minority free places at grammar schools.
6 i.e. private. These quasi-charitable or commercial schools were boarding institutions for the sons of the metropolitan and bourgeois classes.
7 A British scheme similar to the American G.I. Bill which gave studentships to servicemen who had, or were willing to say they had university intentions frustrated by the War.
8 Edward Shils, *Encounter*, V (1955), 25.
9 T.H. Marshall, 'A British sociological career', *British Journal of Sociology*, XXIV (1973), 399–408.
10 T.H. Marshall, *Citizenship and Social Class* (Cambridge, Cambridge University Press, 1950).
11 For a more extended appreciation of Ginsberg by his admirers (especially Professor Maurice Freedman and Professor Ronald Fletcher), see R. Fletcher (ed.), *The Science of Society and the Unity of Mankind* (London, Heinemann, 1974).
12 For an appreciation of Glass and his crucial importance in the drive towards meticulous analysis of social inequality, see John Westergaard, 'In Memory of David Glass', *Sociology*, XIII (1979), 173–8.
13 Tom Bottomore was also a Marxist, but it is significant that he came to be seen after '1968' as tainted with the reformist empiricism of the group discussed here. Thus Martin Shaw (*Sociology*, X: 3 (1976), 510) disparages his 'neutral commentary' style and the use of sources 'rather tilted in the direction of early twentieth-century reformism'. Shaw is shocked to find that 'Bottomore is also capable of statements such as that "Marxism has brought into existence political oppression and cultural impoverishment" – which might have come straight out of *The Open Society and its Enemies*. He obviously feels that Marxism would be better off without its socialist political commitment.'
14 P. Anderson, 'Components of the National Culture', *New Left Review*, 50 (July–August 1968), 3–59.
15 P. Anderson, 'Components of the National Culture', *New Left Review*, 50 (July–August 1968).
16 For an informed account see H. Martins, 'Time and theory in sociology', in J. Rex (ed.), *Approaches to Sociology: an introduction to major trends in British sociology* (London, Routledge & Kegan Paul, 1974), pp. 246–94.
17 D. Lockwood, 'Some Remarks on *The Social System*', *The British Journal of Sociology*, VII (1956), 22.
18 (London, George Allen & Unwin, 1958).
19 (Cambridge, Cambridge University Press, 3 volumes, 1968–69).
20 (Henley-on-Thames, Routledge & Kegan Paul, 1959).

21 For a recent and thoughtful review of Dahrendorf's writings see John A. Hall, *Diagnoses of Our Time*, chapter 5 (London, Heinemann, 1981).
22 *Social Class and Educational Opportunity* (London, Heinemann, 1956), and *Education, Economy and Society* (Glencoe, Ill., Free Press, 1961).
23 (London, Heinemann, 1956).
24 (London, Routledge & Kegan Paul, 1955).
25 *Prosperity and Parenthood* (London, Routledge & Kegan Paul, 1954).
26 Olive Banks' fundamental interest in feminism and inequality gained some expression here, but this was not fully realised until the late 1970s.
27 N. Dennis, F. Henriques, and C. Slaughter, *Coal is Our Life* (London, Eyre & Spottiswoode, 1956).
28. Cf. J.A. Banks, 'The British Sociological Association – The first fifteen years'. *Sociology*, I (1967), 1–10.
29 In 1970 (*New Society*, No. 387) Donald Macrae asserted: 'Empirical research is easy, as well as quite often being genuinely useful. Most of it, like most natural science, could be done by well-designed mechanical mice'. Peter Marris at the Institute of Community Studies replied satirically. Geoffrey Hawthorn (then of the University of Essex) provided the candid and crushing riposte that 'only someone who has never done any can think that empirical research is easy'.

10 On the eve: a prospect in retrospect*

EDWARD SHILS

I

It was bound to come, sooner or later. Once Britain was impelled, reluctantly and slowly, to depart from its Georgian and Edwardian heritage, sociology was bound to find first a foothold, then a niche and now a whole platform. It is not that Britain did not know about sociology. In a sense, sociology, especially empirical sociology, got started in Britain but, like modern industrial technology, it had to be taken elsewhere to be further developed. The sober attempts of a small group of dourly upright reformers and administrators in the nineteenth century to describe in a reliable way the real 'condition of England' were among the first of their kind in history. For the first time men and women sought to arrive at a judgement of their own society through the disciplined and direct study of their fellow citizens, by observing them, and by asking them questions and by systematically recording these observations and conversations. Sociology has certainly grown since the days of the Poor Law Commissioners, of Henry Mayhew, Charles Booth and Beatrice Webb but their mode of learning about their own society is still one very vital element of sociology. Contemporary sociology is more knowledgeable, more sophisticated in outlook, more imaginative in substance, more ingenious in technique than they were, but it would not be what it has become without them. After this great surge, which

* This essay was originally published in 1960 in *The Twentieth Century*. At the request of the editor, I have agreed to its reappearance. I have, however, eliminated some parts of the original which are obsolete and reformulated others to make them a little less anachronistic to a new generation of readers. I would have preferred to write a new paper assessing the development of British sociology over the last quarter of a century but I do not have enough knowledge for that purpose. Such a paper would have been more fitting a testimonial to my friend, Professor Philip Abrams, over whose early years as a sociologist I watched and attempted to help and who, since those early years, did so much to render 'On the Eve' as it was first written so remote from the present situation of sociology in Great Britain.

ran over about three quarters of a century, British sociological powers seemed to exhaust themselves. The zeal of private persons to inform themselves and their contemporaries about the state of British society as precisely as possible waned and faltered. The independent current of more abstract thought about society which reached a very high level in the work of Herbert Spencer fell into discredit. An eccentric movement for the reform of British life in a regional form, in which Patrick Geddes was the leading light, took possession of British social investigation; it aroused no interest in British academic life or in the public opinion of the educated classes. The universities offered no alternative.

In France and Germany, powerful and learned minds thought about the nature of society and tried to envisage modern society within the species of all the societies known to history. In America, sociologists busied themselves in villages and in the city streets, carrying on the work of Booth, finding illustrations of the ideas of Simmel, Tönnies, and Durkheim and developing under the guidance of Robert Park, a few of their own. In Britain, however, for nearly fifty years, while social anthropology and economics flourished as in no other country, sociology gathered the soft dust of libraries and bathed in the dim light of ancestral idolatry. Here and there during these sociologically sterile decades, there was a momentary pulse of life but it never spread and the air of death soon reasserted itself. Graham Wallas on politics, Tawney on the culture of class, Hogben, Laski and Ginsberg on social selection, Marshall in one excellent and forgotten essay on the British aristocracy – published in French and never republished in English – gave off some sparks which no one ever nurtured into even a small flame. Karl Mannheim quickened the pulse of British undergraduate and foreign students for a time but he found little intellectual hospitality among his coevals except for a few educationists, journalists and literary men; he left no mark on British sociology. (Recently his 'sociology of knowledge' has been revived in the work of several British sociologists of science.)

Outside the London School of Economics, where undergraduates had to study sociology, if at all, as a subject subsidiary to economics (except for those who offered Latin for admission), sociology was scarcely even allowed to touch the handle of the university door. One professorship at the University of Liverpool which included in its charge responsibility for social administration was all that could be found in the rest of the country. In the half-world of journalism and politics, there appeared an odd little series called *Fact*, a brilliant popular weekly called *Picture Post* and a wild gypsy crusade called Mass-Observation, a sociological sort of reportage, sociology led a half-life. Under the auspices of Le Play House, two symposia were held, one devoted to programmatic declarations. Political and Economic Planning (PEP) published at least one report which could by generosity of imagination be called sociological. Public opinion polling and market research were making their way and a few sociologists found employment there but their works were unpublished and found no reception in academic sociology.

Since the Second World War, the subject has become established in practically all universities, now greatly increased in number; it has also become established in the numerous polytechnics. Oxford, rolling with the attack, at the end of the 1940s created a lectureship, which, with skill bred of long practice, was then cramped in cold hospitality. After refusing between the two world wars to accept an endowment of a professorship of sociology, Cambridge yielded to the pressure of external opinion, to an internal movement of young and middle-aged Turks within the university and to the enthusiasm of undergraduates, who, inspired by their own liveliness and some American paperbacks, had been carrying on a sociological *guerrilla*. The popular press published the results of sociological enquiries and would have published more if there had been more. *The Times* offered the lofty patronage of its leader columns and its news pages. *The Guardian* made its turnover available to sociologists. *The Spectator* reviewed their work with kindness and *The New Left Review* declared its sympathy with the 'right kind' of sociology although it disapproved of the prevailing kind. So the times changed, and sociologists in a small way joined the ranks of the beneficiaries of these changes, like women, Negroes, working men, young persons and the other outcasts of more spacious times.

II

Why did sociology fail to establish itself in Britain during the first half of the present century except in the furtive, half-starved way which we know? The simplest answer would be to say that sociology was not good enough to fare better. If the world were a scene of justice and of uniformly high intellectual achievement, that answer would be acceptable. It is not, however, a scene of justice and of uniformly high intellectual standards, and to accept that answer is to take, as true, the beliefs of those who defend much that is not very sensible and less interesting than sociology. Much of the resistance to sociology may be attributed to the obduracy, for good reasons and poor ones, of Oxford and Cambridge; some of the responsibility for the intellectual backwardness and the institutional feebleness of sociology in Great Britain falls to Oxford and Cambridge. The complacency of Oxford and Cambridge of the first half of this century, their near-monopoly of the cleverest and liveliest young persons, and their intellectual domination – still far from broken – must bear some responsibility for the institutionally and intellectually retrograde condition of sociology in Great Britain. How could sociologists come into existence in Britain when in Oxford and Cambridge sociologists were looked upon as pariahs, as no better than Americans or Germans? How could sociology establish itself as a subject worthy of a freeborn Englishman when it was a product of German abstruseness and American indiscriminateness, when its practitioners in England were often awkward foreigners or restive lower-class boys and girls and when its chief representative was the London School of Economics, which an Oxford contemporary of Tawney, meeting him after many years, on being told that Tawney was teaching at the School, replied in an attempt to be understanding 'Yes, that's something like Selfridges, isn't it?'

Why were Oxford and Cambridge so resistant? To some extent they were right in their assertion that sociology is no science, that its works are usually painfully inelegant if not outrightly barbarous in presentation and that they were often vehicles for political propaganda. But that is not anywhere near the whole story, nor at all close to the root of the matter. The central fact is that the higher type of British intellectual – the Oxford and Cambridge don or graduate of the first half of this century – was usually a man of acute intelligence and fastidious standards exercised within the constraints of a narrow imagination and an undeveloped heart. Sociology is a study which has for its ultimate object the ramification of the logic of heart. The narrow imagination and the undeveloped heart cannot cope with the logic of the heart as it beats in daily life and in times of crisis.

Sociology is not at present, and is not likely to become in the near future, a subject which can stand up under the fire of intellectual sharpshooters. Too many points can be scored off sociology by those who regard intellectual activity not as the extension of understanding but a game in which the prizes go for rigour and elegance of formulation and proof, and for proving the other fellow wrong. Discoveries are not made in this way, least of all self-discoveries and the discoveries of the self in one's fellow-man. The tutorial system with its emphasis on concise argument and its suppression of the sympathetic understanding of overtones has been a bulwark against the emergence of the sociological way of groping towards the light. The progress of the pure sciences in Oxford and Cambridge in the present century, of meticulous historical and philosophical scholarship, of economic history and latterly of analytic and ordinary language philosophy with their rigorous procedures, subtle and precise distinctions and their imaginative aridity were also uncongenial to the fumbling and inchoate ways of sociology and its frequent loss of itself in winding sidetracks or in the empyrean.

The real obstacles lay, however, in the undeveloped heart, the inability to embrace the condition and state of mind of one's fellow-man through personal contact and imagination, impelled by curiosity. Sometimes this inhibition resulted from respect for the other man's privacy. From another perspective, the few academic Marxists in England had little time for 'bourgeois sociology'. Marxism was a sufficient sociology for them. Furthermore, the most prominent Marxists were natural scientists and ideological aversions reinforced indifference. Repugnance on intellectual grounds and aversion on political grounds, a desiccated capacity for empathy with the disposition of other human beings in one's own society, a sheer lack of curiosity about one's own society all culminated in a conviction of the superfluity of sociology. It was all right, from this point of view, for an Englishman to go to study the Africans in the bush or the natives of the Pacific islands – but even there the chief of those British scholars who did so were from the Antipodes, from Poland and from the Russian-Jewish Pale, several of them via South Africa. (Radcliffe-Brown, the most distinguished English anthropologist of his time lived in one variety of exile or another for much of his career.) The most eminent British anthropologist of the period after the Second World War was of Welsh origin. Audrey Richards and Sir Edmund Leach were among the few leading anthropologists of English stock. British anthropologists did study the natives of the Empire but only a few of them did as much or as penetratingly as the 'foreigners' like Malinowski, Seligman, Firth, Gluckman, Schapera, Freedman, *et al.* To study the natives of Britain was another matter. It was almost unthinkable for an able-bodied and well-educated Englishman in his right mind to study the people of his own country. Tom Harrisson and Charles Madge were thought to be madcaps for starting Mass-Observation, and indeed they had to be to go so far from the boundaries of the academically permissible in the 1930s. (Of the academically established figures, only the Pole, Malinowski, extended a friendly hand to them.)

The proposition sometimes adduced to explain the absence of British sociology is that the United Kingdom was until very recently a traditionally stable society which raised no fundamental problems, unlike Germany or France in the nineteenth century. It therefore did not require sociology to help it to ruminate on its problems; it had no fundamental problems, according to this view, put forward among others by Karl Mannheim. There might be a little truth in this cliché – but not a great deal. It was not that the British social structure and its stability raised no questions; after all, there was a very lively public discussion of quite high intellectual quality about British institutions by politicians and journalists throughout the nineteenth and twentieth centuries. It was rather that once Oxford and Cambridge were established as intellectually respectable institutions, i.e. after the reports of the Royal Commissions on the Universities in the middle of the nineteenth century, and the subsequent reforms, the academic elite of Britain were resolute in their refusal to raise questions about the life of their fellow-countrymen. Adventurous travellers, colonial and Indian civil servants who were curious about societies overseas were not uncommon, but not persons willing as amateurs to explore the lives of their fellow-countrymen. There have been, it is true, since late in the last century, a few university settlements in the working class areas, and before the First World War Oxford men and particularly R.H. Tawney helped to form the Workers' Educational Association to offer instruction to members of the working classes. There was an inhibition about first-hand contact, a shyness about being face-to-face with the lower classes and a plain deficiency of empathic capacity.

In the 1930s, there was a slight animation of sociological interest, a few pieces of reportage of the life of the unemployed. The best of them – Bakke's *The Unemployed Man* – was, however, the work of an American, and Orwell's *The Road to Wigan Pier* was the work of an extraordinary personality who had contracted out of British upper-middle class life and had never been to a university. At that time the London School of Economics was the only academic centre of sociological studies and it, too, despite the presence of Tawney and Malinowski, was not a nursery of the power of sympathetic understanding.

The late Karl Mannheim at the LSE in the 1930s created a stir among churchmen, literary men of Christian bent and publicists. The sociology which he promulgated did not involve contact with the lives of ordinary persons. It was a grandiose disquisition on epochal trends and the enthusiasm which it called forth among students sent very few of them into the field. (I do not recall that there was one native Briton among the few who did a little field-work under his sponsorship.)

There were many Central European refugees at the London School of Economics who were attracted by sociology, but they were also in their special Central European fashion attracted by 'der englische Gentleman'. Those who could tried to pass as such, which meant that they became more British than the announcers on the BBC, they took to tweed jackets, briar pipes and *The Times* and they would not be seen dead with sociology. The others whose appetites for sociology were stronger or more adventurous went to the United States. Those who were left were the less successful, such as the WEA lecturers with their worn briefcases, who were scarcely good advertisements for the dignity of sociology.

When, after the war, the London School of Economics expanded, and sociology expanded with it, the offspring of foreigners and those who had come to Britain as the children of immigrants supplied a quite large proportion of the students of sociology. They were timorous, even if often talkative, outsiders; they lacked the self-confidence to do something which was not generally acknowledged and yet they clung to their subject with a touching affection, with little prospect of becoming professional or academic sociologists and they did not receive much encouragement to try to do so. They were part of a larger group of recruits to sociology – in the second half of the 1940s – who came from the working and lower middle classes. These often gentle, sometimes felinely distrustful young people, for the most part felt themselves ill at ease, uncertain and unconfident of their ability to do something of which their elders and their examiners disapproved. They too felt themselves to be 'outsiders', and a natural shyness was accentuated by a sense of remoteness from the pillars of British society. Only very few of these were able to avoid the defiant suspicion which marks the descendants of Leonard Bast; some of those who succeeded are at present the best hopes of British sociology. The others fell at the wayside; insufficient prospects of employment, insufficient talents, insufficient encouragement from their elders, the indifference of a frightening environment overcame their perhaps too gentle curiosity. Yet this generation was the first generation of a real British sociology. They deserve a loving if belated salute from one of their old teachers.

Bit by bit, in the decade and a half which followed the Second World War, the provinces were populated by sociologists. Professorships were created and filled at Leeds, Manchester, Birmingham, Nottingham, Leicester, Durham, lectureships nearly everywhere. Liverpool had already had a department of social administration, with a smattering of sociological teaching and research under the direction of Professor Simey. The London School of Economics consolidated and enlarged its cheerless but much loved *imperium* and extended its realm into the provinces by sending there its handful of graduates with genuine curiosity about British society and a warm-hearted willingness to make contact with living human beings. Yet, somehow, despite its expansion, academic sociology did not flourish in Britain. A number of modestly undertaken local surveys, some interesting work on educational selection, a judicious study of children and television, an austere review of social mobility in Britain, a study of black-coated workers, a few suggestive surveys of university students, some solid studies of Negro immigrants and dock thefts in Liverpool, the beginning of industrial sociological studies, began to dot the map, but still the sociological study of British society did not catch on. By the early 1960s, there were two sociological journals in Great Britain, each issue filled with articles, but not many of them dealt realistically, or even at all, with contemporary British society. In general, therefore, the academic establishment of sociology in the modern universities did not succeed in those years in overcoming the handicaps to which I have referred.

The practice of sociology outside universities was no more successful.

The Tavistock Institute of Human Relations began after the war with a staff of unusual brilliance and a remarkably diversified and rich experience in the armed forces, but it became very preoccupied with the struggle to survive. It lived from hand to mouth on contracts and fees for consultation and it never succeeded in forming any real connection with the world of academic sociology. At first, it was the object of awed inquisitiveness and malicious gossip; as it settled down to a comfortable career of consultation and research on industrial and administrative problems, it lost its charisma, and its power to disturb.

The chief achievement of sociology outside the universities was the Institute of Community Studies, formed on the initiative of, and inspired by, Michael Young. It carried on from where the urban sociology cultivated at the University of Chicago in the 1920s had left off. Its first books by Michael Young and Peter Willmott were the first results of sociological research to receive widespread attention and appreciation. Neither Michael Young nor his staff had academic sociological training and most of their early work was done without even the friendliness of academic sociology. It was much inspired by Professor Richard Titmuss, who had no university training at all and who was officially the head of the department of social administration at the London School of Economics, and I played a small part in its early life. This history is further discussed in chapter 8.

Michael Young has stood in the tradition of the bold amateur who does what adventurous impulse and moral conviction and imagination dictate, regardless of what the guardians of the official view required and what the dominant prejudices of the time demanded. He was the first of those Labour supporters who renounced the tired phrases of inherited socialist doctrine and sought contact with reality by other roads. Sociology was the road he chose to bring him into intimate relationship with contemporary society; he was much encouraged in this by Anthony Crosland.

Richard Titmuss brought together two unique British traditions, the private amateur scholar and the public servant who seeks to clarify, criticise and guide public policy in the light of systematic empirical study. He represented a sophisticated and deepened return to the tradition of the Webbs, the Poor Law Commissioners and the great Blue Books.

The preoccupation of the New Left with sociology had more resemblance to Michael Young's sociology than to Richard Titmuss's. They too were fed up with the clichés of socialist thought; but unlike Michael Young, the prejudices they have struggled with are Marxian. But, unlike Michael Young, the New Left thought it had found a solution. Although the New Left is critical of Marxism, it also wants to preserve as much of it as it can. It is preoccupied with Marxism, although it is against the Soviet Union – at least on the face. For a time, C. Wright Mills was its man. He has now been forgotten and there are other heroes, drawn from continental Marxism. Such sociology as it does differs not very much from what other sociologists do, although the rhetoric and interpretation differ. The more general orientation of the New Left, as distinct from more specific loyalties to Althusser and others like him, has become widespread and enjoys a pervasive sympathy among some British sociologists of the new generation. This is very different from the undoctrinaire humanitarian socialism of most British sociologists, although the dividing line is a very vague one.

III

The reception, in intellectual circles, of the books of the Institute of Community Studies, of Hoggart's *The Uses of Literacy*, and of the other works of the sociological surge of the 1950s has no single explanation. In part and perhaps fundamentally it was a product of the fact that British intellectuals were beginning to develop some deeper sense of affinity with the sectors of society outside Oxford, Cambridge, the higher civil service, the Church of England, Printing House Square and the House of Commons. The extension of awareness, to some extent, was in part a product of the increased numbers of the offspring of the working and lower middle classes, who, having passed through universities, and entered the civil service and the learned professions, carried with them some memories of life in the outer zones of British society. Such persons had existed around the turn of the century but they were not university graduates and they knew nothing of sociology; their reaching out towards the wide reaches of British society was represented by the novels of Arnold Bennett, H.G. Wells and George Gissing. In the meantime, the attainment of a more widely shared affluence had made for greater visibility of the lower classes; their way of life and their pleasure had simply become more noticeable to the educated. They themselves appeared more often in districts of the large towns into which lower-class persons did not previously enter except in servile capacities. Television made the intellectuals much more sensitive to the existence of the lower classes. As in the United States, the pleasures, the tastes and the outlook of the previously excluded classes forced themselves into the field of attention of the educated. More important than any of this is the growth of the sense of affinity, of the extension of the capacity for empathy. Great Britain is still, like any other great society in the world, far from an egalitarian society but it is more equal internally than it used to be. There is greater mutual awareness of the division and classes of society. Alongside of distrust and hostility, there is a great sense of affinity.

IV

The progress and prospects of sociology in Great Britain appeared to me in the years after the Second World War to rest on whether it could become effectively established. My view at the time rested on the following considerations. The first was that the older universities still got the intellectually best qualified and most imaginatively daring students. In those days, it still appeared that the traditional hierarchy of status in Great Britain was sufficiently firm that membership in those two universities still implanted the nerve of self-confidence in the undergraduates, even if they did not have it when they came up. The modern universities still got the sweet, shy, blanched children, the awkward, the angular, the deferential, the resentful, the hard-working who were intelligent and often very gifted. They were frequently a bit uneasy and their uneasiness was not relieved by the sense that they were members of very distinguished and highly respected universities, which a number of the provincial universities indeed were. Indeed the inclination of their teachers, who came disproportionately from Oxford, Cambridge and London, to look on these provincial universities as the visible evidence of their own exile from the golden triangle, only reinforced the students' vague sense of being cave-dwelling outcasts. (There were, of course, remarkable exceptions among the teachers, who were proud of their universities, outstanding in their own fields and loyal to them and some of these gave much attention and guidance to their students.) But many of the teachers and students remained distant from each other and were not happy about their universities. With this state of mind, little genuinely good sociology can be carried on. Really good sociology cannot be done effectively by those who feel fundamentally alien to their own society, who feel themselves cast out by it and who also feel that the subject they are studying is looked down upon. I thought that this would not occur to sociology if it were taken up by Oxford and Cambridge. Looking back at this belief, after nearly a quarter of a century, it is now clear that despite the acceptance of sociology by Oxford and Cambridge, the beneficial consequences of that acceptance have not been noticeable. Neither Cambridge nor Oxford has had the impact on British sociology which I anticipated. The sociology which has taken root in those two universities, to the extent that it has taken root, does not seem to be markedly different from that practised in other universities. Neither Oxford nor Cambridge has taken a leading position such as Cambridge long occupied in economics. An undergraduate can now specialise in Social and Political Sciences at Cambridge beginning in his second year and at Oxford sociology is now well represented in the PPE course. The opportunities for undergraduate study are there; there are opportunities for university teaching appointments and college fellowships for sociologists. Yet things have not worked out as I anticipated. Why has it turned out this way?

At Cambridge, sociology was introduced by the appointment in 1961 of two lecturers in the Faculty of Economics. After several years the university appointed a committee to examine the status of sociological studies in the university and in due time this committee presented its report and recommendations to the university. The report was not very satisfactory and Philip Abrams, Maurice Cowling and I submitted an alternative proposal. (Philip Abrams was by that time a lecturer.) Our alternative seemed to me much better than the Committee's own proposal and a few concessions were made to us. It was proposed that there be created a Committee on Social and Political Studies, not a full faculty; this was done, and Philip Abrams was its first chairman. A Professor of Sociology was appointed and several lecturers in addition to those already on the ground. Although the syllabus was not what Philip Abrams, Maurice Cowling and I wanted it to be, it was certainly workable. Yet the establishment of sociology in Cambridge did not work out. Why?

Much could be said in answer to this query. I will mention only the fact that the establishment of sociology as a subject in the ancient universities coincided with the aggravation of discontent of the intellectuals in Great Britain following the operation on the Suez Canal in 1956 and the uprising against Soviet domination in Hungary and its suppression by the Soviet armed forces in the autumn of that year. Within a decade, the agitation among students began in British universities. It was, of course, nothing like the agitation on the Continent and in the United States. But it happened in Great Britain and sociologists – both staff and students – were among its most active promoters and agents. Sociology was also one of the prominent targets of the students who demanded fundamental and ill-defined changes in the substance and organisation of their courses of study.

Sociology had for long been part of an oppositional tradition. Werner Sombart had called sociology an *Oppositionswissenschaft* many years before it became firmly placed in German universities and it has remained an 'oppositional science' despite its establishment as an academic subject. It has been that way too in the other countries in which it has become so labelled. It had always been critical; it had almost always been associated with movements for the reform of society. Now it became, at least to many of its students and some of its teachers, especially some of its younger ones, a point of departure for the revolutionary transformation of society.

Cambridge was not immune from this latter development. The undergraduates made outlandish demands and the dons did not resist them firmly and reasonably. This left a deforming imprint on sociology as studied at Cambrige as well as elsewhere in the rest of Great Britain – and throughout the world.

Sociology in consequence began to suffer from a severe malaise. Whereas before this sociology had been riding on a wave of confidence in its merits and its future, it became instead a torn and tattered subject. Its teachers and students became suspicious of its leading lights and its past accomplishments. This was as true of Cambridge as it was in other places. Instead of taking a position in the forefront of its subject, it became like most other places where sociology is studied, a desultorily pursued subject, riddled with accusations of serving 'the interests' in a great variety of forms. Its leaders lost their confidence in the worthwhileness of their subject. Sociology more than most other academic subjects, given its precarious position, needs the faith of its leaders in its potentialities. Even where it is well established institutionally, it needs that faith. In Cambridge, the faith was lost when their subject was only marginally established.

V

Sociology does not require for its progress a whole social class, or an entirely new breed of men. It only needs a few hundred persons at a time, perhaps only a thousand in a quarter of a century. Even in a country of frozen and contracted sentiments, it certainly should be possible for several hundred to be found.

Sociology requires not only curiosity, openness of imagination and high intelligence, it also requires decent institutional sponsorship and patronage. Oxford, having grudgingly created a lectureship in the late 1940s, then, as if by design, prevented it from becoming effective. Sociology failed at Oxford on its early trials, not only because Oxford had high standards which sociology as it then stood could not attain. It failed in part because Oxford was not interested in its success. The subject made no progress in the syllabus. Oxford has now made substantial provision for its study. In Cambridge, its provision is slight, although it is much better provided for than it was twenty years ago. Its old enemies in both universities have declined in number and vehemence. In the present troubles of the British universities, it does not seem to be in any greater danger than much more esteemed subjects like oriental studies and the history of science.

Yet it cannot be assumed that things will continue to be as they have been over the past two decades; it is not desirable that they should be. The visiting professorship of social theory at Cambridge, instituted in the 1950s, seemed at the time to be the opening of the door to sociology. But it turned out in the end to resemble a victory for the patient wisdom of its enemies.

Could not the present situation be like the earlier one, but for different reasons?

The success of sociology in the British universities, ancient, modern and new, now that it is so well incorporated into the budgets of the universities and has numerous teachers and students and entrenched syllabuses, is not so likely to be affected by the contempt and animosity of academic sceptics and detractors. It has acquired a certain amount of respectability in the 'quality newspapers' and is tolerated by the government which supports it financially, even if not wholeheartedly. It has a relatively good standing in the media of mass communication. All this is a pronounced change from the condition of thirty years ago. What it needs now is some measure of mutual respect within the profession. It needs even more, as a condition of that mutual respect, some very distinguished accomplishments around which the sociological profession can rally in a common appreciation.

The qualities which make a good sociologist are moral and psychological as well as intellectual. Good training will make a naturally inclined sociologist better. It can make a person who is not a sociologist by natural inclination into a more useful hewer of wood and drawer of water. British sociology needs more than that. Hence, selection will be as important as training. Whether an aspirant to a sociological career feels at home in the length and breadth of his country and with every class is as important a criterion for a selection committee to bear in mind, as his industry, his erudition, his critical powers and his productivity.

Let me put this proposition in the form of a question: Can the preoccupation with class, the negative snobbery of British sociologists, be lessened? Can it dissolve sufficiently and can British sociologists develop sufficiently to overcome the obstacles of resentment and distrust which narrow their imaginative penetration?

Being an outsider is not a help to sociological understanding past the point of enabling a person to acquire the detachment necessary for sociological observation. To have become a sociologist at all is in some respects a movement away from the outside into the inside of society. The generally sympathetic and even admiring reception accorded to British sociology by some of the important organs of British society shows a similar opening.

I refer to this because I think that British sociology is too 'class-conscious'. Sociologists are sensitive not only to the stratification of status in British society – it is certainly right that they should – but they are too sensitive to their own class status. The two things are connected with each other in both directions. Their sensitivity to their own status, not primarily as university teachers but as having been born into a particular part of the

British hierarchy of status, is itself part of that hierarchy of status and in this sense the sociologists' insight into themselves is of a piece with their insight into British society. But there are other things in British society in addition to its stratification. British society is a society and not just a set of layers of status, one lying on top of the other. It is a 'going concern'; its activities are not just assertions or manifestations of status or the desire to acquire higher status or to maintain one's own status, or to lower the status of others. There are what Professor Dahrendorf calls 'ligatures'. There is some consensus, there are concerted actions cutting across the lines of status. I think that British sociologists are too sensitive to the divisions, which are certainly real; there are also loyalties or self-identifications and collective actions and these too are real.

The situation of the British sociologist as an 'outsider' is composed of many elements. One is the result of the social origin of many sociologists; another is the intellectual standing of the subject. Sociology is now well implanted in practically all British universities, a certain amount of money is available for research, commercial publishers are eager to publish sociological works, there are three British sociological journals; there have until recently been opportunities for employment for graduates in sociology, but institutionalisation is not enough. British sociology still needs some resonant works to establish it as a sound intellectual enterprise. It needs a few persons the corpus of whose works will bring some consensus into the profession of sociology. I do not mean complete conformity with some elaborate theory or some method of research. No intellectual discipline could ever attain such a conformity and if it did it would cease to be an acceptable academic subject. But there is no danger of such complete conformity of theoretical outlook or of practice in research. Indeed, the absence of such an ascendant way of looking at things is a hindrance to the development of British sociology towards a realistic understanding of British society. Without it, chairs, departments, syllabuses will be useless. Similarly, the overcoming of the barriers to understanding in British society and among British sociologists is no substitute for genuine intellectual accomplishment. British sociology still awaits its own Max Weber, or Emile Durkheim, or on a lower level, its own William Isaac Thomas, or Robert Park or Talcott Parsons.

USE

11 The uses of British sociology, 1831–1981

PHILIP ABRAMS

I

Throughout the past 150 years British sociologists have consistently wanted to be useful. The image of a social science for use has been a compelling moving force in the development of the discipline both intellectually and institutionally. From the social statisticians of the 1830s, the social reformers of the 1850s, the social philosophers of the 1880s, through to the Heyworth Committee in 1965 and the campaign for a 'policy science' institute in the 1970s the search has been for social knowledge that would somehow crop usefully into social action. There have been many different versions of what being useful might mean, but one way or another the reference has usually been to some ascertainable contribution to the purposeful improvement of social conditions. Dissenters from this view have been few – unfortunately they do include the only man of genius British sociology has yet produced, Herbert Spencer. There have been moments, such as the very recent past, when the idea of usefulness has seemed oppressively controversial – so that at a meeting of Professors of Sociology in 1981 'the view was expressed' that 'sociology would be unwise to emphasize its immediate usefulness' in any forthcoming struggle for UGC funds. But such hesitations apart British sociology has persistently and ubiquitously wanted to be useful sociology – and has conversely been highly sensitive to the allegation, made with sobering frequency by the various scientific, political and lay audiences for sociology, that it is actually pretty useless.

By way of introduction one voice, appropriately that of Charles Booth, may speak for what I take to be a remarkable historical consensus among British sociologists in this respect. There is no strident positivism here, no utopia of scientific government; there is a quietly emphatic assumption that better knowledge of society can be used to make society better – and that the sort of knowledge that would be needed to make society better can be obtained by better methods of investigation. Booth wrote in 1887:

> It is the sense of helplessness that tries everyone; the wage earners . . . are helpless to regulate or obtain the value of their work; the manufacturer or dealer can only work within the limits of competition; the rich are helpless to relieve want without stimulating its sources; the legislature is helpless because the limits of successful interference by charge of law are closely circumscribed . . . To relieve this sense of helplessness, the problems of human life must be better stated. The *a priori* reasoning of political economy . . . fails from want of reality. At its base are a series of assumptions very imperfectly connected with the observed facts of life. We need to begin with a true picture of the modern industrial organism, the interchange of service, the exercise of faculty, the demands and satisfaction of desire. It is the possibility of such a picture as this that I wish to suggest . . .

What a moderate ambition that seems to be, how reasonable, how decently constructive; not for British sociologists the imperial intellectual projects of the French and Germans. The tone is self-effacing, indeed, in one of its most famous statements almost apologetic; it is just that, as T.H. Marshall put it in an Inaugural Lecture in 1946 (1977:3–25), 'sociology need not be ashamed of wishing to be useful'. Yet what trouble wishing to be useful has caused.

In principle sociology could be useful in a great number of different ways. I shall concentrate on five fairly distinct types of use which seem to have been particularly prominent in the history of British sociology since 1831. Morris Janowitz (1970:243–59) has established a basic distinction between 'enlightenment' and 'engineering' models of applied sociology and my five types can be thought of as an elaboration of that distinction. For Janowitz the difference between engineering and enlightenment conceptions of the use of sociology seems to be in large part a matter of focus: 'the engineering model focuses on the necessity of identifying specific cause and effect relations', is 'concerned with definitive answers to specific questions . . . particular hypotheses . . . concrete recommendations', whereas 'the enlightenment model assumes the overriding importance of the social context, and focuses on developing different types of knowledge . . . the emphasis is on creating the intellectual conditions for problem solving'. Yet behind such differences in the immediate outcome proposed for sociological work lie deeper differences, rooted in assumptions about the nature of the social and of sociology as a science of the social and in inferences from those assumptions about the nature of the gap between social knowledge and social action and about the possibility of closing or joining it sociologically. To follow the working-out of these deeper differences a refinement of the basic engineering/enlightenment distinction such as that envisaged in my five types of use seems helpful.

To begin with, one can identify two significantly different versions of the engineering view of the uses of sociology which I shall call (1) Policy-science and (2) Socio-technics. Similarly, the enlightenment view can be seen to contain two fairly distinct perspectives which may be termed (3) Enlightenment-as-clarification and (4) Enlightenment-as-advocacy. And then, separate from and cutting-across each of these first four positions there is a further conception of the proper use of sociology as (5) Education. I shall briefly outline what I take to be the main features of each of these five understandings of the use of sociology; then, in the second part of the chapter I will consider the experience of trying to use sociology in Britain since 1831, noting the overlaps, disjunctions and interactions as well as the fluctuating fortunes of each of the five types in different historical situations; and in a final section I will examine some reasons for the non-use of sociology suggested by the historical record (as well as by recent sociological theory) and suggest a possible strategy for anyone setting out to be the 'compleat' (and useful) sociologist today.

My five types of use are of course related not only to the distinction between enlightenment and engineering but to some other well known classifications of both the applications of social research (such as those of Scott and Shore (1979), Bryant (1976), Fay (1975), Cherns (1979) and Podgorecki (1979)) and the basic modes of research (for example, those of Lazarsfeld (1975), Dainton (1971), Donnison (1972), Bulmer (1978) and Payne et al. (1981)). This is hardly surprising since what one makes of the possible uses of sociology has to be bound up with what one thinks of the status of sociological knowledge as knowledge in the first place. Distinct notions of the use of sociology have to involve distinct notions of both the nature of social knowledge and the relationship between social knowledge and social action. Thus, the *Policy-science* conception of the use of sociology involves what might be called a 'strong' engineering model. It envisages the possibility of authoritative social knowledge and hence a firm closing of the gap between knowledge and action. The appropriate outcome of social knowledge is planning, an increasingly purposive and concerted movement toward a better society. Whether presented as facts or as prescriptive recommendations sociological knowledge effectively pre-empts politics – that pre-emption may indeed be seen as a principal use of sociology since politics will probably be understood as inherently irrational and the new combination of social-scientists and policy-makers as imperatively rational. By contrast, *Socio-technics* involves a relatively 'weak' engineering model. The target of activity is still government rather than politics and in principle the sociologist is still seen as capable of generating conclusive (if not now authoritative) knowledge across a wide range of specific social problems (if not now the whole range). But certain difficulties of communication and practicability are also likely to be recognised. The tendency will be either to see the need to negotiate with policy-makers or to adopt the role of technician in relation to them. In either case the closure of the gap between social knowledge and social action achieved by sociology is significantly less than perfect. The Socio-technician sees sociology as supplying 'intelligence' for policy-makers but also recognises that intelligence is not irresistible. The ideal of the rational plan is still there but the world is full of unintended consequences, conflicts of value, overriding interests; there is after all some legitimate space for politics; and politics is not the business of the sociologist. In this conception the sociologist tends to become a technical functionary for the policy-maker – but a functionary who reserves the right to a small but crucial grain of scepticism. When that scepticism comes to be directed to the process of policy-making itself it can have invigorating results, turning the technician into an alarmingly political animal. Meanwhile, however, the watchword of Socio-technics is Method. Useful work is defined in terms of the reliable, proficient servicing of policy-makers – whether in the form of basic information, analytic data, advice on data-gathering, technical problem-solving, identification of technically-best courses of action or evaluation of the effectiveness of policy after the event.

As against all that, the *Clarification* model of the use of sociology is a strong but ultimately passive version of Janowitz's conception of sociology as enlightenment. Enlightenment in this view is interpreted as a matter of competently creating a knowledge-base (whether or not that is understood as incorporating theory) for a sociological view of the world – and then more or less leaving it at that. The learned article or book is published and, according to its scientific merits, sociology enters the world by a gentle osmosis of public opinion. Typically, clarification is seen as taking the form of demystification, dispelling illusions and unmasking myths, of reformulating issues or problems by elucidating assumptions or revealing hitherto unperceived realities of social structure or meaning, or of changing the possibilities of social action by changing the language of public discourse. There is a certain optimism, or perhaps just a certain patience, built-into this model in its tendency to treat the world as a reasonable place, a place in which non-sociologists will be interested in what sociologists have to say and probably respond to it sensibly. Building the bridge from knowledge to action is understood as a political matter in the Clarification model but also as one that can be left to others because on balance others are likely to treat the knowledge sociologists produce with due respect. It is all rather reminiscent of A.V. Dicey's view of how social reform happened in the nineteenth century.

By contrast again, the *Advocacy* model is thoroughly un-sanguine about the wisdom and goodwill of others. Sharing the basic enlightenment view that the relationship between knowledge and action is an argumentative, or political, matter – that authoritative social knowledge is not to be had – it actively enters the arena of argument. In effect, this view of the use of sociology impels the sociologist to become a lobbyist for a preferred reading of sociological evidence. Taking-up Booth's view that a coupling of evidence and intensity of feeling is needed if sociology is to move the world aright the sociologist adopting the Advocacy model of use will seek to treat sociological knowledge as a means of political persuasion. The advocate, like the socio-technician will have close relationships with policy-makers but they will be relationships of argument or partnership in argument rather than of service. The assumption that policy-making is at bottom a matter of technical rationality will not be a prominent feature of this way of using sociology. What will be prominent is a sense of the propriety of bringing good evidence to the support of a good cause.

And finally, there is the *Education* model. The reason for treating this as a distinct conception of the use of sociology is (quite apart from the fact that it is widely advocated by contemporary British sociologists) that it combines elements of the other models in a curious mix of its own, leading to a quite distinct image of good sociological practice. Eschewing both politics and government, sociology is aimed instead at the innocent. The justification for this may be either that sociology is a corpus of authoritative knowledge (or authoritative scepticism, which is more difficult) obstinately not acknowledged as such by politicians or government, or that it is a corpus of methods and techniques of social inquiry and analysis which, widely disseminated, would powerfully help politicians and government to solve the various social problems with which they are faced in a more rational, efficient, sensitive (one may pick one's own enthusiastic adjective) manner. Either way, whether it is seen as a way of producing policy-scientists or advocates, socio-technicians or clarifiers, whether understood as method, knowledge or scepticism the distinctive use of sociology in this conception is teaching. It is a matter of changing the world through the next, or the next twenty, generations. Education is seen as a conduit for understandings which for whatever reasons cannot flow through society more directly.

II

In the 1830s a Policy-science conception of the uses of social inquiry and analysis was rapidly giving way to a Socio-technical one. It is fortunate that this historical discussion can begin at a moment of such relative clarity. As we shall see, British sociologists have for the most part resolutely declined to attach themselves to any one of my five conceptions of how social knowledge might be used – have insisted, rather, not just on mixed patterns but on something not far short of an attempt to implement all five simultaneously. Nevertheless, there are discernible patterns of selection and emphasis at different periods and sometimes, as in the 1830s, these do crystallise very one-sidedly.

Empirical social inquiry and analysis were launched in Britain under the auspices of political economy – a putative policy-science if ever there was one. The appetite for an authoritative closure of the gap between knowledge and action was indeed quite frankly admitted in the way social inquiry – the collection of social statistics and the conduct of social surveys – was promoted in the early 1830s. Such work was seen as the necessary means of perfecting the hold of political economy on policy. For Malthus, for example, the need was simply 'to prepare some of the most important rules of political economy for practical application by frequent reference to experience'. Unfortunately, the theoretical net of political economy was showing signs of strain. Rifts in the form of theories pointing towards mutually exclusive lines of policy were beginning to threaten its intellectual ascendancy in and around government. The assumption was that meticulously conducted social inquiry, assembling a body of facts uncontaminated by theory, would authoritatively resolve theoretical differences, simultaneously validating correct theoretical positions and opening the way for their implementation by government. An intellectually authoritative package of theory, evidence and policy seemed a serious possibility.

Unfortunately, however, social inquiry at once started to loosen the package. Much of the information gathered was plainly not of the sort any variety of political economy expected – it was, from the first, information suggesting the existence of complicated social structures impervious to the ministrations of the Invisible Hand and profoundly challenging the atomistic model of society on which political economy depended. And as facts became more multitudinous and less easy to accommodate, theoretical rifts widened, policy became more controversial, the hoped-for unity of knowledge and action dissolved. The first response to all this was to retreat from policy-science to socio-technics. Perhaps, after all, social inquiry could not lead immediately to definitive resolutions of policy questions; but at least if pursued with sufficient rigour it could provide policy-makers with a firm basis of information from which to make what would have to remain their regrettably difficult decisions. For this purpose a severely empiricist conception of the nature and use of social research was adopted. Social inquiry was formally separated off from social theory (in the form of political economy) as a service technology (very aptly named statistics) which 'neither discussed causes nor reasoned upon probable effects, but sought only to collect, arrange and compare the class of facts which can alone form the basis of correct conclusions with respect to social and political government'.

And this separation in turn had curious effects. On the one hand the attempt to subordinate social knowledge to government as intelligence encouraged a concentration of information-gathering activity in and around government, a sustained cultivation of the Socio-technic model. At the same time the very information that was gathered also led to increasing uncertainty, both in and out of government, about the reliability of facts, the nature of society and the cogency of political economy, a sustained subversion of the credentials of Socio-technics. We begin to find statisticians being warmly thanked for their invaluable work in 'comforting' Ministers with regular accounts of 'the progress of the nation' (a slightly special mode of Socio-technics, this). And we also find increasingly virulent debates among statisticians as to how the nation is to be understood and as to what is to count as a fact about it. Thus, even in the pre-history of British sociology one can see a strange ambivalence of use. The effort to use social inquiry in the manner of Policy-science and Socio-technics was generating a body of knowledge, and a body of doubt, which was actually being used to undermine Policy-science and Socio-technics alike by calling in question the rational continuity of knowledge and action on which such uses of social knowledge must depend.

Nevertheless, Socio-technics once launched in the 1830s proved impossible to suppress. Alone among my five models of use, it has a continual actual history in British practice from 1831 to the present. Indeed, the history of British sociology as a whole has been permanently tied to an interest in augmenting and advancing this particular type of use of social knowledge. As statistical monitoring with or without an associated survey component, it has been a regular and until 1981 regularly expanding activity of government – and not just as a device for enabling Mr Gladstone (or whoever) to sleep soundly. British government has become increasingly attached to the idea of putting its authority on a Socio-technical basis. As part of a general legitimating myth for government the supposed objectivity and impartiality of quantitative intelligence obviously fits well with the supposed anonymity and neutrality of bureaucracy but there is more to it than that: at the very least a small number of senior officials and politicians have always worked strenuously to get the best quantitative intelligence they could, apparently from a genuine commitment to Socio-technical ideas. Already by 1885 it could be said that 'statistics have become parliamentary and administrative' and that as a result 'order, method and precision' had been injected into 'all branches of legislation on social subjects'. And already by that time one could see both that the appeal to quantitative social intelligence had come to be a widely approved way of silencing, or at least trying to silence, political opponents, and that government of that sort was sufficiently widely believed-in for the normal response to demonstrations of the uncertainty, unreliability or error of intelligence not to be to abandon the approach but to seek to improve its method and scope. The two great drives to develop the social sciences after 1945 associated with the Clapham Committee and the Heyworth Committee both sprang directly from that concern.

However, the history of encouragement for a Socio-technical use of social knowledge is not just one of unwavering progress. There have been suggestive fluctuations, too. They are particularly apparent if one looks away from Whitehall. And what they suggest to me is that Socio-technics flourishes best in the absence of principled argument about social purposes. Argument of that sort is, in turn, muted either when there is a dominant consensus about social objectives or when people simply do not know what to do. There is, for example, an evident relationship between the fortunes of Socio-technics and the state of party politics. The years of confident alliance between Whigs and philosophical radicals in the 1830s were good years for Socio-technics; so were the years of Liberal ascendancy after 1905; and the years from 1945 to 1950; and also the years of the Second World War. In each of these periods of relatively strong purposeful government the demand for social intelligence tailored to the implementation of goals was that much keener within government and social knowledge generated outside government was the more likely to take the form of, and be taken up as, such intelligence. To date, the clearest version of this particular pattern is perhaps to be found just after 1945. The Inaugural Lectures of Professors T.H. Marshall and David Glass at the LSE, calling for stringent methodological training to equip people for useful social research; the Clapham Committee interpreting the problem of providing for social research almost entirely as a matter of recruiting skilled professionals to service government; the creation of a Central Statistical Office; the enthusiasm with which the Wartime Social Survey was perpetuated; the authority with which Professor Mannheim identified the tasks of sociologists in the process of social reconstruction – all add up to a quite unprecedented assertion of the viability of using social inquiry and analysis in the manner of Socio-technics. It was, as Marshall saw, a moment of special demand for sociology, of a 'realisation that sociology is not only desirable but essential' for action, a 'partner in a common task which cannot be fully accomplished without its aid'. But, as he also saw, it was a demand of a special sort: 'we find that those who are preparing for the day when . . . reconstruction . . . can begin in earnest . . . are looking to sociology to help them . . . . Planning is taking place on an increasing scale and is arousing . . . a demand for sociological investigations'.

But, oddly perhaps at first sight, Socio-technics has also flourished in times of party-political disarray and general confusion of social purpose. It had a long period of ascendancy by way of the National Association for the Promotion of Social Science following the virtual dismantling of the party system by Sir Robert Peel through to the revival of deeply principled partisan conflict in the 1880s. It enjoyed a distinct revival of its own, marked not least by the formation and early activity of PEP (cf. Pinder, 1981), in the years of social uncertainty, economic crisis and fumbling bi-partisan government after 1931. And it was noticeably taken-up again in the 1960s and 1970s as post-War political certainties evaporated and the new values and projects that displaced them (including some quite new types of sociology) were found to be precipitating confusion rather than a new sense of direction. At such moments it is the supposed ad hoc problem-defining and problem-solving capacity of Socio-technics that appeals. In the absence of well and politically defined alternative strategies the British seem regularly to have discovered an interest in using social inquiry and analysis to bridge social problems and public administration and so cope with what one of the Presidents of the National Association termed 'the mass of sin and misery' that continues to surround them. What Socio-technics cannot withstand is principled political conflict. It rests on the assumption that failure to solve social problems is a matter of intellectual incompetence not of the irreconcilability of legitimate interests. The great successes of the National Association, when year after year its investigations culminated in amendments of the law, like the great successes of PEP, its *Report* on the Health Services in 1937 which became 'a sort of Bible at the Ministry of Health', or its study of racial discrimination in 1966 which was acknowledged as 'decisive for legislation', depended on the posibility of persuading a relatively de-politicised political and administrative elite that competent intelligence was what mattered and that that was what had been provided. It was not just that the whole exercise tends to be highly elitist, 'our object', as one of the founders of PEP put it, 'was to influence key people'; it also depends on key people sharing a belief that policy disputes are attributable to nothing more important than silliness. Lord Brougham was in many ways the very model of a Socio-technician and he spoke clear and loud for the whole tendency when he told the National Association for the Promotion of Social Science not only that 'there is less diversity of opinion than might be supposed', but that where disputes did occur 'ignorance or misinformation, or inattentive, and therefore inaccurate, observation, or careless reflection and hasty declaration, is the cause of most of these differences'. For the rational plan conception of the use of social knowledge to work structured social conflict has to be irrational. Even in its most reasonable forms, such as that espoused by Albert Cherns today, Socio-technics requires a certain suspension of politics.

Which is not to say that Socio-technics has not, within its own terms, achieved some remarkable successes. But from the perspective of an overall view of the uses of British sociology it is its unintended consequences which are most striking. One could well argue that the most useful thing research conducted under the aegis of a Socio-technical conception of the use of social knowledge has accomplished is regularly to discredit the assumptions on which yesterday's Socio-technics was based. Throughout the nineteenth century, for example, it is clear that the attempt to generate social knowledge for Socio-technical purposes was rooted in a thoroughly atomistic conception of society. And yet what even the research most tightly governed by that conception tended to discover was the social not the individual; socially structured connections, the interdependence of groups, the facticity of social relationships. Expecting to account for poverty in terms of the weakness of personal character the pioneers of survey research, as early as the 1830s, found their inquiries leading them to explanations of the condition of the people couched in terms of the structural concomitants of poverty. Eager as the moralists who crowded the meetings of the National Association in the 1860s were to seize on palpable, simple causes of social problems – causes that would succumb to equally simple, direct fiscal or punitive or educational counter-action – even they could not resist the more complicated, and more sociological, message of their own investigations. 'Do we not find', as one of them put it, 'that each of the social problems we have been in any way at pains to unravel strikes its roots into the substance of the nation, ramifying through a hundred secret crevices into classes apparently the most remote from its influence?' Of course that is just what they did find. Facts accumulated for Socio-technical purposes served to frustrate Socio-technical action by revealing a quite unexpected connectedness, complexity and ambiguity. The attempt to use social knowledge to supersede politics by presenting government with a basis for uncontroversially correct legislation produced research which, insofar as it was technically good research, tended to subvert the very social theory which had justified and sustained Socio-technical ventures in the first place – and so to both renew and transform politics. It would not be absurd now to consider those uses at least as useful as the intended uses which for the most part failed to materialise.

And perhaps a similar judgement could be made of more recent experience as well. Might we not now appreciate the way in which the self-conscious Socio-technical projects of the last twenty years have ended-up producing highly sceptical evaluations of the claimed rationality of the policy process they were designed rationally to serve? Will the rational plan model of the relationship between sociological knowledge and policy-making ever again be taken as a serious or acceptable possibility for a democratic society? And if not, is not the gain in terms of Clarification well worth the disappointment in terms of Socio-technics? Or consider the accomplishment of sociological work addressed to the long list of urgent social problems needing investigation (as a basis for solution) produced by the Heyworth Committee as a major part of the case for a great expansion of the social sciences in 1965. Although much of that work was undertaken with the best of Socio-technical intentions, hardly any of it culminated in studies on which solutions to the Committee's problems could be straightforwardly based. Instead, it produced a literature (widely stigmatised by disappointed politicians and administrators as 'useless') which has commanded a drastic re-definition of many of those problems and an appreciation of the complex ramifications and ambiguities of all of them. Perhaps we should embrace the thought that one of the principal uses of attempts to use social knowledge for Socio-technical purposes seems to be to reveal the limits of Socio-technics. In unexpectedly discovering the fact that the social world is genuinely social, awkward, fluid, multi-valued and elusive, Socio-technics turns into Clarification. The failure of one use is the success of another.

For if the hope of using social knowledge Socio-technically has been the pivot and trigger of the history of British sociology, other models of use have also always been in play. Policy-science, the strong engineering model, has probably fared least well. Despite lurid assaults on the supposed 'positivism' of British sociology in the last twenty years, British sociologists have never been whole-hearted positivists and Policy-science has only appealed in moments of peculiarly intense distress. Harriet Martineau, whose many mistakes included that of translating Comte into English, understood that the turn towards Policy-science was an act of desperation. Faced with the intellectual chaos into which political economy (not without help from Socio-technics) had degenerated by 1850, faced with a resulting 'supreme dread' of finding her contemporaries 'adrift for want of an anchorage for their convictions', she found comfort in a sociological utopia of authoritative knowledge. Twenty years later, faced with a baffling welter of social information and the generally agreed utter uselessness of economics, large numbers of her intellectual peers were unfortunately ready to follow her. The positivist delusion did not last long – although it did compel Hobhouse and his successor Morris Ginsberg to waste too much of their lives in a tortured return to common-sense. But calamity as it (like any other Policy-science conception) was, the British discovery of Comte did have one totally beneficial result. It entailed a recognition of the central importance of social theory; that is to say a recognition of the fact that social knowledge is not in the last resort a product of facts but, rather, a product of reasoned judgement and values.

Addressing the British Association (Section F) in 1883 R.H. Palgrave was to articulate (under the influence of Comte) for the very first time what I would regard as the authentic voice of an authentic sociology. 'Endeavour to avoid the conclusion as we may', he told what must have been a largely astounded audience, 'we are drawn to admit that our science must be founded on theory'. Although his own idea of the potential authority of theory was grossly overdrawn, his assertion of the theoretical basis of social knowledge – of theory as the mediating bridge between knowledge and action – was of fundamental importance. It repudiated Socio-technics and, once the fantasy of Policy-science had been dispelled, opened the door to a quite new recognition of the idea that the proper use of sociology might be Clarification, empathy not planning.

Actually, the discrediting of Policy-science was not all that difficult. Quite apart from Herbert Spencer's splendid, and enormously Clarifying albeit grossly overstated, analysis of the absurdity of planning in the face of the unmanageable complexity of social processes, a veritable army of economists, statisticians, statesmen and ordinary sensible people was on hand to point out that sociological theory was not a single lucid voice but an incomprehensible babel of tongues and accordingly of absolutely no use as a means of determining or legitimating social action. There was really no answer to the sort of criticism Henry Sidgwick advanced against the Policy-science pretensions of positivist sociology at the British Association meeting of 1885; in the face of the 'portentous disagreement' among would-be sociological Policy-scientists, Sidgwick's audience needed little urging when he begged them 'that our Association will take no step calculated to foster delusions of this kind'. Positivism retreated to its own private church and so far as I can judge strong engineering conceptions of the use of sociological knowledge have not convinced anyone except a few official research managers, bureaucrats, politicians and, sadly, writers of textbooks, since that time.

On the other hand the Clarification model of use has been enormously attractive. The vital germ of wisdom in the appeals of Palgrave and other positivists of the 1880s was their sense of the need to understand society as what they termed an 'ensemble' of relationships. It was on that now obvious but then thoroughly radical idea that sociology proper was to develop – not the least of its Clarifying uses has been to make the idea of the reality of society as an ensemble of relationships commonplace of course. And it was initially at least very much in terms of the elaboration and specification of that idea that its use as Clarification (for better or worse) was consolidated. The first British sociologist overtly to espouse the Clarification model as an adequate and proper conception of the use of sociology was probably Hobhouse. Although the effect of Spencer's work had been, by reaction, to Clarify drastically, his intention after all had been to establish a compelling Policy-science: 'My ultimate purpose, lying behind all proximate purposes, has been that of finding for the principles of right and wrong in conduct at large a scientific basis'. Hobhouse was one of many who used Spencer's work to see-through the pretensions of Policy-science. His own series of books was addressed to the business of unmasking the Policy-science ambitions of Spencer, Galton and the Eugenicists and Social-Biologists who followed them. But not proclaiming an alternative Policy-science in the old nineteenth-century manner. Rather, his case – the case for an optimistic, interventionist humanism, perhaps – was overtly based on and subjectively conditioned by values, deploying evidence and argument within the framework of values. His sociology was intended to be reasonable, not definitive. And Hobhouse thus realised the distinctive feature of 'enlightenment' models of sociology – that the subject is necessarily argumentative, that the public form of sociology is likely to be one of diversity and dissensus since enlightenment can in the end (given the subjective implication of sociologists in their own object of study) only to be the outcome of many different accounts of the social world. The task of clarification is always to correct the partiality of others as best one can within the limits of one's own partiality. Sociology can therefore perhaps only proceed by way of disagreement – a state of affairs which easily leads those who secretly hanker after Policy-science or Socio-technical uses of social knowledge to judge the whole enterprise useless.

Hobhouse has had many distinguished successors and, although Clarification normally works both slowly and painfully, one can hardly deny that they have had considerable success. By way of the endless, useless crises and debates and fragmentations of British sociology since 1914 the terms of social thought, the language of politics, the basic concepts of social understanding have indeed been changed, and changed in ways directly traceable to the diffusion of sociological wrangling as well as in ways that have made public thought, language and concepts themselves steadily more sociological – not least in their understanding of the relations of social knowledge and social action. The net result is a state of affairs in which – in my view – society is generally understood more sensitively, more realistically and more sceptically. Simplistic reactions to social problems – such as the view that feckless parents can be held responsible for the involvement of juveniles in urban riots – are rendered generally incredible. We are not given an easier social world, but we are given a social world in which it is easier for people to be sympathetically and rationally responsive to one another.

Such uses, the effects of demystification, are not always easily observed. From time to time it has been necessary for the devotees of Clarification to pause and take stock of just how much has been achieved – as A.F. Wells in effect did in his report on social surveys in Britain in 1935, or T.H. Marshall in 1960 or John Rex in 1974, or John Eldridge in 1980 or the BSA conference in the same year (Abrams 1981). Invariably such reports have convincing things to say about the usefulness of sociology in obliquely, cumulatively, dialectically changing the world through Clarification. Wells, for example, could point both to a widespread acceptance of the connectedness of social conditions (as opposed to horror stories of personal failure) and to the specific recognition (eventually) of the authority of some findings in Parliament, or the Newcastle Chamber of Commerce, as consequences of the two hundred surveys (from Booth to Caradog Jones) which he reviewed. But the most impressive stock-taking is surely that offered by the Webbs in 1932. The conclusion that follows their long list of the subterranean workings of social inquiry and analysis in social consciousness (from the diffuse establishment of standards of objectivity in public life, to the recognition of society as a structured system of relationships – *Poverty: a Problem of Capitalism*, *Unemployment: a Problem of Industry* – and to the acceptance, in the face of the work of Booth and Rowntree, of 'guaranteeism' as a basis for social policy in place of the Poor Law) is surely irresistible:

> The sociologist cannot ignore the fact that many people . . . are sceptical about the value of sociology. The sociologist, they declare, may, by what he calls his science, accumulate a mass of knowledge, but can it be made useful? We think that the commonly expressed scepticism on the subject is unwarranted and that it is due partly to ignorance of what has already been achieved, partly to misconception of what science is and how it is applied and partly to impatience with a new science. It can scarcely be denied that it is the steadily increasing knowledge of social facts that has, during the past 100 years, led to one change after another in social structure. Whatever the mathematicians and physicists may feel about it, this, in fact, is how sociology becomes increasingly an applied science (Webb, 1932).

If, as seems to be the case, the majority of sociologists (or at least of those in academic posts) in Britain today are wedded to Clarification as the principal use of sociology, if they see contributing piecemeal through publication to the slow and erratic formation of a more sociological collective consciousness as the proper end-term of their work, they can cite imposing historical evidence to support the view that that is both a useful and effective thing to do. If I may invoke one American example, Daniel Patrick Moynihan was right when looking back on his own attempt to use sociological research as a basis for social policy, for a Socio-technics for the ghetto as it were, he said 'I was wrong, hopelessly wrong'. But the sociological knowledge he tried to use was not wrong – only the Socio-technical translation of it. The sort of knowledge we now have of the political sociology of race relations might have saved him from *ab-using* sociology in the way he did. The need is plainly for more Clarification, the diffusion of a richer, more complex and theoretically deeper knowledge base. There may still be a lot to be said for the view advanced by J.A. Hobson in 1911 in the face of urgent demands for sociology to be useful that 'it may be a better economy of our resources . . . not to concern ourselves too closely or too clearly with the practical uses to which the knowledge may be put when it is got' – but to concentrate on getting it.

However, most contemporary sociological enthusiasts for Clarification turn out to be enthusiasts for other uses as well, particularly for Education or Advocacy. The commitment to Education is not just a recent phenomenon; what is recent is the view that Education is something that should be largely practised within and governed by the norms of educational institutions. From 1900 to 1940 the most energetic exponents of the Educational uses of sociology directed their efforts quite differently. Just because institutionalised education was based on a firm dissociation of knowing and doing (in almost all subjects except medicine, law and theology anyway) the first educational enthusiasms of British sociologists were firmly extra-mural. The surveys sponsored by the Institute of Sociology and inspired by Patrick Geddes and Victor Branford were meant to be instruments of local community action, a nexus of learning and planning rooted in Geddes' conviction that social science 'is lived not written', an answer to the 'fundamental question of how to direct the attention of men and women to the natural conditions and social possibilities of the world around them'. Unfortunately, this project was something of a disaster. Although the Institute was to build-up a huge file of local surveys, the attempt to popularise survey work (coupled with the originally highly eclectic idea of what surveys involved favoured by Geddes) made for a rapid loss of discipline. Arguably, the handful of carefully designed and professionally executed surveys that were carried out, together with the personal influence of Geddes, did contrive to convince some geographers and planners of the value of social inquiry and so to sustain a further pattern of Socio-technics in town planning after 1945. But so far as strictly educational effects were concerned the glut of do-it-yourself surveys were to leave little mark. One unintended consequence they have had, since they were associated loudly and vehemently with the contempt of Geddes and Branford for the wizened, lifeless and from their point of view useless chastity of the universities, was to make it easier to justify excluding sociology from the more formal educational settings. Not that Geddes and Branford were altogether wrong. There seems little doubt that throughout this period, the weight of senior academic sentiment in Britain favoured the view that social inquiry and analysis would need to be wholly dissociated from any sort of practical interests or applications if they were to hope for legitimate educational standing. As Lancelot Hogben was to put it, resigning in despair from the Chair of Social Biology in London in 1938, 'the academic value of social research in our universities is largely rated on a futility scale . . . the Idol of Purity ensures "innocuous aimlessness" when social inquiry makes contact with the real world'.

All of which makes it the more surprising that efforts to develop sociology as a useful science (in the Socio-technical, problem-solving sense) after 1945 should have been directed almost entirely to the end of funding sociology as a teaching subject in universities. What is perhaps not so surprising is that the sociologists then recruited to the universities should in many cases themselves have become devotees of the Idol of Purity. From 1960 onwards, with the formidable support of the Heyworth Committee and the appetite for practical, policy applications which it represented, British sociology was turned towards formal education. The idea of contributing to the general education of the young now emerged as a distinct, and for some paramount, proper use of sociology. And at the same time, suitably socialised in its new setting, sociology came to be understood as a discipline embodied in teachable knowledge and techniques and significantly disengaged from other, more immediate, uses. Much energy was devoted to winning space for sociology in the educational system at all levels; and integral to that effort was a good deal of concern to demonstrate the respectability (purity, perhaps) of sociology in terms of existing educational criteria. It is not irrelevant that the main effort to 'professionalise' sociology in this period came from the Teachers' Section of the BSA, nor that the main intellectual components of professionalism were thought to be a rigorous training in largely quantitative methods and a grasp of sophisticated general social theory. None of this was necessarily a mistake. But it did tend to aggravate a certain confusion about uses. Public support for the development of sociology in the universities sprang from the hope that it would prove useful, Socio-technically. Indeed, many sociologists themselves justified and urged the development in just those terms. But to succeed in the universities sociology had to be largely useless in just those terms. A first intellectual responsibility was to accommodate the longstanding critique emanating from other disciplines of the very idea of Socio-technics, let alone Policy-science.

It is hardly surprising that the first generation of university sociologists after the expansion was thoroughly ambivalent about the uses of sociology. Or that there was a dramatic turning towards the exploration of every conceivable mode of theory, a search for some sort of specifically academic intellectual grounding for the pursuit of whatever other uses might more furtively have been cherished. Nor perhaps is it very surprising that the one body of theory other than traditional positivism which claimed to be able to bridge the gap between knowledge and action authoritatively – Marxism, of course – should have appealed widely to teachers and students alike. In 1960 there was a great deal of ground to be cleared before theory and evidence could be brought together in a basis of knowledge for a cumulative sociology. Placing sociology in the universities at that juncture and defining its uses as educational probably ensured that the theoretical aspects of that problem would be given precedence. What ensued was in turn probably a necessary turmoil – and certainly one from which in retrospect and synthesis much Clarification has emerged. But initially it seemed to give much comfort to those committed to the idea of sociology's uselessness. Instead of the skilled and professional problem-solvers hoped for by Heyworth, sociology as Education seemed to mean – not least in the transformation of syllabuses that took place between 1960 and 1975 – a subversion of the whole idea of that sort of usefulness.

My final conception of the use of sociology, Advocacy, has always existed alongside the others and has usually been thought slightly disreputable. Repudiating both the claims to authoritative knowledge implicit or explicit in engineering models of use and the Weberian schizophrenia about the gap between knowledge and action which seems to afflict many devotees of Clarification and Education alike, the Advocate joins knowledge and action concretely and often without too much theoretical finesse in her or his own avowedly political practice. Exponents of Advocacy seem to me to be distinguished by their determination to insist on the proper continuity of sociological work beyond the printed page; recognising sociological knowledge as argumentative knowledge they follow their arguments through to the point of action in ways which the devotees of other models of use seem unwilling or unable to do. Among our present generation of senior sociologists Jean Floud and A.H. Halsey, Dorothy Wedderburn, Peter Townsend and Michael Young would be prominent among those whose attachment to an Advocacy model of the use of sociology could most easily be documented. However, I suspect that most of us, certainly most of us who have done enough empirical research to have something to advocate, are likely to be at least part-time and occasional Advocates. After all, even when most lost in the 'foggy labyrinth' of facts he had created, Booth could always find time to make the case for old age pensions. And even when most taken up with the clarification of Weberian theory, and the inhibition of action it entails, John Rex has always been ready to make the case for decolonising race relations. The problem about Advocacy is not that it precludes other uses, although it does in principle make nonsense of some, as that most sociologists who engage in it still tend to do so a little shamefacedly, a little as though it was not quite professionally proper, not a sociological thing to do. There is, as it were, no professionally acceptable rationale for Advocacy – although in different ways sociologists such as Ray Pahl (1977) and Ralf Dahrendorf (1968:256–78) have begun to work towards one; and Christopher Bryant (1976) and others have made clear our need for one. I shall come back to this question of strategy shortly but at this point I would simply stress that Advocacy is not just a matter of personal bloody-mindedness any more than it is just a matter of one's social connections. David Donnison (1972) seems to me to have done much less than justice to his friends and colleagues when he suggested that 'the influence of sociology has been largely by diffusion through the social networks of eminent academics', above all through the networks of 'a London-based liberal left'. Certainly Fabian summer schools, WEA classes and Anthony Crosland's 'salon' may have provided the places and occasions for making the case against the 11+, but the sociologists who turned those places and occasions into opportunities were not just 'there', they were actively pursuing a sociological argument in what they took to be an appropriate way. Similarly, they were not just being a nuisance; they had made judgements about the use of sociology and were implementing them in duly considered ways.

So much, very crudely, for the history of my five types of use of sociology since 1831. What can we make now of the situation today? In the first instance we have achieved a modicum of wisdom and, usefully, have disseminated it through Education and Clarification quite widely. Policy science in all its varieties including its marxist varieties is more or less thoroughly discredited. Socio-technics survives but in an encouragingly sceptical revisionist mode. Some part of that revision is certainly attributable to intense sociological criticism of the intellectual basis and practical achievements of Socio-technics, culminating in works such as Scott and Shore's *Why Sociology Does Not Apply*, Boudon's *The Crisis in Sociology* or Payne et al.'s *Sociology and Social Research*. Some is certainly a result of the day-to-day experience of sociologists working in different capacities for policy-making bodies and so demystifying themselves about the nature of policy-making, coming to appreciate policy as itself an enigmatic social process needing to be understood sociologically – the increasing use of sociologists in research or administrative posts in and around government, and on advisory committees and commissions of inquiry has been very important in this respect as an occasion for mutual learning and 'concept trading'. But perhaps the greatest source of change has been the sheer development of political and social democracies as the context in which Socio-technical uses have to be accomplished.

As Cherns has pointed out, Socio-technics has to operate in a real world in which as in any other 'the relations possible in any situation are bounded by the state of the system'; and for Socio-technics that system has changed dramatically. It is not that the sort of elite networks discussed by Donnison have ceased to exist, or that social intelligence agencies no longer have access to key people over lunch in Belgravia, or that sociologists with imposing track records of 'relevant' research no longer win advisory posts at the highest levels of government as Rowntree or Halsey or Abel-Smith did. All these points of entry remain and some have become more genuinely open. But the system as a whole has grown and diversified, spawning a host of what Cherns calls 'mediating institutions' between policy-makers and the public which function as both filters and amplifiers for social knowledge. Special interest groups, parliamentary Select Committees, specialised research institutes, the device of the Green paper, pressure groups, organised local communities and many other agencies have all helped to democratise the environment for Socio-technics and blur the role and the ascertainable impact of the Socio-technician. A policy process that contains a mass of such institutions is one that both permits social knowledge to enter the field of policy-making relatively easily and diffuses its impact very considerably. It 'prevents the muffling of research', but it also militates against direct engineering uses of research. Probably, by forcing the sociologist to think more reflexively about sociology-in-society, it encourages a shift of self-image for the sociologist from Socio-technician to Advocate.

For there is little evidence that British sociologists have turned away from their traditional hope of contributing to social amelioration and of doing work that is somehow useful for policy. None of the evidence suggests that the enthusiasm of British sociologists today for using their subject to Educate and to Clarify marks a simple retreat from older concerns. Those concerns seem to have remained strong even in the university teaching departments – as Perry found in 1972 (Crawford & Perry 1976). According to his figures not only were Departments of Sociology very much more heavily involved in externally funded research than Departments in most other social sciences, but the general pattern of the research, even though most projects had been generated and designed internally, was plainly intended to be useful, somehow, for policy. It was mostly focused on information-gathering or description rather than on, say, the refinement of method or the elaboration of theory. And it was mainly aimed at an audience of policy-makers or decision-makers rather than at fellow researchers, students or general public opinion. Unfortunately, having documented this continuing strong desire to be useful for policy among even the most academic British sociologists, Perry was not able to go on to explore his informants' view as to how such usefulness was to be accomplished.

My own recent attempts to pursue that question suggest a quite pronounced move away from engineering and towards Advocacy – and a related recognition of the new mediating institutions as peculiarly apt sites for Advocacy. Of the sociologists I interviewed, three-fifths saw the proper use of their work in terms of some combination of Clarification and Advocacy. The common pattern was one that united elements of 'I publish and if the work is any good its relevance is obvious – people will take it up', with 'If I think my work has policy implications I try pretty hard to get the message across to the relevant people'. Obviously, the way in which these two themes were combined, the fine blend and balance varied greatly. Nor did the pattern typically exclude some commitment to Educational and Socio-technical uses. Indeed, the existence of a further combination of Advocacy with Socio-technics – particularly among those who had had some sustained experience of working with or for policy-makers – a sense of the possibility of using sociology both to service and to contest policy, was perhaps the most intriguing and in some ways the most encouraging of my findings. What I did not find was either any great enthusiasm for Policy-science, for using sociology as an authoritative instrument of government, or much Weberian anxiety about the propriety of using sociology as a resource for politics, about the possibility and legitimacy of treating it as a cogent basis for argument. What was missing – except at the level of personal experience reflected in tranquility – was much sense of just how sociologists in general might go about using sociological knowledge as Advocacy. Whereas the ground rules for Socio-technics are well known and consolidated in a substantial and critical literature so that the more obviously crass versions of the model, such as the one-sided discipline-based idea of rational-plan application stigmatised by Scott and Shore, are recognised and widely repudiated, the strategies appropriate and inappropriate for the business of using sociology as Advocacy seem still to remain a mystery.

Clarification, Advocacy, Education and a revised Socio-technics, Socio-technics as dialogue rather than as planning, seem then to constitute the preferred pattern of uses of sociology among British sociologists today. Given that this represents a considerable advance in science and self-awareness when compared to some of the patterns of the past, two questions remain. How can one account for the continuing impression that sociology is not much used? And can one begin to identify strategies that would make pursuit of the preferred pattern of use more effective?

There are, to begin with, some quite straightforward institutional reasons for non-use. There is actually not all that much sociology to be used. The establishment of an extensive theory-saturated and self-conscious basis of knowledge is the crucial conditon for any of the uses of sociology I have discussed to flourish. We know very well that the creation of cogent social knowledge is a laborious and very expensive business: Booth had a research force comparable to 'a whole Department of State'; Rowntree could afford hundreds of investigators over many months; since the 1930s it has been generally accepted by British sociologists that only government has the resources to investigate any major social issue in a comprehensive, let alone a definitive way. The funding of sociological research nevertheless remains derisory. The SSRC, which is estimated to provide about 20% of the total funding for sociological research in Britain at present, produced a total of £266,000 for both sociology and social administration in 1979 – about the equivalent at adjusted prices of the cost of, say, one of Booth's seventeen volumes; and also to be compared to the £36 million of government money provided for research and develoment in sociology in the United States in 1972. It is widely agreed that British sociology would be more useful (in almost any of the possible senses of usefulness) if British sociologists did more good empirical research. What is hardly ever acknowledged is the order of the bill that would be involved in taking that requirement seriously.

But there are subtler reasons for non-use as well. I will mention just a few. First, insofar as we recognise sociology as politically involved in society we can hardly expect sociology to receive the sort of fair deal 'on its scientific merits' which a Policy-science view would assume. The well-documented exclusions and repudiations of 'troublesome' research become understandable, even probable, as does the common appropriation of whatever is judged good research as educational research, psychological research, criminological research, research on poverty or old age or health care – indeed, as anything but sociology. One cannot have argument without adversaries. Then there are problems related to the deviousness of the take-up of social knowledge. Unlike the rational plan the actual world of social politics is thoroughly untidy and erratic, a world of contingencies. Even when determined Advocacy carries a sociological argument to the relevant decision-making centre, even when decision-makers overtly acknowledge the force of such argument the precise contribution of argument to outcome is likely to remain obscure, embedded in a mass of other factors and forces. The role of work in the sociology of education in dismantling the selective tripartite secondary system is often mentioned as one of the conspicuous success stories of sociological Advocacy in Britain. Yet, although most of those involved, researchers and policy-makers alike, have been quite forthcoming about what happened it seems fairly certain that we shall never know with any precision just what the sociological contribution was to the process that culminated in Anthony Crosland's famous Circular. All one can say is that almost all of the participants judged it to have been important. But it is in the nature of political processes (as distinct from the rationalistic model of policy) to conflate and confuse specific influences rather than to isolate and specify them. And finally, there is the Cheshire Cat problem. Insofar as sociology is successfully used as Clarification it tends, as fast as it is used, to disappear as sociology. Insights, concepts, language which began life as sociology filter into the world of taken-for-granted common-sense and common discourse and to the extent that they are indeed used in that world are no longer perceived as sociology. At any given moment – as Mackay has demonstrated very convincingly in the context of industrialists' odd 'double image' of sociology in which all sorts of particular studies are recognised as having been extremely valuable while sociology as such is thought to be either laughable or subversive – what is seen as sociology is likely to be that which has not yet been found useful. When demystification fails the demystifier is an irritant; when it succeeds the demystifier is redundant.

How then, would the compleat sociologist use sociology in 1981? The work of Education is probably the most clearly defined and many certainly find it the most directly rewarding – we do after all in education impose tests to demonstrate that sociology has indeed got into the minds of others, perhaps that it is even being taken seriously there. The work of Clarification is well-established and academically respectable – even though the remoulding of the language and categories of common-sense occurs in ways which tend to eat-up sociology without acknowledging the nutritional debt. It is in the ill-defined and slippery territory of Advocacy and Socio-technics that appropriate ways of using sociology are least clear and most need to be made clear. As yet we have little more than a few possible clues as to the direction in which we might go. Bryant (1976) has reviewed a number of options – not very optimistically it must be said: it is clear enough from his analysis of 'sociology in action' that 'sociologists who seek to influence social development' more immediately than through the circuitous channels of Clarification 'need to elaborate strategies for the realisation of their ideas', and that 'strategy elaboration is the most neglected dimension of sociology in action'. It is clear, too, that he is right to find the Weberian separation of science and politics and the resulting arbitrariness of sociological Advocacy less than intellectually adequate. And perhaps he is right, too, to remain dissatisfied with Dahrendorf's rapprochement of science and politics on the strength of the common uncertainty of both –

since there again just what the sociologist does then seems in all respects to be alarmingly indeterminate and whimsical.

The travellers' tales we have from a few battle-scarred practitioners of Advocacy can perhaps take us a little further. In particular, Pahl's account (1977) of his experience as a high-level sociological adviser is instructive and helpful. Not the least of its merits is his recognition of the way in which establishing oneself as an Advocate for sociology involves one to a considerable extent in taking the role of the Socio-technician. One can, as he points out, find that that in turn means many things and opens-up many possible short-range uses for sociology – he lists the following: gatekeeper for the literature, filterer of the literature, advocate for a focus of interest, advocate for a political element, watchdog or demystifier, managerialist or technocrat, fall guy, social statistician, legitimator and token underdog or as he puts it 'woman'. But the important thing to emerge from his account is that over and above such service functions it is perfectly possible for a clear-minded and determined sociologist also to act, and in a quite statesman-like way, on behalf of sociology. Building on 'the sociologist's basic scepticism' as a cardinal resource he was able to secure a position in which, perhaps as the price for providing the social intelligence his policy-making colleagues required, he was also able to plant in the policy process basic Educational and Clarifying messages of sociology – messages about unintended consequences, about the relativity and diversity of social interests, the uncertainty of planning, the latent functions and implications of policy. Sometimes one needs to be or can afford to be less Machiavellian than that – as was the case in forcing on government the message of Cole and Utting's findings about the non-take-up of welfare entitlements, where what was needed was simple persistence. But, however devious or direct Advocacy may have to be in particular contexts the point that emerges from the accounts of it that we have is that the process of sociological Advocacy is not at all arbitrary in either Weber's or Dahrendorf's sense. The model for the role is neither that of the 'mouthpiece' for any client who comes along, nor that of the 'community lawyer' accepting only the briefs of the deserving downtrodden. Rather, sociological Advocacy is the advocacy of sociology. As the work of sociological Education and Clarification goes on, as the distinctive basis of social understanding which those uses build and disseminate develops, it becomes clear that it is precisely that sort of understanding of the social world that sociological Advocacy is also promoting.

Sociological Advocacy carries into the arenas of power and policy, perhaps on the back of Socio-technics, perhaps in the guise of a shared political enthusiasm, a social wisdom that has been slowly acquired in a hundred and fifty years of sociological work – a wisdom that is sceptical in its defence of empirical social inquiry, reflexive in its pursuit of objective social analysis, disenchanted in its support for purposive social action. Twenty years ago, W.J.H. Sprott (1962) pointed out that since the time of Hobhouse, since, that is, the earliest institutionalisation of sociology in this country the central message of British sociology had been that two themes run consistently through the best evidence one can accumulate about the social world: the messages of 'increased rationality and widened sympathy'. In the last twenty years sociology has usefully demonstrated something of the limits of rationality and of the complexities of sympathy. The repudiation of Policy-science as a proper use of sociology and the growing acceptance of Advocacy in its place seem to me to mark a significant step, a step that builds on sociological knowledge and brings sociology realistically into the realm of social action, in the advancement of both increased rationality and increased sympathy. Perhaps that is useful enough.

REFERENCES

Abrams, P. et al. (1981) *Practice and Progress: British Sociology 1950–1980* (London: Allen & Unwin).

Boudon, R. (1980) *The Crisis in Sociology* (London: Macmillan).

Bryant, C.G.A. (1976) *Sociology in Action* (London: Allen & Unwin).

Bulmer, M. (ed.) (1978) *Social Policy Research* (London: Macmillan).

Cherns, A. (1979) *Using the Social Sciences* (London: Routledge).

Crawford, E. and Perry, N. (eds.) (1976) *Demands for Social Knowledge: the role of research organisations* (London: Sage).

Dahrendorf, R. (1968) *Essays in the Theory of Society* (London: Routledge).

Dainton, F. (1971) *The Future of the Research Council System* Cmnd. 4814 (London: H.M.S.O.).

Donnison, D. (1972) 'Research for policy', *Minerva* 10, 1972, pp. 519–36, reprinted in Bulmer (1978), pp. 44–66.

Eldridge, J. (1980) *Recent British Sociology* (London: Macmillan).

Fay, B. (1975) *Social Theory and Political Practice* (London: Allen & Unwin).

Janowitz, M. (1970) *Political Conflict* (Chicago: Quadrangle).

Lazarsfeld, P.F. and Reitz, J.G. (1975) *An Introduction to Applied Sociology* (New York: Elsevier).

Marshall, T.H. (1960), 'Sociology – the road ahead', lecture in Cambridge, 25 November. reprinted in Marshall (1977):26–45.

Marshall, T.H. (1977) *Class, Citizenship and Social Development* (Chicago: University of Chicago Press).

Pahl, R.E. (1977) 'Playing the Rationality Game: the sociologist as hired expert', in C. Bell and H. Newby (eds.), *Doing Sociological Research* (London: Allen & Unwin), pp. 130–48.

Payne, G. et al. (1981) *Sociology and Social Research* (London: Routledge).
Pinder. J. (ed.) (1981) *Fifty Years of Political and Economic Planning, 1931–1981* (London: Heinemann).
Podgorecki, A. and Los, M. (1979) *Multi-Dimensional Sociology* (London: Routledge).
Rex, J. (1974a) *Sociology and the Demystification of the Modern World* (London: Routledge).
Rex, J. (ed.) (1974b) *Approaches to Sociology* (London: Routledge).
Scott, R.A. and Shore, A.R. (1979) *Why Sociology Does Not Apply: a study of the use of sociology in public policy* (New York: Elsevier).
Sprott, W.J.H. (1962) *Sociology at the Seven Dials* (London: Athlone Press).
Webb, S, and Webb, B. (1932) *Methods of Social Study* (London: Longman).
Wells, A.F. (1935) *The Local Social Survey in Great Britain* (London: Allen & Unwin).

12 Informants, respondents and citizens

CATHERINE MARSH

In the past, social research has generally been done by the powerful on the powerless, the poor, the underdog (Becker 1967; Barnes 1979). The collection of social intelligence about the contours of the population was born, with capitalism, in Britain's industrial centres, and it was quickly taken over by the state apparatus. Indeed, the very root of the word 'statistics' is the 'state' – items of information gathered by German statesmen, to help them rule; the connection between statistics and mathematical theory developed much later. These three historical features of social statistics – its concentration on the powerless, its close link with the capitalist mode, and its centrality to the state – have all had important consequences for the relationship between researcher and researched. Furthermore, as changes have taken palce both in the technology available for conducting research and in the relationship of the state to both the economy and to social relations, so we might expect and indeed do find developments in the way the subjects of research are characterised.

In this chapter, I intend to trace the development of ideas about the relationship between the researcher and the person from whom the researcher collects his or her information. My argument is that there have been three discernible stages in the evolution of the relationship. The first view, predominant in the nineteenth century, was that social researchers should only interview other professionals, acting as *informants*, giving proxy information to the researcher. This gave way to the second idea, that one should research directly those about whom one wanted to make generalisable statements, and treat them as *respondents*, providers of data who are, nonetheless, still 'subjects'. The growth of egalitarian ideas since World War Two seems to be encouraging a third view of the subjects of study, namely as *citizens*, status equals of the researcher, whose attitudes are not just of scientific curiosity but of important political significance. However, it should be stressed that these three, informants, respondents and citizens, are analytic categories, and history will not allow us to draw neat time boundaries around them.

Informants

The only occasion on which systematic social investigation was undertaken in pre-capitalist, pre-urban Britain, was after the conquest of new territory – the Domesday Book after the Norman invasion and the Down Surveys after Cromwells's invasion of Ireland. The ignorance of the invaders forced them to conduct such special investigations in order to rule the new countries efficiently. The feudal social structure was otherwise relatively open to inspection; the face-to-face relations which existed between people made features of the social structure 'obvious', and precluded the necessity for purpose-built exercises in social investigation.

But the breech birth of capitalism, the success of the factory system based on 'free' wage labour, and the erection of the textile mills, iron foundries, and railways of early capitalism, with their surrounding shanty towns, all happened so fast, violently, and anarchically, that it was impossible to detect the social contours of this new development without special effort. 'No-go' areas fast developed in all Britain's early industrial cities, and anyone who could escape the conditions of the labourers' slums did so gratefully and set up more respectable residences on another side of town. 'Every city', said Engels in 1844, 'has one or more slums, where the working class is crowded together. True, poverty often dwells in hidden alleys close to the palaces of the rich, but in general, a separate territory has been assigned to it, where, removed from the sight of the happier classes, it may struggle along as it can' (1844; 1969: 60). These working class areas could not be ignored, however; the ruling class feared that the ideas of the French Revolution might be spreading abroad, and, even if Chartism was not as revolutionary as they feared, it was a new and worrying phenomenon.

Intervention, however, was out of favour with the laissez-faire, anti-corn-law lobby of the early industrialists; poor relief could not be handed out on a charitable basis, since it could undermine the operation of the labour market. Chadwick, the architect of the new Poor Laws, devised the 'less eligibility' principle which seemed a brilliant solution to this problem: the workhouse was to be so unpleasant that people would prefer any kind of work to it. Individuals could only fall back on the Poor Laws by effectively placing themselves outside the labour market and, indeed, outside civil society, for the workhouse was tantamount to prison. Laissez-faire could remain intact as the principle elsewhere (Finer 1952).

There were, however, obvious limitations to this early method of dealing with the poor by punishing them; the very size of the problem precluded incarcerating everyone. If the demands for intervention were to be steered away from the factory system, then the responsibility for the conditions had to be laid at some other door.

In the early decades of the nineteenth century, statistical societies sprang up in most of the industrial towns. Their membership was mainly composed of the new industrialists themselves, those who shared their commitment to utilitarian ideology, and those philanthropists, some of whom were clearly motivated by deeply-felt religious conviction, but who were also determined to find outlets for their philanthropy that did not tread on the toes of the emergent industrial order.

The problem, everyone agreed, was at heart a *moral* problem. The working class was often viewed with fear which bordered on hatred; a common argument against seeking improvements in wages was that the effect would only be to increase the amount the working classes spent on drink. Moral decay was to be attributed to urbanism, to the physical conditions of the city, to overcrowding, and not to the wages system, not to the factories. The early Victorian social investigators set out to map the physical and moral features of the slums, and to enter territories considered as almost foreign lands; Engels writes, for instance, that 'before the Bishop of London called attention to this most poverty-stricken parish [St Philip's, Bethnal Green], people at the West End knew as little of it as of the savages of Australia or the South Sea Isles' (1844; 1969: 62).

This distrust and fear of the new objects of research was not conducive to a methodology which allowed the researchers to interview directly those in whom they were interested. The statistical societies that flourished in early Victorian Britain used two different modes of enquiry. The Statistical Society of London experimented on a large scale with the use of questionnaires ('interrogatories') distributed to relevant authorities – the police, hospitals, poor-law administrators, school boards, factory commissioners, insurance societies, landlords, newspaper editors, magistrates and prison governors (Abrams 1968: 18). Having no authority to force these officials to respond, the results were disappointing. The early statisticians therefore turned instead to the method of direct observation, using it to an extent that was not repeated until the phenomenon of Mass-Observation in the middle of this century (see chapter 7). The beliefs and values of the working classes were usually inferred from such things as the type of reading material that they had in their houses, the type of pictures they had on the walls. The researchers' great concern was with the physical conditions of life in which the early industrial proletariat lived, especially with their physical and moral hygiene. Government regulation was sought only in public health and education.

The statistical societies proved to the authorities the value of collecting intelligence on the 'social problem' and, although they withered as organisations and failed in their major attempts to prevent factory legislation, they achieved one major success, in that, by the mid-century, they had persuaded the state to take over many data-gathering functions (Cullen 1975). These included, not just civil registrations of births, deaths and marriages, but also a regular Census of Population, routine collection of crime statistics, and a quite unprecedented number of *ad hoc* enquiries into aspects of life, into different industries, into education and religion, and so on.

It is to the various Royal Commissions and Parliamentary enquiries that we must look for the development of the idea that if systematic and reliable information was to be collected about the state of the working class, it had to be ascertained from systematic and reliable individuals, informants who had claim to expertise on the poor, not the individuals themselves.

The evidence on which the Poor Law Amendment Act of 1834 was based, for example, was the detailed reports of thirty itinerant Assistant Commissioners, who were instructed either to observe the Petty Sessions directly or to convene meetings of the magistrates or overseers in a division, to take down their evidence on the operation of poor relief.

Chadwick himself did actually draft a questionnaire several pages long, which he proposed that the Assistant Commissioners should administer directly to the poor. He wanted to know such details as women's parity histories, and whether their first child was born within a year of their marriage. The enquiry was to be held behind closed doors. There was, however, an outcry from the working class themselves to this proposal, especially to the proposed secrecy, and they made organised attempts to subvert the collection of this information (Finer 1952: 52–4). The terror and suspicion engendered by the new Poor Laws is eloquently illustrated by the rumour circulating at the time that the investigations were designed to help the government implement a policy of reducing the number of working class children by killing one in every ten of them (Webb 1955). One reason, therefore, for the concentration in subsequent Parliamentary enquiries on expert informants, rather than working class witnesses, was the practical difficulties of collecting the information. (Chadwick cooled off the idea of formal interviews with the poor, but visited Manchester later to see how the Poor Law was operating; he claimed that he systematically visited homes, factories and meetings to discuss the scheme, but the quality of his evidence is called into question on reading his conclusion that the new law was popular!)

A second and overlooked reason for the prevalence of informant interviewing was also the very simple fact that the urban working class were working very long hours to earn even a subsistence wage. If the views of these labourers were to be considered, someone would have to enter the factories to do the talking. This the Factory and Mines Inspectorate actually did. But the usual pattern for official enquiries was to summon witnesses to attend either Parliament or an urban administrative centre. Expenses, when they were paid, had to be claimed in arrears, and sometimes, as in the second enquiry into the plight of the handloom weavers, they were not allowed at all (Richards 1979).

The third reason for the use of informants was, however, more straightforwardly ideological, stemming from the attitudes of the urban bourgeoisie and their fellow-travellers towards the poor, who were the 'objects' of research, in the manner of biological specimens. Experienced mayors and district councillors were the experts on the causes and consequences of unemployment in the Select Committee on Distress from Want of Employment in the 1890s, and their conclusion that the main problem was the weather rather than a trade depression was accepted and repeated. Clerics and employers, teachers and magistrates were summoned to pronounce on what education the poor needed, what effect it would be likely to have on them, and what problems might be faced in terms of attendance. Johnson, reviewing the major official nineteenth-century investigations about education, says that 'a careful combing reveals only a scattering of examples of working class witnesses' (1977: 8) and the occasional 'representative of the working classes' was usually a deferential artisan.

There was also a major practical stumbling block to researching the poor directly in these days before the major discoveries about sampling had been popularised; social research of this period still carried with it the encyclopaedic drive of the Enlightenment, namely to document *all* knowledge. In the absence of sampling, informant interviews acted as a necessary short-cut. The sheer problems of size are best illustrated in Charles Booth's monumental study of the *Life and Labour of the People of London*. Booth, a wealthy shipping magnate, devoted seventeen years of his life to the production of the same number of volumes of statistical information about the extent of poverty in London. This massive enquiry led to generalisation about 80% of the population of London.

There is a great deal of mythology about Booth and his study. He is often hailed as the founding father of British survey research, whereas, in reality, survey investigations of an equally sophisticated nature had been performed since the early Victorian period. He is often credited with providing the basic information which made obvious the need for state intervention into insurance, wage and factory regulation and other educational and welfare provisions. In fact, his methods were so imprecise, and his classification systems of classes and poverty so impressionistic that he was able to interpret his own statistics as a *refutation* of the 'sensationalists' among the Social Democrats who argued the need for political redress of grievances (Hennock 1976).

In the main, Booth did not elicit statements from the inhabitants of London themselves but relied instead on a variety of school board visitors, police, rate collectors, sanitary inspectors and almoners for the information, supplementing these with qualitative impressions gained from visiting and observing the subjects. His calculation of the numbers in poverty was done by aggregating the number of people various professionals believed to be in various impressionistic categories of poverty. The potential for error in this process was denied by Booth:

> Most of the [School Board] visitors have been working in the same district for several years . . . they are in daily contact with the people, and have a very considerable knowledge of the parents of the school children . . . No-one can go . . . over the description of the inhabitants . . . full as it is of picturesque details noted down from the lips of the visitor to whose mind they have been recalled . . . and doubt the genuine character of its information and truth. (1892: I.5–6)

Beatrice Webb, a worker on Booth's study and from whose autobiography we get not only an account of the methods used but also an interesting appendix on interviewing, was aware that these impressionistic methods could produce problems, but declared optimistically that this proxy method, which she called 'wholesale interviewing',

> blocked the working of personal bias. Each of the two hundred school attendance officers had doubtless his own predilections . . . but with so large a group of witnesses, these different types of prejudice cancelled out. (1926: 198)

The appendix makes it clear that she believed that interviewing was a method to be used on competent informants; she admits that these are not always those at the head of an organisation, and urges students of society to make 'speculative investment in queer or humble folk' – but by this she soon makes it clear that she meant it was worth interviewing foremen as well as managers!

Beatrice Webb never came around to the idea that there was anything to be gained from administering a questionnaire to respondents. In *Methods of Social Study*, the Webbs report that they tried sending a postal questionnaire to trade union officials, with little success (Webb and Webb 1932; 1975). Their response rate was very low. They had asked questions that they thought would make sense – 'Do your members work at piece rate or at time rate?' – but discovered that this question was unanswerable to the majority of officials who got their questionnaire. They joined the early

Victorian statisticians in deciding that questionnaires had nothing interesting to offer, instead of concluding that if you intend to ask people structured questions of this kind you must do some very careful piloting.

The distinction between informant and respondent is analytic, not temporal. There certainly are examples in the nineteenth century of direct investigation and interrogation of the poor. One important exception among official enquiries is the *modus operandi* of the Factory Inspectorate, which made a much more regular feature of talking to operatives directly. Some of the early factory inspectors undoubtedly had a genuine concern for the physical conditions of work in the factories; even Karl Marx considered that Leonard Horner, the chief factory inspector, had 'rendered undying service to the English working class' (Marx 1886; 1970: 225). It is certainly true that the inspectors visited workplaces directly – they had to in order to perform their job. And activists like Horner even surveyed thousands of workers directly in 1848 to discover what factory workers thought of the Ten Hour Act, interviewing over 200 of them himself (Lyell, 1890: entry for 26 October 1848). But we must not mistake the exceptional for the normal; even among some of the most activist inspectors we find a contempt for the working class, and a concern more for their moral than their physical condition.

This can be illustrated by looking at the activities of Tremenheere, one of the most influential of the nineteenth-century reformers because of his great energy and prodigious pamphleteering (Corrigan 1977: 263). He started his career in the schools' inspectorate, investigating the state of education in South Wales after John Frost's Chartist uprising at Newport, and then became one of the chief mining inspectors; he is credited with inspiring fourteen acts of Parliament (Webb 1955: 352). To be sure, he did talk to workers, and worse, trade unionists, even once meeting with a strike committee while a strike was in progress (Corrigan 1977: 251). As he pointed out in his own defence, however, despite the Home Secretary's alarm at his meeting with 'the most violent of agitators' his reports never substantiated that alarm (Webb 1955: 359). Indeed, the trade unionists were disgusted with his disproportionate reliance on the word of the coterie of 'enlightened' employers with whom he kept most common consort. *The Miners' Advocate* denounced him unreservedly, claiming that not a whisper was heard by the miners of his first visit to Durham until he reported, and his 'single source of information seems to have been the after-dinner conversation of the owners, composed as it was of the well-worn strictures on the extravagance of the pitmen, the conventional picture of their prosperity, and the regret that so excellent a body of men should be so prone to combination and so open to the persuasions of dishonest, self-seeking demagogues' (Welbourne 1923: 102).

It was only the radical sympathisers with the working class who regularly obtained information directly from them. Cobbett's *Rural Rides* and Engels' *Condition of the Working Class* make it clear that these individuals did spend time listening as well as watching. Even Karl Marx did a survey; he recruited a volunteer sample from the *Revue Socialiste*, and asked them to fill in one hundred open-ended questions about their conditions of work (Weiss 1936). The intention of this questionnaire was to raise important questions in the minds of those who answered them, as well as to provide information for the investigator, so the questions are not at all neutral. One question, for example, asked workers to consider whether those who worked in the so-called profit-sharing industries could go on strike 'or are they only permitted to be the humble servants of their masters?' Marx had in mind that the results could be presented as *cahiers du travail* like the *cahiers de doléances* of the French Revolution, and would form an agitational basis for 'preparing a reconstruction of society'. In point of fact, there were so few returns to the 25,000 questionnaires sent out that they were not worth analysing.

Those who did interview the poor directly were usually frankly disbelieved. Mayhew's claims that a vast majority of London's needlewomen and journeyman tailors subsisted on twopence halfpenny per day was rejected by *The Economist* as 'entirely false and irreconcileable with known, recorded and public facts, being based on the statements of the poor themselves whose "utter untrustworthiness" was well known' (Thompson 1973: 43). In one *official* attempt in the 1880s, to collect information about wages and rents from over 25,000 men in one area of London, the investigators tried out the bold initiative of asking the men directly to supply the information by handing them a questionnaire which they had to fill in. The results were published, but William Ogle, the then superintendent of statistics at the General Register Office virtually dismissed them in his introduction to the report:

> after devoting much time and labour to a careful examination of the returns, and after informing myself fully as to the conditions under which the data were collected, I have come to the conclusion that these returns are of small statistical value. (Board of Trade 1888)

Respondents

Although we saw examples of respondent interviewing in the nineteenth century, it did not become the predominant method until quite a profound change had occurred in the practice and ideology of the state. The Victorians agreed that the social conditions were pathological, but not that they were curable. Once a consensus was established about the need for the state to intervene to modify, to some extent, the otherwise too brutal hand of the market, the stage was set for a partnership between the state and the social researcher which has been a predominant feature of British survey research. To quote Mark Abrams' introduction to social surveys of 1951:

> Occasionally surveys originate in an abstract desire for more knowledge about the structure and workings of a society; more frequently, however, they are carried out as an indispensable first step in measuring the dimensions of a social problem, ascertaining its causes, and then deciding upon remedial action . . . Most surveys have been concerned with curing obviously pathological social conditions.

In order to understand the political milieu of social research, it is important to have an understanding of the forces shaping the foundations of the welfare state and its subsequent development. The early history of the welfare state is sometimes written as a development of the sensitivity and humanity of a benevolent government. A counter-view which has been more popular recently portrays it as a series of attempts at social control by a wicked bureaucracy. It is probably best understood as the result of an interaction between popular demands for forms of social insurance and the state's adaptation to these pressures to suit its own needs as well as possible. The decisive factor was the formation of an organised labour movement capable of formulating demands, and eventually capable of sustaining a powerful enough struggle to achieve them. In the previous section, four obstacles were identified to the development of respondent interviewing: suspicion by the working class of the social researchers, a reciprocal distrust of the working class by the researchers, difficulty of contacting the working class and lack of developed sampling methods. It was the enhanced strength and respectability of the labour movement which removed three of these four. The early responses of the labour movement, often primitive and violent but appropriate to a period in which the working class was having to fight for its survival, gradually gave way to more organised and peaceful forms of struggle. This is a process that has been interpreted in many different ways, from conspiratorial theories of incorporation to comfortable assertions about the inevitability of gradualism. Whatever the truth is, one effect was clearly a declining distrust of the state apparatus. The growth of literacy perhaps also helps to explain the ebbing of the more violently expressed suspicion of the educated.

Furthermore, people were not working such long hours. The turn of the century seems also to have been the nadir of female participation in the labour market; most married women were at home and therefore available to the survey investigator. Valuable wages were not lost by the imparting of information (although one still suspects that valuable time and even more valuable patience may have been lost by the visitations of the solicitous middle class investigators!).

The same forces which shaped a new political approach to the problems of chronic illness, unemployment and old age, an approach which did not directly blame the victims for their own conditions, was reflected in a new respect for the subjects of research, and led to the acceptance that they should be approached directly. The respondents to social enquiries were no longer treated as 'objects' to be studied in a social laboratory, but rather as 'subjects'. They were respected as human beings, but were still at the powerless end of the relationship between researcher and researched: the researcher asked the questions, the respondent provided the answers.

This shift in practice marked one of the most significant changes in the history of social research. Great improvements were made possible in the factual accuracy of the data collected; we know today how unreliable proxy information provided by one individual about another can be (Martin and Butcher 1981). Every intervening buffer between the researcher and his or her question, and the subject who can provide an anwer to that question, increases the possibility not just of random error but also of bias. Respondent interviewing also greatly increased the scope for the investigation of the subjective; subjectivity is irreducibly individual, so, if one is interested in beliefs, attitudes and value, one must ascertain them directly from the individuals concerned.

One of the most important figures in the transition from informant to respondent interviewing was Seebohm Rowntree, a wealthy industrialist, who, in the course of his lifetime, conducted three surveys into poverty in a 'typical' English town, York, in 1899, 1936 and 1950. His family, Quaker philanthropists, had made their money in the cocoa and confectionery trade, and York was a major centre of the chocolate industry. Booth and Rowntree are frequently spoken of in the same breath, as though their enquiries were very comparable. In fact, Rowntree's was born of a different spirit of enquiry altogether, organised by an individual who promoted working class housing projects, and later became a champion of the welfare state. Methodologically also it was an advance on Booth's; it set the stage for survey investigators obtaining information directly from the families they studied by using interviewers and structured schedules.

Rowntree points out that the method of using informants was not open to him, since there were not sufficient voluntary workers, district visitors and clergy to perform that function. He discovered that the respondents were willing to supply the information; the checking of statements by neighbours and others convinced him that the information obtained was substantially correct. Even wage information was solicited directly in the 1901 study, although only when the respondent's wages could not be inferred directly from his occupation. (In the second survey in 1936, Rowntree reverted to using informants on wages, claiming that the information culled from respondents on this topic was unreliable. Detailed methodological investigations conducted for post-war expenditure surveys have not vindicated this view.)

Once the tradition of direct interviewing was established, other important methodological breakthroughs were made possible and necessary. The use of standard question-wording and standard definitions became vital. Because Rowntree's interviewers approached the poor directly, he could not rely upon shared middle-class assumptions about what constituted poverty, and so was forced to define it clearly for the first time. He tried to give a physiologically-based definition, spelling out how many calories were required in a meagre subsistence diet, and then calculating the sum necessary to buy it. He defined 'primary poverty' as a situation in which the family did not have enough income to meet this standard, and 'secondary poverty' as the situation where money was being diverted to strictly inessential items like drink or furniture. He was probably the first to combine Le Play's method of collecting detailed family budgets with systematic interviewing of a cross-section of people. His findings agreed strikingly with Booth's, but where Booth had suggested vaguely that casual labour was associated with poverty, Rowntree pinpointed the effects of family circumstances; the understanding that every family, not just the feckless and undeserving, was at risk of severe deprivation at critical stages of the life cycle was a much more humane and productive view of poverty, for it pointed the way to effective intervention.

The move to respondent interviewing, pioneered by Rowntree, was consolidated by Arthur Bowley, perhaps the single most important figure in the development of survey methodology. He was responsible for a much more rigorous attitude towards the precise questions to be asked, the definition of the unit under investigation and qualities sought of these units. *The Measurement of Social Phenomena* (1915) was ahead of its time in an effort to standardise definitions of such things as income, poverty, household and other commonly used terms. The need for such standardisation still plagues survey research, and several international organisations have tried to lay down standards in the way that Bowley did in order to ensure compatibility across time and across nations.

But Bowley is more commonly remembered for his development of a practical sampling scheme for selecting respondents, which removed the final block to acceptance of the idea that they should be interviewed directly; in his famous Five Towns study (Bowley and Burnett-Hurst 1915), a random sample of households was selected from a list stratified by areas. The early social researchers often saw their job as filling in the cracks of knowledge in a general intellectual division of labour. This meant that when they did an investigation, the idea of considering only one in ten households was as unthinkable as it would have been for a cartographer to map one square in ten on his grid.

One rationale behind Booth's use of wholesale interviewing was that it enabled him to cover a much wider area with his enquiry; his expert informants provided the information already aggregated and thus solved what would otherwise have been a tremendous problem of volume. Random sampling provided a much more secure solution. It took a very long time to become accepted; Rowntree, for example, did not use it in his 1936 enquiry, and was only persuaded of its value for the 1950 survey by empirically taking 10% samples from the 1936 schedules and confirming that the estimates obtained from these samples were accurate predictors of the statistics in the whole enquiry.

For the most part, the shift from informant to respondent interviewing occurred in the early twentieth century. But there is one important exception. One major source of social statistics, the Census of Population, had, before the middle of the nineteenth century, turned to self-completion questionnaires as the way to collect the vast quantity of information required. In order to understand why the census was such an early exception to the more general pattern, it is instructive to look at the reasons for the shift to householder schedules in the 1841 census.

The first four censuses in 1801, 1811, 1821 and 1831 were mainly conducted by the overseers of the poor, whose suitability for the job was doubted both by opponents of the census and also eventually by its organisers (Drake 1972:11). The enumerators had to report upon the total number of males and females, and the numbers engaged in agriculture, trade, manufacturing or handicraft in their parish. Precisely how they set about collecting that information is not clear, for all they had to present was the aggregated result of their enquiries. In some areas the census took days to complete, resulting in much error and double-counting, and there was reason to believe that some cheating occurred: it had been possible under this system for an enumerator 'to sit at home and make *marks* and no examiner could detect his errors' (History of the Census of 1841: 5). The overseers of the poor were used as suitable informants in these early enquiries because they were 'officially cognizant of every individual and the number of children of every individual, who from poverty and consequent obscurity may be supposed often to escape particular notice in other nations' (Drake 1972: 24). In the 1841 census, the organisation of census-taking was made the responsibility of the new local registrars, and they had to recruit and train suitable local enumerators.

The decision to use householder schedules and to restrict the task of the enumerators to transcribing the information was taken late in the day. Lister, the first Registrar-General, was originally opposed to the idea, 'for the majority probably would either not fill them up or would fill them up wrong' (History of the Census of 1841: 6). The Population Act of 1840 made no provision for householder schedules. When Thomas Mann took control of the plans for the census, however, he was determined that it should only take one day to complete; he organised some piloting to see how much one enumerator could do in a day, and how many enumerators each District could provide. The results are reported without comment in the History of the Census of 1841 (p. 17), but they must have made Mann realise that in around one quarter of Districts there would not be sufficient enumerators to do the job if they had to question every household directly. An effort was made to entice more enumerators by raising the fees to be paid to them, but, eventually, the practical arguments in favour of printing individual household schedules for self-completion became overwhelming. A second Amendment Act was put before the House which introduced the individual schedules, and made it compulsory for household heads to complete them.

The 1841 census was thus the first modern census, and no-one has tried to change the methods employed in subsequent censuses. The reason for this early recourse to respondents was the practical problem associated with surveying an entire population at one point in time; just as with Rowntree's survey in York in 1899, an insufficient number of informants pushed the researchers towards the respondent mode. It is hardly surprising that this breakdown occurred first of all in an enterprise on as large a scale as the census.

Citizens

Since the Second World War, there are signs that a further change in the relationship between researcher and researched is beginning to take place. While it is always much more difficult to see the important contours of the landscape immediately surrounding one, there is evidence to suggest that we are moving towards a new conception of the subject as a citizen. The subjects of research are increasingly accorded equality of status, and with it a *right* to speak, to have their views heeded. The apparatus of social research is used not just for the collection of intelligence but increasingly as part of a process of public consultation. On occasion, social investigation is treated as tantamount to a petition or a referendum on some topic, and survey results are presented as if they were the result of a due process of democracy, as the voice of the citizenry.

It is hard to determine whether this shift is comparable to the move from informant to respondent interviewing. It could be argued that it is just a change of emphasis in the way in which respondents are treated rather than a replacement of that status. There is reason, however, to believe that something more profound may be at work. The argument in the previous section was that the form of the relationship between researcher and researched was conditioned both by the practice and ideology of the state and by the technical apparatus available for the conduct of research. Large changes in both since World War Two can be documented.

No-one can deny that the post-war welfare state has brought with it a change in the practice and ideology of the state, especially in the concept of citizenship. Marshall traced the development of an equality of status among all citizens through three phases, the early establishment of civic rights, through to the formal establishment of political rights, and, in the twentieth century, to the consolidation of citizenship through the establishment of qualitative social rights (Marshall 1950). The 'citoyens' of the nineteenth century, whose putative rights Marxists have traditionally contrasted with the *de facto* powers of the 'bourgeois', have since the Second World War established tangible rights to income, housing, health care, legal aid and so on. With the hindsight afforded by the spectacle of industrial decline and attempts to reduce the scope of the welfare state we may now question Marshall's confident statement that the development of citizenship was independent of, and cut across the boundaries of, social class, but nevertheless he was clearly documenting a very real social process whose effects have permeated society at all levels.

There have also been major changes in the technology of social research which have mainly stemmed from the general decrease in cost and increase in access to respondents, and the speed and reliability of collecting information. Furthermore, changes are occurring so rapidly that we cannot yet know their full effect. The spread of automated data processing, the telephone, cable television, computer-assisted interviewing and automatic character recognition is transforming the practice of social research. The increase in the speed with which research can be conducted means that the pronouncement of public opinion on a current issue of concern can be virtually instantaneous. The decrease in the cost means that access to social research could become wider.

These changes, both ideological and technical, have also altered the meaning of many important political concepts. The idea of public opinion, which to conservatives like Burke, de Tocqueville or Bryce meant the opinions of '. . . a body of men [sic] . . . agreed on the ends and aims of government and upon the principles by which those ends shall be attained' (Lowell 1913 cited in Nisbet 1975: 185), now involves a much more democratic conception of the views of all members of society. Furthermore, it is now social researchers who are held to have access to that public opinion: 'Public opinion, whatever that phrase once meant, now is taken by most people most of the time to mean poll findings' (Gollin 1980).

The subject matter of surveys has become increasingly evaluative. The modern survey textbooks no longer declare, like those of the 1930s and 40s (e.g. Jones 1948), that their subject matter is rigidly factual; all the modern survey textbooks have chapters devoted to attitude measurement and scale construction. Local authorities and other public bodies increasingly conduct surveys as part of a process of public consultation, to help decide where to site a bus station, what facilities are needed in a city centre and so on. There is, on average, at least one poll report cited in every edition of a national or local newspaper in the UK and the USA. (This estimate is made from a clipping study conducted for the US National Academy of Sciences Panel of Survey Based Measures of Political Phenomena; see Turner and Martin (forthcoming), appendix 2B.) Gallup, Market & Opinion Research International and NOP Market Research in Britain do monthly polls in which they assess how well people think government is doing, what they think of the Prime Minister, the Leader of the Opposition, and so on. The European Commission runs a regular series of 'Eurobarometer' surveys which are solely concerned with how the citizenry of Europe evaluates various aspects of its life. The Organisation of Economic Cooperation and Development has a social indicators program which includes some subjective measures (although not as many as originally intended, after a strong protest from the Swedes that this was not a suitable subject matter for governments to investigate). The suggestion has even been made in *Social Trends* that the government should conduct regular surveys of the subjective well-being of the nation in order to calculate the evaluative equivalent of the gross national product, to calculate individual utilities directly.

It is hard to decide how enthusiastic to be about these developments. One thing, however, is clear. We should not view the information explosion simply through Orwellian spectacles, for there is no way that Big Brother will manage to retain centralised control over the processing of legitimate information. Opinion polling is clearly not exhaustive of the new developments in survey investigation; it probably represents the tip of the iceberg of all social and market research. But we can estimate that it accounts for over 90% of the surveys which enter the public domain via the mass media; it has become the public face of the survey industry, and it is the one area of social research that everyone in society is familiar with. For this reason, we may expect its populist rhetoric to become associated more generally with survey research.

However, there are strong reasons for distrusting the idea that opinion polling, at least as currently practised, could provide a major fillip to democracy. The enthusiasm of the opinion pollsters for their role as champions of the common people, and the predilection of the mass media for presenting opinion polls as if they were part of the political process – referring to results as 'votes' or even 'mandates', for example – are rather misplaced. The line between true democracy and populism is of course hard to draw, democracy being an 'essentially contested concept', but there are several aspects to the way in which opinion polling is currently practised that lead to the conclusion that much of it is better placed on the populist side of the divide.

What, briefly, are the reasons for saying this? The argument is not that it is intrinsically manipulative or coercive to discover directly from individuals how they evaluate different aspects of their life, their views on government policy, their individual preferences, beliefs, values. The argument relates to the particular form that this research takes at the moment, the actual relationships that are involved between people as opposed to the ideal ones. The arguments boil down to four.

In the first place, opinion polling still continues the tradition, noted at the outset, of social research being done by those with power and resources sufficient to buy research expertise. The majority of polls are sponsored by the national mass media, who find that telling their consumers what the average person thinks is almost as good copy as telling them their individual horoscope. But a large minority of the published polls are done by a variety of partisan organisations who often present the results of their surveys as a sort of scientific petition; examples range from lobbying groups concerned with abortion to organisations advocating Sunday-trading, employers' associations and so on. Some organisations are brought into being specifically to sponsor this type of research. The Committee for Research into Public Attitudes, a grouping of industrialists, surveys attitudes to wage increases and public expenditure (Marsh 1982); the Institute of Atlantic Affairs, based in Paris and funded by a large number of different national newspapers and other organisations, monitors attitudes of Europeans to NATO and other defence matters (*International Herald Tribune*, 25 October 1982). Social research is becoming much cheaper in relative terms now (although still beyond the reach of many), but old patterns linger after real changes have taken place in the cost of doing research.

Secondly, the current sponsorship of polls is probably responsible for the selectivity in terms of the subject matters chosen to be polled about. Figure 1 shows the results of a clipping study conducted into published poll reports in August 1980.

The preponderance of trade union and pay-related issues among the subject matter put before the public is striking. One reason for the particularly heavy emphasis during August was the coming Trades Union Congress;

Figure 1. *Broad subject matter of polls*

Unions and pay increases	43.0
Other economic	7.1
Election	14.7
Political (other than election)	17.1
Other social	5.9
Other non-social	12.3

Notes
1. Taken from 31 July to 11 September 1980
2. Total number of clippings on which the estimates are based is 168.
3. Percentages are weighted by the circulation of the newspaper in which they appeared.
4. For full documentation of procedures and results, see Turner and Martin (forthcoming), chapter 2 and Appendix 2B.

indeed, many of the cuttings made explicit reference to this, most pointing out to the trade union leaders that if they did not endorse pay restraint they would be acting undemocratically, since the majority of trade unionists, they claimed, were in favour of restraint. However, it is doubtful that this concentration of items is restricted to this pre-Congress period.

One is justified in calling this a bias in the selection of issues. There was a time when the public did think that the trade unions and their pay demands were one of the most important problems facing the country, but this has not been true in recent years. In August 1980, 53% in fact named unemployment and 25% named the cost of living as the most important problems; only 4% gave replies which were coded as 'other economic' and could have included trade unions and pay increases (*Gallup Political Index*, September 1980). The newspapers, and others with the money to buy this kind of research, however, have managed to create the impression, through publishing polls on the subject, that public opinion is as strong and vociferous as ever on the subject. There is nothing very democratic about claiming that you speak for the citizenry when there is no serious way in which the citizenry can place items on the political agenda. Unemployment has been by far the biggest concern to the public recently, but there have only been a handful of polls on the topic.

Thirdly, the pressure of the mass media for good copy, for punchy headlines, encourages the boiling down of political issues to one single question, the answers to which are then presented as 'public opinion' with no further qualification. The trouble is that most political issues are complex, and most people's views of them are equally complex. Single questions may appear to boil an issue down to one simple stimulus, but we know from split-ballot trials that many seemingly innocent words carry a stimulus all of their own: 'not allowing' is different from 'forbidding'; 'leaving' the Common Market is different from 'not staying in' the Common Market, and so on.

The technical solution to the problem is to combine answers to several different kinds of question so that the stimulus associated with the wording of individual items can be filtered out, leaving only the common element. While the subject of how index construction and scaling should be performed is still hotly debated in academic circles, there is agreement that reliance on single items is very dangerous. Yet the press can rarely be persuaded to report upon more complex scaling exercises, and so these are rarely performed in opinion polls.

The political solution to the potential problem of bias in the way that issues are reduced to simple questions is to reply to opinion polls with further opinion polls, perhaps with a different bias. One good example of this concerns a survey done on the 'new right' in American politics by the CBS News – New York Times Poll (see Turner and Martin (forthcoming) for full details), which alleged that conservatives were moving to the left, on the basis of a series of questions about what federal government should be expected to provide. The North American Newspaper Alliance was worried about the way the issues were presented, so it commissioned another poll in which it presented the same questions substituting 'private enterprise' for 'federal government'. The exercise served to demonstrate that people had not been focusing on the *agency* which might be expected to provide medical care, jobs or housing, but had been simply agreeing that somebody should do so: the percentages endorsing both forms of the question were very similar.

Since the search for genuinely unbiased forms of question-wording is probably misplaced, and our understanding of the technical difficulties associated with artefact in question-wording still so meagre, this poll and counter-poll approach is to be applauded. It is sadly a very rare occurrence. The response of the trade union movement, for example, to the barrage of anti-trade union polls of recent years has been the growing conviction that there is something ideologically unsound about polling, rather than a determination to join battle.

Finally, those with the money to buy this kind of research not only get to choose the subject matter to poll about and get away with asking potentially tendentious questions which they can present as 'public opinion', but they have the final trump card in being able to decide whether or not to publish the results. Holmberg (1980) has shown, in a disturbing systematic study of four major Swedish newspapers, that the likelihood of a poll result showing a swing towards one party being reported in a newspaper was strongly correlated with the political allegiance of the newspaper. No similar systematic study has been undertaken in Britain, but examples of selective reporting in advocacy polls sponsored by a pressure group can be documented when the results of the entire survey performed can be obtained.

One small example of selectivity in reporting can be shown in an opinion poll sponsored by the National Water Council and conducted by Market & Opinion Research International during a strike by water workers in early 1983. The example will also allow some illustration of the previous arguments as well. The reason for this choice of example is simply that it is reasonably typical of this style of polling, and it happens to be current at time of writing; for other examples, see Marsh 1982, chapter 6.

Tom King, Secretary of State for the Environment, is reputed to have rebuked Sir William Dugdale, the Chairman of the National Water Council on Thursday 27 January for losing the propaganda battle with the unions. Later that day, Dugdale commissioned MORI to do a survey of public attitudes to the dispute (although he denies that the two events were connected). The details were worked out with MORI on Friday, on Saturday the interviewers went into the field, on Monday the results were presented to the NWC and on Tuesday they issued a press release, carried by the national media later that day and on Wednesday, which was reported under such headlines as 'Public say: Take water pay offer' (*Daily Mail*). The poll cost £7,500.

Public perception of the cost of meeting the water workers' claim (estimated to be around 3p per household per week) and the general run down of finance for the water industry were not investigated. The poll asked questions about perception of the seriousness of the dispute, the extent of personal inconvenience, the steps people were taking to save water and public perception of the NWC's advertising campaign. However, the questions which attracted the heaviest media coverage were the public's knowledge of the NWC's offer and their views on whether, how and when the water workers should accept it.

The sponsors have the power simply not to include some of the questions in their press release. In answer to an open-ended question in this poll, over 60% of the public demonstrated that they knew the amount of the offer, but over 90% of them did not mention, and may not have known, the fact that this was spread over sixteen months. The press release did not report this second finding, and claimed that awareness of the latest pay offer was high. This criticism of the press release does not invalidate the result of the question about whether the water workers should accept the offer, for the interviewer was instructed to tell everyone the full details before sounding opinion on whether the offer should be accepted. It simply illustrates that there are many gatekeepers guarding the route between information sources and destinations, and many of them are not disinterested parties to the information they are processing.

It may appear contradictory to characterise the most recent developments as a move towards treating the subjects of research as *citizens* of equal status, and then to proceed to argue that power and resources to commission polls on particular topics, to decide how the issue should be presented and whether the results should be made public are all very unequally distributed in society; the fact that the results of this process can then be presented as the *vox populi* could be seen as a further enhancement of the power of those commissioning the poll. Some may explain the paradox by seeing as sham many of the other developments of modern citizenship, of the various push-button 'rights' now being thrust upon us.

I remain convinced, however, that the recent developments in information processing will, in time, make possible a very much more profound change in our capacity to understand and communicate with one another, which is what social research has always been about; opinion polling, rather than being paradigmatic of the new research mode, may in retrospect seem to be a rather quaint early response to the information revolution. The idea of institutions and groups in society using social research as a way of coming to a more objective view of themselves and their members has been around for a long time, but the community self-survey of the 1930s is now becoming a more practical possibility. One very good example of this is the effort being made by the Centre for Educational Sociology at the University of Edinburgh to train anyone who wants to to gain access to and to analyse their databank on features of Scottish schools.

Only when a broader section of society can have a say in research agendas, can have access to the apparatus of social research and can have some control over the means of information dissemination will the subjects of research really be accorded citizenship status. The technology is making this increasingly possible. The right to private ownership of and control over social information of this kind, however, conflicts with the citizen conception of the researched. For a real democratisation of social research to occur, there will have to be changes not just in the status of the researched, but also in the right to be the researcher.

REFERENCES

Abrams, M. (1951) *Social Surveys and Social Action*. London: Heinemann.
Abrams, P. (1968) *The Origins of British Sociology: 1834–1914*. London: University of Chicago Press.
Barnes, J.A. (1979) *Who Should Know What*. Harmondsworth: Penguin.

Becker, H. S. (1967) 'Whose side are we on?', *Social Problems* 14: 239–47.
Board of Trade (1888) *Statements of Men Living in Certain Selected Districts of London in March 1887*.
Booth, C. (1892) *Life and Labour of the People of London*, Vol. I: *East, Central and South London*, London: Macmillan.
Bowley, A. L. (1915) *The Nature and Purpose of the Measurement of Social Phenomena*, London: King.
Bowley, A. L. and Burnett-Hurst, A. (1915) *Livelihood and Poverty*, London: Bell.
Bradburn, N. M., Sudman, S. and Associates (1976) *Improving Interview Method and Questionnaire Design: Response Effects to Threatening Questions in Survey Research*, San Francisco: Jossey-Bass.
Corrigan, P. (1977) 'State Formation and Moral Regulation in Nineteenth Century Britain', PhD thesis, University of Durham.
Cullen, M. (1975) *The Statistical Movement in Early Victorian Britain*, Hassocks, Sussex: Harvester Press
Drake, M. (1972) 'The Census 1801–1891' in E. A. Wrigley (ed.), *Nineteenth Century Society*, Cambridge University Press.
Engels, F. (1844; 1969) *The Condition of the Working Class in England*, London: Panther.
Finer, S. E. (1952) *The Life and Times of Sir Edwin Chadwick*, London: Methuen.
Gollin, A. (1980) Editorial, *Public Opinion Quarterly* 44 (4).
Hennock, E. P. (1976) 'Poverty and social theory in England: the experience of the eighteen-eighties', *Social History* 1, January: 67–91.
History of the Census of 1841, manuscript in the library of the Office of Population Censuses and Surveys, London.
Holmberg, S. (1980) 'The breakthrough of opinion polls on the editorial pages of Swedish newspapers', paper presented at the 58th European Society for Opinion and Marketing Research (ESOMAR) seminar on opinion polls at Bonn, 23–26 January.
Jahoda, M., Lazarsfeld, P. F. and Zeisel, H. (1972) *Marienthal: the Sociography of an Unemployed Community*, London: Tavistock Publications (first published 1933).
Johnson, R. (1977) 'Elementary education: the education of the poorer classes' in G. Sutherland (ed.), *Education: Government and Society in Nineteenth Century Britain*, Dublin: Irish University Press.
Jones, D. C. (1948) *Social Surveys*, London: Hutchinson.
Lyell, K. ed. (1890) *Memoirs of Leonard Horner*, Vol. II, London: Women's Printing Society Ltd.
Marsh, C. (1982) *The Survey Method*, London: Allen & Unwin.
Marshall, T. H. (1950) 'Citizenship and social class' in *Citizenship and Social Class*, Cambridge University Press.
Martin, J. and Butcher, B. (1981) 'The quality of proxy information – the results of a large scale study'. *OPCS Survey Methodology Bulletin*, 12, April.
Marx, K. (1886; 1970) *Capital; a Critique of Political Economy*, Vol. I, London: Lawrence and Wishart 1970.
Nisbet, R.A. (1975) 'Public opinion versus popular opinion', *Public Interest* 41, Fall: 166–92.

Nisbett, R. E. and Wilson, T. D. (1977) 'Telling more than we can know: verbal reports on mental processes', *Psychological Review*, 84 (3): 231–59.
Richards, P. (1979) 'The state and early industrial capitalism: the case of the handloom weavers', *Past and Present*, 83, May: 91–115.
Rowntree, B. S. (1901) *Poverty; a Study of Town Life*, London: Longmans.
Rowntree, B. S. (1941) *Poverty and Progress; a Second Social Survey of York*, London: Longmans.
Rowntree, B. S. and Lavers, G. R. (1951) *Poverty and the Welfare State*, London: Longmans.
Teer, F. and Spence, J. D. (1973) *Political Opinion Polls*, London: Hutchinson University Library.
Thompson, E. P. (1973) 'Mayhew and *The Morning Chronicle*' in E. P. Thompson and E. Yeo, *The Unknown Mayhew*, Harmondsworth: Penguin.
Turner, C. F. and Martin, E., eds. (forthcoming) *Survey Measurement of Subjective Phenomena*, New York: Russell Sage Foundation.
Webb, B. (1926; 1972) *My Apprenticeship*, Harmondsworth: Penguin 1972.
Webb, B. and Webb, S. (1932; 1975) *Methods of Social Study*, Cambridge University Press.
Webb, N. (1980) 'The democracy of opinion polls', paper presented to the 58th European Society for Opinion and Marketing Research (ESOMAR) seminar on opinion polls at Bonn, 23–26 January.
Webb, R. K. (1955) 'A Whig inspector', *Journal of Modern History*, XXVII: 352–64.
Weiss, H. (1936) 'Die "Enquête Ouvrière" von Karl Marx', *Zeitschrift für Sozialforschung*, Vol. 1: 76–98.
Welbourne, E. (1923) *The Miners' Unions of Northumberland and Durham*, Cambridge University Press.

13 Surveys of poverty to promote democracy

PETER TOWNSEND

My intention is to reflect critically about the limitations and potentialities of social surveys. It is a supreme irony that in the months following the choice of theme for the York Symposium on which this book is based, the present British Government decided to cut its statistical services by 25 per cent and has threatened to cut resources devoted to surveys by approximately 40 per cent (Sir Derek Rayner, 1981; *Government Statistical Services,* 1981; Hoinville and Smith, 1982). Part of this chapter will be concerned with explaining, indirectly as well as directly, why this should have happened. The social survey is not only a technological instrument of service to the administration of the modern state: it symbolises forms of power, and it embodies and not only represents necessarily partial values drawn from the historical development of the culture of this country and other countries. On attaining office some political administrations therefore find that the routine compilation and publication of the reports of surveys is embarrassing if not objectionable and steps may be taken to restrict them or control their scope more carefully. This I will endeavour to explain, followed by a discussion of some of the more general functions of social surveys and going on to illustrate certain possibilities from my own work on poverty.

The history and general characteristics of social surveys have been carefully summarised in other chapters by Marsh, Whitehead, Kent and Hakim. They have been the subjects of a growing literature (see, for example, Moser and Kalton, 1971; Leggatt, 1974; Bell and Newby, 1977; Bulmer, 1977; Hoinville and Jowell, 1978). But we have to explain the forms taken by surveys and the functions which they serve, and that will bring a better understanding of their limitations and the part they can be expected to play in national life.

The social influences which define surveys are strong. They are brought to bear upon the initiators or organisers of surveys as well as upon members of the public who participate in them. There are currents of opinion among professional social scientists both about subjects which lend themselves to the survey method and the merits of that method. It is believed, sometimes on spurious grounds, that certain subjects, like the distribution of wealth (Royal Commission on the Distribution of Income and Wealth, 1979; Knight, 1980), do not lend themselves to the survey method. Again, at the present time the survey method has become rather unfashionable among some groups of sociologists. In the words of one group of writers the 'conventional' survey 'typically counterposes expert enquirers against isolated, passive informants' (Griffiths, Irvine and Miles, 1979, p. 373). And a sympathetic specialist in research methodology recognises that the survey method is 'more applicable downwards than upwards, and for that reason better as an instrument of control of underdogs than of topdogs' (Galtung, 1967). The sociologists are fearful of being trapped into time-consuming exercises which they consider may produce merely descriptive statistics which happen to conform with conventional views about the structure and nature of society.

The influence of the professions

Some of the elements to which they are objecting deserve to be isolated. First, there is an excessive professional influence. Social scientists who administer surveys belong to professions which contribute to the definition of the scope and nature of those surveys. What is professionally respectable is not always wholly rational or scientific. Certain subjects may be avoided because they are politically contentious, and others because they are insufficiently categorised by discipline. The general values of professions tend to be adopted in developing social survey techniques. I mean that professions tend to assume heavy-handed and sweeping responsibility for the job in hand, which involves adopting rather cavalier attitudes towards consultation, communication and accountability. Terminology and techniques may be chosen less on their merits than on grounds of professional acceptability. There is an ambivalence between imperious practice of a professional role and the supposition of service for the public good, which deserves a lot more examination and analysis. On the one hand, survey professionals exercise extraordinary power. On the other hand, they acquiesce in the restriction by their political and managerial masters of the roles they play. They believe they are scientists who influence neither administration nor policy. But this abrogation of independence can too easily become a kind of subservience to the status quo. Survey professionals see their roles not so much in terms of rigorously independent work which brings out the real causes and nature of economic and social conditions for purposes, if necessary, of reorganising the whole basis of society, as slotting into a hierarchy of occupations managed by others and helping to smooth out some of the rougher consequences of existing structures.

A more critical literature of professionalism has been developed in recent years, particularly of professions like medicine, teaching and law (Friedson, 1970; Johnson, 1972; Illich, 1977; Larson, 1977; Abel, 1979; Parry, 1979; Wilding, 1981). This begins to allow the survey 'tradition' to be re-interpreted in terms of the likely biases and conventional assumptions of the practitioners.

The influence of the funding agency

Secondly, there is the excessive influence of the commissioning or funding agency. Surveys could be carried out in earlier days by wealthy philanthropists, partly because they could be done relatively more cheaply than today but partly because different forms of the sponsorship of social research had not yet been institutionalised. Today surveys are primarily funded directly or indirectly by government, through central departments, and the research councils, and by major foundations and Trusts, such as the Joseph Rowntree Memorial Trust, the Nuffield Foundation, and the Leverhulme Trust. Little attempt has been made to assemble information about the structure and trends in funding of survey research. From both scientific and democratic standpoints, however, at least two major problems can be identified. One is that a great deal hangs on the predispositions and composition of funding bodies. It is difficult for funding bodies within government or dependent upon government to act contrary to government interests and values. They are bound to be sensitive not just to the main thrust of Government policies, but also to the kind of issues and of people governments are likely to support.

It is, of course, difficult to assess the full consequences of such bias. A simple examination of all applications for grants in relation to the decisions reached would tell something, but not enough. Many of those likely to apply for research grants will not go ahead if they know their chances are minimal. Many who believe their first choice of research topic cannot attract financial support will resort to a second or third choice.

For such reasons bias in research funding is unlikely to be properly exposed. What can be said is that only a small minority of those taking the financial decision on applications will be professionally equipped to assess them. While it is true that predominantly unspecialist funding committees will often obtain professional opinions on applications upon which they will to some extent base their decisions, the choice of people to give those opinions can be unreasonably selective. The network of membership of research councils, and departmental research grant committees – such as the Research Liaison Groups of the DHSS – are represented among the ruling elites of the 'State' or the 'Establishment' and the extent to which they are in harmony with comparable commercial bodies is a matter of controversy. Companies commission market research and opinion polls and thereby influence the scope and subject-matter of surveys and hence the kind of supplementary tasks, or questions, that can be fitted into the programme for academic purposes. The sociology of research funding is itself a neglected area of research. What has to be recognised is that the commissioning agency is a rather different element from the profession in defining the history and present functions of the social survey.

The influence of the bureaucracy

Thirdly, there is the organisational or bureaucratic influence and this too can distort the scope and nature of the survey. Here we have to examine modes of organisations within which surveys are administered. Few social scientists can attract the means to build up their own organisation even temporarily to administer a single survey in a small area, still less a variety of areas. Market organisations are predominant. In understanding what kind of surveys are carried out we have to understand the mixture of commercial and bureaucratic principles on which the procedures are based – for example, the standardisation of methods of interviewing to suit a particular corps of interviewers; the simplification of sampling; the concentration on housewives as respondents; and the pre-coding of questions. Sweeping assumptions are made about the uniformities of information and culture and the homogeneity or limited range of styles of living, family type and everything else. In some important respects the survey is what the organisation has been modelled to undertake and there are severe limits on its flexibility to accommodate differing management demands.

Academic social scientists often find that commercial research organisations just cannot cope with sample surveys of certain minorities in the population, or questions on sensitive or complex subjects, or the production of data for analytic purposes. With one or two exceptions these research organisations cannot match in range or quality the survey work of the Office of Population Censuses and Surveys – which has been developed on the basis of the work of the former Government Social Survey.

Nonetheless, within both Government and commercial survey organisations certain habits of thought and administrative programmes become engrained. Those in charge allow their objectives of a qualitative and technical as well as substantive kind to be governed by administrative or bureaucratic priorities. They forget the influence of hierarchical modes of control and routinised practice upon their direction of survey research. Cutting corners on cost, now enforced as well as generally approved by the Treasury, tends to take precedence over the reliable measurement of need. It is with dismay therefore that outside research workers sometimes regard government and commercial survey capacities. When exploring the possibilities of commissioning a survey or undertaking joint research they find the situation overlaid by organisational needs and constraints. Among other things the capacity to do original research is seized with bureaucratic constipation. I mean not just that there are procedural rigidities but a kind of corporate condescension about the terms under which an outsider, however reputable or skilled, will be tolerated.

The corporate threat to independent inquiry

A disturbing feature of the administrative concentration and control of surveys, therefore, is the growing difficulty of those who are not directly employed by Government or private companies to obtain access to this method of research on their own terms. In Britain there is an urgent need for an independent survey research centre and for radical social scientists to have an opportunity to administer their own surveys. In relation to current Government and UGC policy this possibility has receded even further into the distance. The most serious need is for opportunities for independent management of national social surveys. I was very fortunate to secure the support of the Joseph Rowntree Memorial Trust in the mid-1960s to carry out a national survey of poverty (Townsend, 1979). There was a historically unique combination of favourable factors. A Conservative Government had launched a large number of new universities. The social sciences, and particularly sociology, were expanding rapidly and were regarded as functional for the expansion of the national economy. The study of poverty was not yet regarded as a threat to governments of different political persuasion (cf. Banting, 1979). Indeed it has a very respectable history as an occasional occupation practised by a few capitalist entrepreneurs – albeit uncommon entrepreneurs. Seebohm Rowntree himself had studied poverty in 1899, 1936 and 1950 and there had been no large-scale study since his early post-war study.

It is not easy to see the circumstances in which a critical social scientist would be likely to be given the same opportunity to embark on a national survey of poverty in the 1980s. Yet the case for it is powerful. Unemployment is over three millions. The urban riots have called attention to worsening social and environmental conditions among large sections of the population. There are major problems of deprivation among children, ethnic minorities, disabled people and the elderly as well as the unemployed.

What is extraordinary is that the Government does not recognise the importance of fostering really independent national examination of the causes of our contemporary problems. Far from recognising the value of using independent research as a form of Government accountability and using the knowledge derived from that research to evolve the right set of policies, it has been cutting back university incomes, reducing research money for the social sciences, closing bodies such as the Centre for Environmental Studies and the Personal Social Services Council, cutting its own statistical and research capacity to review social conditions and generally seeking to bury its head, ostrich-like, in a desert of its own making.

We witnessed in 1981 the spectacle of a distinguished non-sociologist, Mr Michael Heseltine, conferred with the duties of a kind of roving commissioner of urban squalor, touring Liverpool to reach a verdict on the causes of the riots. He has sought neither to utilise specialised survey evidence nor to consult professional sociologists who have studied the relevant issues. The irony of this behaviour will not be lost on a future generation. Although the Government's management of the economy is heavily criticised, at least it bases its strategy on the prescriptions of professional gurus: there are economists in the Treasury and elsewhere and there is always Professor Milton Friedman on hand to stiffen the Chancellor of the Exchequer's resolve. Imagine Mr Heseltine being invited to make an individual study of the control of the money supply or the level of the pound against the dollar!

This example of concern about the 1981 riots helps to bring us back to the more positive features of social surveys and the expertise associated with them. They represent a potential bulwark of democracy. Once we understand the structural forces which can powerfully dominate or circumscribe the so-called survey tradition we can also appreciate how those elements might be offset or minimised in order that that tradition may increase in importance in relation to national life. The social survey represents an attempt to extend bases of comparison to geographically distant sections of the population, and to the propertyless as well as the propertied. That exercise necessarily poses questions about the variation in the human condition which requires convincing and rigorous explanation. The human condition is given a central place in our attention and therefore our scale of values. Individuals selected for interview are accorded approximately equal rights to representation in the aggregation and analysis of results. All of us must appreciate that this methodology cannot occupy the entire stage. There have to be scrupulous studies involving participant observation of social behaviour, inquiries into the structures and modes of control of governing institutions of a society, like state administration and giant corporations, and the unravelling of links or patterns of contact among families, communities and ruling elites. But in undertaking surveys a democratic value is being asserted. By choosing this means of investigating a problem and searching for an explanation for its existence, priority is being given, over organisations, political power and process, to the human situations and predicaments of a cross-section of the population.

The survey method applies the value of equality of respect in obtaining information about the functioning of society. That is why it can help to fulfil democratic values. There is the possibility of conditions, and attitudes, coming to light which have been neglected by elites. The richest and poorest participants in the survey are treated, in principle, as equals. Of course the survey can be used to manipulate and oppress. But it can also be used imaginatively to reveal the consequences of manipulation and oppression and the complexities of political and social problems.

This Government would be advised, especially in relation to unemployment, inner city deprivation and racial conflict, but primarily the more generalised problem of poverty which underlies these problems, to take a long, hard look at the desirability not of stultifying but of building upon the survey tradition. This will involve expansion of facilities for survey research and associated types of social research outside as well as inside Government. We need reasoned if not inspired management of our social as much as our economic problems. The social survey is one of those regulators of a modern democracy which we can ill afford to be without.

REFERENCES

Abel, R., 'The Rise of Professionalism', *British Journal of Law and Society*, June 1979.

Banting, K., *Poverty, Politics and Policy*, London: Macmillan, 1979.

Bell, C. and Newby, H. (eds.) *Doing Sociological Research*. London: Allen and Unwin, 1977.

Bulmer, M. (ed.) *Sociological Research Methods: An Introduction*. London: Macmillan, 1977.

Friedson, E., *Professional Dominance: The Social Structure of Medical Care*, New York. Atherton Press, 1970.

Galtung, J., *Theory and Methods of Social Research*, London: Allen and Unwin, 1967.

Government Statistical Services, Cmnd 8236, London: HMSO, 1981.

Griffiths, D., Irvine, J. and Miles, I., 'Social Statistics: Towards a Radical Science', in Irvine, J., Miles, I. and Evans, J., *Demystifying Social Statistics*, London: Pluto Press, 1979.

Hoinville, G., Jowell, R. *et al., Survey Research Practice*, London: Heinemann, 1978.
Hoinville, G. and Smith, T. M. F., 'The Rayner review of Government Statistical Services', *Journal of the Royal Statistical Society* 145(2) (1982): 195–207.
Illich, I., *Disabling Professions*, London: Boyars, 1977.
Johnson, T., *The Professions and Power*, London: Macmillan, 1972.
Knight, I., 'The Feasibility of Conducting a National Wealth Survey in Great Britain', London: OPCS, January 1980.
Larson, M. S., *The Rise of Professionalism: A Sociological Analysis*, Berkeley: University of California Press, 1977.
Leggatt, T. (ed.), *Sociological Theory and Survey Research: Institutional Change and Social Policy in Great Britain*, London: Sage, 1974.
Moser, C. A. and Kalton, G., *Survey Methods in Social Investigation*, London: Heinemann (2nd edition), 1971.
Myrdal, G., *Objectivity in Social Research*, London: Duckworth, 1970.
Parry, N. *et al., Social Work, Welfare and the State*, London: Arnold, 1979.
Royal Commission on the Distribution of Income and Wealth, Report No. 7, Cmnd 6999, London: HMSO, 1979.
Sir Derek Rayner's Report to the Prime Minister, London: Central Statistical Office, 1981.
Stouffer, S. A. *et al., The American Soldier* (4 vols.), Princeton University Press, 1949.
Townsend, P., *Poverty in the United Kingdom*, London: Allen Lane and Harmondsworth: Penguin Books, 1979.
Wilding, P., *Professional Power and Social Welfare*, London, Routledge and Kegan Paul, 1981.

14 Reading the palm of the invisible hand: indicators, progress and prediction

LORRAINE F. BARIĆ

Introduction

The nature of indicators is probably not a topic of overwhelming interest to the average citizen concerned with the many problems of modern industrial society, alarmed or exhilarated, as the case may be, by hazy visions of the future. Nevertheless, indicators play an increasingly influential part in shaping those visions, sometimes, as I shall argue, distorting them in not immediately obvious ways.

The ideas on which the arguments of this chapter are based arose as a result of exploring the form in which influential people – shapers of public opinion – put forward views in the mass media about the current status and future direction of society. Their utterances can be studied as texts exemplifying the rhetoric of persuasion, which involves types of 'clinching arguments' that vary according to time, place and context. Over recent years, the use of indicators has played a notable part in this rhetoric. Exploration of the aims and purposes of the users of indicators, and the way in which the indicators themselves channel thought and argument thus emerges as an important topic and one that the ordinary consumer of the mass media and the social researcher alike might consider more than a matter for specialists.

It is the aim here to examine the ramifications of just one aspect of the growth of the use of indicators. The main theme could be called the '*inertia*' of indicators. It appears to me that this *inertia*, which is the result of a number of processes, has far-reaching consequences and, in particular, affects the way ideas of progress are used in exhortation, persuasion and evaluation. It also affects the nature of prediction, by encouraging the unexamined extrapolation of the past into the future.

Looked at from this angle, indicators are seen as part of everyday language; they shape our socially constructed reality in the same way that the categories of language tend to do. A relevant aspect here is the quality of reification (Berger and Luckmann, 1967: 106), which shrouds the origins of institutionalised cultural inventions in mystery and eventually gives innovations the power of familiarity and inevitability.

Indicators of all sorts are likely to become more and more a matter of public concern. Research workers, short of resources to collect original data, may turn increasingly to other people's indicators and the statistics prepared as a by-product of administration, in order to make sense of society (Hakim, 1982: 170). Furthermore, governments everywhere are coming to be treated as huge management teams, to be evaluated in terms of indicators of their own or others' choosing. Sometimes the observer of political point-scoring might ask whether governments wish to improve the state of things or the status of the indicators: a case of improving the weather by fiddling the barometer. Whatever the case, indicators have a much greater impact on argument and image than is frequently recognised.

The nature of indicators

There has been a great deal written about the nature of indicators, their possible flaws, and the problems of using them (see, as samples, the classic collection edited by Bauer, 1966; influential studies by Mark Abrams, 1976, Shonfield and Shaw, 1972; and a thorough recent study by Carley, 1981). Yet, in sociology, it is hardly possible to do without social indicators. In the first year of their university courses, sociology students are likely to learn that we cannot trace the changes in any feature of society without using indicators, since the features of a society that interest us are often not directly available to our observation, and we require some form of correlate to allow us to talk about them. There is no special problem in the idea itself as far as students are concerned; they readily accept, for example, that if we are interested in the health status of some community, we might look at morbidity and mortality statistics.

Despite the large amount of work concerned with indicators (including the overlapping categories of economic, social, demographic, health and science indicators) the terminology has not really settled down. It is possible to find 'index' and 'indicator' used interchangeably, although there is a great deal to be said for restricting the term index to a composite constructed measure (see Zeisel, 1978: 253–4).

There is also some objection to the idea that statistics are in themselves indicators (see Moser, 1973, reprinted in Bulmer, 1978). I do not want to become embroiled in questions of definition. By 'indicator', I mean any feature of society that is apparently easy to identify, that reveals noticeable variations in its nature or magnitude over time, and that is supposed to be directly related, in a known way, to some feature that is of interest to us. Although some statistical series should, as Moser points out, be excluded, others, on this definition, qualify as indicators.

In recent years, some of the trenchant critiques of the use of indicators in the study of society have been associated with anti-positivist and anti-quantitative approaches to society (a good example is Hindess, 1973). In some instances, justifiable criticisms have been pushed to excess, since there can be no objection to measuring what can legitimately be measured (cf. Bulmer, 1980). It is sometimes forgotten that Cicourel (1964), who greatly influenced the anti-quantitative critics of the 60s and 70s, coupled his attack on gullibility in the face of figures with a wish to improve measurement in sociology, not destroy it altogether.

It is not necessary to assume that a search for indicators must be confined to social scientists of a statistical bent. In the broad sense, indicators may be used by a researcher of any persuasion, who realises that, to see something clearly, it may be necessary to direct one's gaze to the side of the object. For example, Max Weber, least quantitative of sociologists, used indicators. If we consider his notion of charisma, or natural leadership arising from special gifts, which he developed in detail, we discover that the reaction of people is an indicator of charisma in a leader. No recognition and following, no charismatic claim (*Wirtschaft und Gesellschaft*, pt III, ch. 9 (quoted by Gerth and Mills, 1948: 246)). Weber used something that he could see – and perhaps could even have counted – to show the presence of something that could not otherwise be identified.

Some of the most amusing indicators can be rather off-beat. In a splendid book, *Unobtrusive Measures: Non-reactive Research in the Social Sciences* (Webb, Campbell, Schwartz and Sechrest, 1966) the authors show what can be done with imagination and ingenuity in identifying promising indicators. They borrow (ibid: 28) the notion of 'outcropping' from geology, and look for external signs of underlying substance. A theory can only be tested at those points where available observations and theoretical predictions coincide. Their argument is that theories are more complete descriptions than any data, 'transient superficial outcroppings of events and objects' (ibid: 29) as these are, but that stubborn outcroppings may prove enough to force the abandonment of a theory. Examples of unobtrusive measures include the wear on floor tiles around a particular museum exhibit as compared with wear elsewhere; accretion rates (level of whisky consumption in a 'dry' U.S. town as indicated by empty bottles in rubbish bins); library withdrawals as indicators of levels of interest. In fact, the study of the discarding of rubbish as an indicator subsequently went a little far in the United States and led to some wry thoughts about sociology. Nevertheless, this is not so pointless as it might seem to the uninitiated. After all, a good part of the activity of the most respectable archaeologists consists of the interpretation of the rubbish left by people in the past.

Despite the entertainment and enlightenment to be derived from some of these unusual indicators, the most familiar types of indicators are those taking the form of published series, usually created and issued by, for example, research bureaux, statistical offices, government departments and academic researchers. Some of these are not, as mentioned earlier, specifically designed with some social theory in mind; they nevertheless may be turned to good use in ways not originally considered. Olson (1976: 96) provides a good example derived from Glaser and Strauss (1964), whose theory concerning the extent of social loss felt at death identifies age at death as the main indicator of disruption. Age distribution is a census statistic collected for other reasons than theory testing, but becomes an indicator within the framework of a particular theory.

Other sets of indicators and indices are, however, created in order to provide illumination, in the context of an explicit or implicit social theory. A great deal of early work, especially that related to economic indicators, was concerned with the appropriateness of the construction of index numbers. The complex problems of the weighting of aggregated components have been described by Webb et al. as 'heroic' (1966: 8), and the conceptual and mathematical aspects of index numbers have been explored in great depth.

In the case of simpler indicators, critiques have been made of their validity, on the grounds of whether the indicator in question indeed measures the feature of interest, in view of the fact that indicators are not 'natural' but are created by people with purposes. The mystique of the 'objective' social indicator has been heavily under attack; Irvine, Miles and Evans (1979) is a good example of the demystifying genre. Nevertheless, it is not my purpose to examine indicators or sets of index numbers from this technical point of view, important though it is. My aim is rather to take a sociolinguistic approach towards indicators in context and look more closely at some of their social and cultural aspects.

It is obvious that all indicators are not idiosyncratic to researchers nor do they remain the intellectual property of their producers; indicators gain a good deal of their value from the fact that they can be readily used by others. They form published series and come to be institutionalised. The business of statistical institutes and organisations around the world is to devise, safeguard the collection of, and promote the use of necessary indicators. It goes almost without saying that policy-makers rely to a great extent on the nature of available indicators both in framing their policies and in evaluating them.

The inertia of indicators

I should like to return now to the question of the inertia of indicators. From the preceding discussion, it can be seen that the types of indicators most in question are those that are officially produced, usually with quite specific policy intentions.

There are two important reasons for inertia, which we may think of as the inertia of production and the inertia of consumption. The inertia of production arises because the way the indicators are produced follows a pattern established in the past. The procedures and set-up are arranged to make it feasible for those concerned, enumerators, interviewers and statisticians, to follow a standard way of going about things. Everything does not have to begin afresh every time an updating is necessary. Schedules are to hand; returns come in from respondents; the standard procedures of collating and aggregating are followed. This is absolutely understandable.

On the consumption side, it is highly frustrating for anyone whose task it is to use or interpret statistics to find a hiccup in the series or a sudden restructuring of the nature of the data. The pressure from consumers is very much to continue the series that have been started some time ago and regularly issued; the need for continuity is very great. This also is understandable, and, speaking as one whose job once was to write state-of-the-art reports on various industries, based on published data, I can confirm there is nothing more annoying than a bland footnote announcing that the basis of a certain table of data has been changed.

Such forces help to maintain indicators in current forms: they contribute to the inertia of indicators. I do not suppose that these pressures are anything but the mundane result of processes that arise when any activity is routinised. Furthermore, the rectification of any patent nonsense, on the one hand, or innovations to provide more useful data, on the other hand, are both likely to be slow, given the layers of participants in decision-making.

The inside story of the creation of inertia (if it is possible to express the process in this way) really calls for a participant observation study, since producers of statistical series, like scientists everywhere, are not accustomed to write up the struggle to produce data, warts and all, but follow the cleaned-up convention of setting out the description of data-production using the logic of hindsight. Among the few studies of statistics production, one field study stands out (Government Statisticians' Collective, 1979) as providing unusual insight. Some of the implications of apparently simple procedures, such as the decision to treat a part-time worker as equal to one-half of a full-time worker, can have quite important implications (ibid: 140).

The main aim of the Government Statisticians' study is to emphasise the political aspects of the production and use of indicators. Among other accusations they include those of changing the definitions of terms, unjustifiably extrapolating trends, and manipulating adjustments (ibid: 148–9). Other students of indicators have also looked at the political context of identification and measurement. Ezrahi (1978), for example, has looked at this aspect of science indicators in the U.S. Science indicators are particularly sensitive because of their international and military aspects. Ezrahi has identified the role of the self-fulfilling prophecy in science indicators in the following terms: '... we can understand that as the publication of science indicators constitutes an attempt to fix the parameters of public definitions of the "state of science" in the context of public policy, that act inevitably becomes a part of the political process. With indicators functioning as a means of altering public definitions of "reality" and thereby influencing the priorities and direction of public action, professional considerations of their merits are not likely to be divorced from their behavioural implications' (1978: 309).

Whether the inertia of indicators is a political ploy or a by-product of the process of their production is a matter for determination in any specific case, and cannot be answered in a general sense. It is just the way things go on – probably unintended and unnoticed – that interests me. Indicators are produced and used when they are manifestly not relevant any longer or do not mean what they are intended to mean. The net to catch reality may be too coarse and cast in the wrong spot. The relationship between concept and indicator is sometimes very tenuous: the easily measurable replaces the truly relevant. There is some analogy with the man who drops his key in the gutter on a dark night and who looks under the lamp on the other side of the road for it because the light is better there. Some of the complaints about emphasis on quantitative, apparently concrete, measures simply because they are available are justified. Even when political considerations are not made explicit to or by anyone in the system, the really relevant indicators may be too painful or risky to take note of, while others may be more easily manipulated.

The recognition of the problems of inertia lurking in the process of institutionalisation does not imply that indicators should not be institutionalised, still less that they should not be used. As I mentioned at the outset, they can hardly be dispensed with by any professional researcher concerned with social change. Carley, for example, makes it quite clear that institutionalisation is vital if policy-makers are to be persuaded to use indicators (1981: 109). He underlines the point made by Caplan and Barton (1978) and de Neufville (1978) concerning the institutional prerequisites for making the existence and legitimacy of indicators sufficiently salient for them to make an impact on decision-making. Furthermore, the risk of an indicator being used as propaganda ('indicator/vindicator') may be *lessened* by institutionalisation, as Carley argues (ibid: 109–10).

Despite these considerations, the phenomenon of inertia is an important aspect of the use of the language of indicators, and emerges quite vividly when looked at in the context of publicly conducted policy-making and evaluation related to particular issues.

The state of the nation

One issue of great importance is the position of any social entity – group or aggregate – in an imagined scale of progress. Is it going up or down? As a nation are we scrambling onward and upward or sliding back? The fact that this may be an unanswerable question formulated in such a way does not prevent the topic from being a main concern of economic, political and other social commentators, who must, perforce, base their views on some set of indicators.

It might appear that there is a close relationship between ideas of progress and the nature of indicators, and to some extent that is the case. But the relationship is not that of appropriate indicator following closely the changes in the concept of progress, but, since the institutionalisation of the indicator business, quite the other way round. The indicator, through the strength of its inertia, influences the concept of progress. Furthermore, since progress and prediction are inseparable, in that anyone who talks about progress implies that we are moving towards a goal (or failing to), indicators are used not only to provide evidence of progress, but also to direct attention in prediction.

The notion of wealth has been central to arguments about human progress since *The Wealth of Nations* was published in 1776. Adam Smith's recognition of the importance of the division of labour in creating a country's wealth was linked specifically to factory operations (see Hollander, 1973: 239) and the wealth itself was purely material. The 'invisible hand' that ordered arrangements in the free market was one that dealt out material satisfaction. There have been so many definitions of wealth subsequently that it is truly risky to try to bridge sociologists', anthropologists', economists' and historians' views. Many would agree that it should include the physical goods that human societies value. Nevertheless, when pressed, few would accept that only such physical goods are the basis of wealth. Services are part of wealth and all sorts of non-material things might be included. Indeed, it has been cogently argued, by the economist Lancaster (1966), that it is impossible in any case to consider goods as such to be the basis of wealth, but only particular combinations of goods and services which yield particular satisfactions. In this sense, 'goods are not goods', the theme of his article.

Still, we cannot escape the inertia of indicators. Repeatedly, statistics used to identify forms of wealth include records of material production. Indeed, whole theories of wealth-producing sectors are posited on the view that wealth is things, stemming possibly from Adam Smith, but routed through Marx, an odd genealogy but explicable considering the extent to which Marx accepted many concepts of classical economics.

That is not to say that attempts to widen concepts of wealth and the indicators of wealth have been lacking. Most important here have been the efforts to identify subjective social indicators, which are really pointers to other sorts of wealth. Some of the research on life concerns has been rather simple (or even simple-minded) but some has been sophisticated and thoughtful (see Carley, 1981: 33–45). It must, however, be agreed that rather rough treatment has been given to some quality-of-life studies, thus revealing the way in which concentration on the countable and the material, in the form of standard indicators, has come to be the epitome of so-called sensible hard-headedness in assessing both wealth and progress in its acquisition. If it can be counted easily and if it can be enshrined in conventionally accepted indicators, then it is solid and serious. If it is qualitative, hard to objectify and to circumscribe, then any project taking this approach is considered to be hazy, relying on 'soft' data and only the woolly-minded would pursue it.

None of this is surprising to social scientists, to whom the argument about hard and soft data is an old story. But it returns again and again in policy statements and judgements about progress by influential people. It is only necessary to turn to the financial, business or political commentary in the respectable mass media of the late 70s and early 80s, to note the extensive use of the phrase 'wealth-producing sector' to apply to manufacturing industry, with the implication that it is more virtuous to produce a refrigerator, say, than provide a good tourist attraction. There is a world of social and economic theory behind the assumption: that wealth is material wealth, that what one can see and count easily is of primary importance, and that the whole of the economy rides on the back of the manufacturing sector.

Some semi-popular writing on economic policy has strengthened the ready acceptance of this idea of wealth-creation. The notion has tended to be used in discussion as an argument-clincher, brooking no dissension. Among confirmers of this concept of wealth, we must include the writings of Bacon and Eltis who, in *Britain's Economic Problem: Too Few Producers* (1978), provided an argument relating economic performance to industrial production, in order to account to their satisfaction for Britain's economic decline. Yet decline is only relative to the indicators selected from those to hand and the economic model adopted. With different theories and different indicators, another picture would have emerged.

My aim here is not to explore the 'decline' of Britain (quite another problem), but to emphasise the fact that available and readily accepted indicators – the 'hard' ones – slant assessments in a way that imposes itself. Policy-makers using these indicators may be out of step with what members of the population, or large segments of it, think, feel or value. Satisfaction with life in this country often emerges as higher than that of comparable industrial countries (cf. recent Gallup polls, 1981). Allowing for flaws in subjective indicator studies, a social observer might still pause and think about the alternatives missing in contemporary discussions about progress and decline. Someone hooked into the current system of indicators of progress will identify this satisfaction as complacency. But of course it is possible, as I have argued, to turn the whole set of values on its head and view the accepted indicators as irrelevant and misleading signposts.

This is not a naive plea to return to some alternative life-style, a mythical ur-communal world that is the negation of our present one. I do not think that such a return (if such it is) is feasible in the light of increasing population, dwindling resources and growing organisational complexity. Perhaps some elements of the past, though suppressed in public consciousness, are still there, ready to burgeon, like the domestic household economy, more powerful in economic affairs than is as yet generally realised (see Burns, 1975; Mount, 1982). It is, on the contrary, a realistic suggestion to take seriously the fact that policy-makers and evaluators are largely caught in a system that makes sense to them, but is circumscribed by, amongst other things, the inertia of indicators.

Progress

A question to take up here is whether we have always been influenced by the concrete and measurable in our concepts of progress. Has there always been a tendency to be led by the institutionalisation of indicators in view of the fact that students of society have always had to look for some correlate of many of the things they were interested in? I think not. I believe it is to a large extent the product of the growth of established statistical services. It is not my intention to denigrate the services; they do a remarkable and valuable job. It is only necessary to look at a sympathetic study of the products of statistical services, such as Hakim's (1982) to be aware of this fact. It is only the channelling occurring as a by-product that is dubious.

An interpretation of progress in purely material terms is partly a reflection of the ethos of our times, which is a direct heritage of the eighteenth and nineteenth centuries, in this as in so many other things. It is also, as I have argued, partly a reflection of the terms in which we identify trends.

It was not like this in the past or elsewhere. Ideas of progress have existed for a long time in the Western tradition. On the whole, the notion of social and cultural progress, from the Greeks on, has been a distinctively Western cultural notion. The same sort of idea does not seem to have figured in the Eastern tradition. For example, when the *I Ching*, the Chinese *Book of Changes*, and a much-used guide to prediction, speaks of progress, it is progress in a personal sense, that is, betterment of an individual's career *vis-à-vis* ruler or people, that is in question. The idea of moving towards a general societal goal is lacking.

Nevertheless, earlier ideas of progress drew more freely on indicators of moral as well as material progress. The concern was frequently that society should become 'better' in some ethical or spiritual sense, as Nisbet has shown in his masterly book *The Idea of Progress* (1980). Think for example of the idea of progress as freedom. It is described in one of Nisbet's chapters (6), together with some of the variety of indicators involved, from rotation of office to land ownership. Nisbet is a 'fox' not a 'hedgehog', to borrow Berlin's distinction (a fox knows many small things, a hedgehog knows one big thing) and his grand design to explore the idea of progress in society grows all sorts of side shoots and irrelevant though interesting thickets. It is not possible to use his work as a source for the study of the relationship between the idea of progress and its more pedestrian indicators, although he offers many clues – some of which are frustrated by his extraordinary decision to provide neither footnotes nor references in his book.

Of course, going back in history, the straws in the wind, the vague signs of progress, were qualitative, impressionistic and often highly personal to the observer. But they permitted speculation about many more types of progress than we are, on the whole, concerned with in our standard policy-making. It would perhaps be difficult and certainly odd in some cases to use the signs of some of the thinkers in the past. We can, however, learn from them a lesson, that indicators and statistical series are valuable tools of modern planning, but they are not neutral signs fitting well-worked-out universal theories and concepts of which they are the objective correlates. In particular they have tended to tie us down to a view of progress which is narrow and unimaginative, and one that must surely change in the future.

Predictions

I should like now to look at the implications, for prediction, of accepting consensus indicators of progress. It is very difficult to break out of the trap. Policy implies prediction; a policy or plan is devised to meet a situation in which it is foreseen that we are going off-course with respect to some desirable quality or feature of society. Predictions are produced by predictors, and these predictions have consumers. The demand for predictions is insatiable, which is why we have so many, even though they are manifestly unreliable to a greater or lesser degree. It is fortunate that misleading people and causing them to lose money or worse through following wrong predictions is not an indictable offence or our gaols might be even fuller. But the immediate consumers of a prediction are usually firms or organisations, or a conglomerate of subscribers. They come to recognise familiar indicators, which are doing familiar though sometimes unwelcome things. The predictors oblige.

Indicators in series provide trends, and the extrapolation of trends, by any means, is a form of prediction. There are other forms of standard prediction, such as cross-impact analyses, cost-benefit studies and Delphi techniques, ably discussed in, for instance, the Science Policy Research Unit's book on prediction (Encel et al., 1975). But all techniques rely to some extent on knowing where things have been in the past and where they seem to be heading in the future. It may be argued that prediction is in principle impossible, as Popper did (1977). In the pure case, of perfect prediction, this would seem to be so. If one argues that the future is influenced by our knowledge, and if one cannot know what future knowledge will be, or one would know it now, then it is not possible to predict. All the same, rough and ready prediction is needed in order to live in society; so we have the paradox of doing all the time, however imperfectly, what we really cannot do. I would maintain that extrapolation is what we work with: the past is the best predictor of the future that we have. What is extrapolated is in effect what is identified as being important in the signs of progress; this is formulated in terms of indicators. Since the indicators suffer from inertia, they tend, as discussed earlier, to hold us to views of progress that may be inappropriate or conventionalised.

A vivid instance of the practical advantages of liberalising the signs of progress was presented to me in the course of a study of the industrialisation of the countryside and the economic growth of communes in Yugoslavia in the early 1960s. This study was based on fieldwork and on other data, including the use of official published statistical series. Through fieldwork, it was clear that the advantage of the industrialisation of the countryside lay not so much with the actual increased production of rural factories as in the spin-off or multiplier effect of the operation of the factory on the surrounding countryside and the increased market and opportunities for the peasant farmers. However, the data officially collected and published reflected the usual formulations and series that had been produced in the past, based directly on received socio-economic theories. Only factory workers were counted as productive workers. No one in any service or related industry formed part of the workforce of the commune. The reality of what was going on could not be formulated and therefore recognised within the 'respectable' framework of accepted analysis.

In centralised economies, predictions and plans cannot be separated. Since the indicators have solidified (probably to a much greater extent than in market economies) and must accord with a particular doctrine, they can hardly be changed, and the 'invisible hand' that patterns individual actions in aggregate cannot be given any recognition. In the pure case, the prediction *is* the plan, the plan *is* the prediction. Hence, as things inevitably go awry, the plan must be constantly rewritten. Endless meetings involving innumerable officials, write and rewrite 'the plan'. The activity of such organisations is not to do, but to re-work the plan acceptably. Progress is achieved by redefinition and adjustment.

Admittedly, this was in the early 1960s. Even in centralised economies, the unbiddable nature of society is now recognised in a more sophisticated way. Nevertheless, this does not stop failures of planning piling on failures. Perhaps they can never be avoided; but they could be helped by the recognition of two things: the necessary role of unpredictability in human affairs, and, still more, the underestimated role of the inertia of indicators in preserving irrelevant and rigid interpretations of progress.

Prediction shaped by indicators from the past is usually thought of as quite distinct from large-scale historical prophecy; yet there is some overlap, and the study of indicators and historical sociology are linked. The issues here go far beyond modest questions concerning the inertia of indicators. There certainly is a sense in which the past is a launching pad for future trajectories, but we can do rather little about guidance in flight. Philip Abrams, in his last book, put the point succinctly: 'Historical sociology can hope to show everything is inevitable once it has happend. But it is constrained to assume that nothing is inevitable till then' (1982: 146).

There is, however, another aspect to history in this context, based on the idea that the past is another country. We can not only recognise the rhetoric of past time (and its categories, labels and indicators) where it threatens to constrain us unnecessarily, but also look outside the ethnocentric present for other ways of conceptualising where we are and where we might be going. Kumar, in *Prophecy and Progress*, argues cogently against the narrow view of the past projected into the future, when he says (1978: 309) that we are ill-advised to allow categories appropriate to early industrial societies to shape our views, and still more foolish, I suppose, to apply categories we *think* are appropriate to such societies which are not really so.

One might suppose that the most free-wheeling and imaginative professional predictors might be able to escape such tunnel vision, but the same process can be seen to operate even in extreme and highly critical predictions, when the whole of our current social system is coming under attack, as in the global predictions of such futurological studies as the famous *Limits To Growth* (Meadows et al., 1972) with its many followers and opponents (see Freeman and Jahoda, 1978, for a good summary of the debate). The characteristics taken into account here are again the material and countable. A suggestion that strength of religious feeling or sense of global responsibility should have been included in their study would have seemed strange and probably unmanageable to those concerned, and also to those forming part of the 'invisible college' of global predictors.

In the sphere of this great debate (important as much for the image of the future it projects, with its concomitant effects of promoting optimism or pessimism, as for actual success in prediction) the lines of the permissible indicators have been drawn. The 'problematique' that Waddington identified in his book *The Man-Made Future* (1978), as the complex of problems concerned with population, resources, food, standards of living and environment, together with the growth of technology, has by now had its standard set of indicators thoroughly institutionalised. Yet values connected with religious beliefs are patently important in, for example, population growth, and ideas concerning responsibility similarly important in the use of resources. It is unlikely that the crude models global predictors are working with will yield appropriate predictions; furthermore some are so carried away by the power of computers in modelling that they often concentrate on manipulation to the detriment of input or output; and their problems are compounded by the obvious fact that some policies are framed in order to stop some predictions coming true.

The most telling point here is not so much the problems of the bold global modeller as the speed with which the indicators defining the 'problematique' have come to be institutionalised both in production and use. This might make us more wary of the force of indicators in prediction and more successful in being prepared for the inevitable shocks of the new.

REFERENCES

Abrams, M. 1976. *A Review of Subjective Social Indicator Work, 1971–1975*. S.S.R.C., London.

Abrams, P. 1982. *Historical Sociology*. Open Books, Shepton Mallet.

Bacon, R. and Eltis, W. 1978 (2nd edn). *Britain's Economic Problem: Too Few Producers*. St. Martin, London.

Bauer, R. A. 1966. *Social Indicators*. M.I.T. Press, Cambridge, Mass.
Berger, P. and Luckmann, T. 1967. *The Social Construction of Reality*. Allen Lane the Penguin Press, London.
Bulmer, M. (ed.) 1978. *Social Policy Research*. Macmillan, London.
Bulmer, M. 1980. 'Why don't sociologists make more use of official statistics', *Sociology* 14(4): 505–23.
Burns, S. 1975. *The Household Economy: its Shape, Origins and Future*. Beacon Press, Boston.
Caplan, N. and Barton, E. 1978. 'The potential of social indicators: minimum conditions for impact at the national level as suggested by a study of the use of Social Indicators 73'. *Social Indicators Research*, vol. 5, pp. 427–56.
Carley, M. 1981. *Social Measurement and Social Indicators*. George Allen and Unwin, London.
Cicourel, A. 1964. *Method and Measurement in Sociology*. Free Press, New York.
de Neufville, J. I. 1978. 'Validating policy indicators'. *Policy Sciences*, vol. 10, pp. 171–88.
Elkana, Y. et al. 1978. *Toward a Metric of Science: the Advent of Science Indicators*. Wiley, New York.
Encel, S., Marstrand, P. K., and Page, W. (eds.) 1975. *The Art of Anticipation: Values and Methods in Forecasting*. Martin Robertson, London.
Ezrahi, Y. 1978. 'Political Contexts of Science Indicators', in Elkana, Y. et al. (1978).
Freeman, C. and Jahoda, M. (eds.) 1978. *World Futures: the Great Debate*. S.P.R.U., Sussex: Martin Robertson, London.
Gallup, G. H. 1981. *The International Gallup Polls: Public Opinion, 1979*. Scholarly Resources Inc., Wilmington, Delaware.
Gerth, H. H. and Mills, C. W. 1948. *From Max Weber: Essays in Sociology*. Routledge and Kegan Paul, London.
Glaser, B. and Strauss, A. 1964. 'The social loss of dying patients'. *Amer. J. of Nursing*, vol. 64, pp. 119–21.
Government Statisticians' Collective. 1979. 'How official statistics are produced: views from the inside', in Irvine et al., 1979.
Hakim, C. 1982. *Secondary Analysis in Social Research: a Guide to Data Sources and Methods with Examples*. George Allen and Unwin, London.
Hindess, B. 1973. *The Use of Official Statistics in Sociology: a Critique of Positivism and Ethnomethodology*. Macmillan, London.
Hollander, S. 1973. *The Economics of Adam Smith*. Heinemann Educational Books, London.
Irvine, J., Miles, I. and Evans, J. 1979. *Demystifying Social Statistics*. Pluto Press, London.
Kumar, K. 1978. *Prophecy and Progress: the Sociology of Industrial and Post-Industrial Society*. Penguin Books, Harmondsworth.
Lancaster. K. 1966. 'A new approach to consumer theory'. *Journal of Political Economy*, vol. 174, pp. 132–57.
Meadows, D. et al. 1972. *The Limits to Growth*. Earth Island, London.
Moser, C. 1973. 'Social indicators: systems, methods and problems', *The Review of Income and Wealth*, 19, 1973, pp. 133–41, in Bulmer, 1978.
Mount, F. 1982. *The Subversive Family*. Jonathan Cape, London.
Nisbet, R. 1980. *History of the Idea of Progress*. Heinemann, London.

Olson, S. 1976. *Ideas and Data: the Process and Practice of Social Research*. The Dorsey Press, Homewood, Ill.

Popper, K. 1977 edn. *The Poverty of Historicism*. Harper and Row, New York.

Shonfield, A. and Shaw, S. 1972. *Social Indicators and Social Policy*. S.S.R.C., Heinemann, London.

Waddington, C. H. 1978. *The Man-Made Future*. Croom Helm, London.

Webb, E., Campbell, D. T., Schwartz, R. D. and Sechrest, L. 1966. *Unobtrusive Measures: Non-reactive Research in the Social Sciences.* Rand McNally, Chicago.

Zeisel, H. 'Difficulties in indicator construction: notes and queries', in Elkana Y. et al. (1978), pp. 253–8.

Index